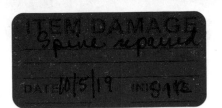

RUN JANE RUN

RUN JANE RUN

A True Story of Murder and Courage

BY JANE WELLS

New Horizon Press   Far Hills, NJ

Requests for permission should be addressed to:
New Horizon Press
P.O. Box 669
Far Hills, NJ 07931

Wells, Jane
    Run Jane Run: A True Story of Murder and Courage

Library of Congress Catalog Card Number: Pending

ISBN: 0-88282-140-7

New Horizon Press

Manufactured in the U.S.A.

2000 1999 1998 1997 1996 / 5 4 3 2 1

To Johnny, and the extraordinary memories
no one can take away from us.

To my children.

To all survivors of domestic violence.
I hope that by making people aware, more efforts will be
made to help them.

To the educators and those who work in the trenches to end
the violence and all forms of oppression.

Author's Note

This book is based on my experiences, and reflects my perceptions of the past, present and future. The personalities, events, actions and conversations portrayed within the story have been reconstructed from my memory, court documents, letters, personal papers, and press accounts. Some names and events have been altered to protect the privacy of individuals. Events involving the characters happened as described; only minor details have been altered.

Acknowledgments

The author wishes to thank the following people for their assistance; Kristi Alsop; Amanda Baker; Dr. Joanne Belknap; Dianne Cimosz; Mel Cole; Robert Collins; Tonya Covington; Thelma Dillow; Lesta Cooper-Freytag; Dana Gilbert; Shelly Graff; Lou Harris; a special thanks to Pat Herold for her writing assistance and advice; Kathy Huff; Teresa Hundemer; my great friend Candy Johnson; Stephanie Jones for her legal expertise; Tommy Jones; The Kentucky Foundation for Women; Dr. Andrea Kornbluh; Melinda Mayo; Sandy and Ken Matthews; Sherry Minwalla; Patty Monahan; Michele Morgan; Big Jane Mowry; Dr. Joseph McClusky; Leslie Bennet McNeill; Jamie Newsome; Allegra Nicodemus; Our Place gang—especially Carla, John, Natalie, Karen; Laverne Poole; Tricia Rampley; Megan Richards; Randy Rupp; Kathy Schmadel; Dennis Schoner; Mary Sergent; Nichole Smith; Bobby Stern; Tina Tompkins; Shannon Tuzzi for her help with the early writing and the humor and patience to keep the project going; Karen Welch; Betty Widmer; My agent, Frank Weimann; Danny Williams; Janet Winters; Women's film Project of Cincinnati; Peg, Tim, Pete, and Dan W.; a very special thanks to Dr. Jim Wilson for his editing, encouragement, and enduring support. Thanks to Dean for helping me keep my sanity; my family who helped me through the ups and downs of school and publishing; and most of all, to my children who gave me love and hope.

Contents

CHAPTER 1

The Nightmare

The early morning sun streamed through the bare bedroom window, soothing my aching body but threatening another steamy July day for the inhabitants of Lexington, Kentucky. I lay in a deep but troubled sleep beside my infant daughter, Megan, on a makeshift bed, exhausted from working two jobs, moving into a new home, and from a physically and emotionally punishing fight with my estranged husband, Michael. Before twenty-four hours would elapse, my life would be threatened, my children's lives endangered, and a murder would occur before our very eyes. But as I lay sleeping I had no idea that when I woke up a nightmare would begin.

Within moments Erica, my six-year-old daughter, dressed in a bathing suit, began to shake me gently, "Mommy, it's gonna be lunchtime, you sleepy head, wake up."

I opened my eyes. Still unfocused, I looked around the strange room, not recognizing it at first, and then sighed thankfully, believing at last we were safe.

The new apartment was a godsend after the ramshackle hotel we'd been living in. Now that Johnny, my first husband, was here to help us, things seemed to be looking up, but I still missed my old home. I'd worked hard for that three-story frame house with its ivy walls and leaded glass windows. I had fixed it up just the way I liked, painting the walls antique white with carpet to match and arranging my dark cherry and mahogany furniture so it looked beautiful. Most of the furniture had been handed down to me by my family. They always told me it was real important that I'd have something to start housekeeping with when I got married.

Things were always done a certain way back home. Furniture and whatnots were passed down to the daughters while money, land, and attention were handed to the male heirs if the family had them to give. You learned not to question these traditions, because if the family was to run out of simple answers they'd backhand you, and that was bound to bring fire to your face and forgetfulness to your brain.

Most of the furniture was long gone now because of Michael. He took from me all the material things I had, but I still had what was most important—my children. My children and I couldn't even live in our own house anymore. It was too dangerous with Michael on the loose. He'd find us there. And even if he was stopped now finally, it was too late. The bank was about to foreclose. The children and I had lived at a half dozen different addresses since we stayed at the abuse shelter. I was always told I shouldn't cry over spilt milk, but spilling milk doesn't bother me like losing my house did.

I grew up in the hills of Kentucky. On both sides of U.S. 23 there were worn out school buses converted to houses and considered marvelous mansions. No running water. No bathroom. Maybe a two-holer outhouse built close by. You could tell when the owner of the bus was on the road to prosperity. They'd have newfangled miniblinds installed on the very windows that children used to stare out on their way from school. Thank goodness I never had to live like that. Dad's job at the railroad afforded us enough to get by on. Of course we weren't rich but we weren't dirt poor either and could hold our heads up, at least until now.

For, among my people, a girl can't go home once she's been married. No matter what she has to endure. That must be written in stone somewhere. They should've made it plain by just stamping "No Return on Used Goods" on us somewhere or maybe on the marriage license.

The customs of Appalachia favor men and even lawmakers uphold them. After the police took the girls and me to the shelter, Michael made off with almost everything I owned except the living room set my grandmother started housekeeping with and some clothes he couldn't sell. My most prized possessions—a house full of furniture, keepsake jewelry and my record album collection—all gone. Everything but the living room set which was in Mom and Dad's basement.

The smell of fresh paint on the walls and clean carpets underfoot gave me a feeling of new beginnings. How long it'd last was hard to tell. I tried to look on the bright side of things, though I was sad and angry about having to move so often.

Nevertheless, the fact that I didn't own this new place unnerved me. Who knew when I'd get on my feet enough to buy another place of my own. I was dog tired. I was barely twenty-seven years old and already felt like a worn out plow horse. I couldn't remember my back hurting as badly as it hurt now, except maybe the time Michael threw me down the stairs the week after I gave birth to Megan. He drop-kicked me like a football, and I felt the stitches snap, pains shoot, and joints jolt as I bounced and banged to the bottom of the stairs and slammed onto the floor. I laid there crumpled up for what seemed like hours till the throbbing went away. Then the soreness set in.

It seemed like I'd been sore and tired ever since, tired from the demands of working two jobs after just giving birth and the strain of being bashed and bruised by Michael and then by the courts. The goal of gaining a safe place for the girls and me to stay while getting my divorce paid off kept me going. I still haven't figured out how my mind stayed in place during the whole ordeal.

Poor little Megan. It was hard to believe she was six months old and had already lived at more than five addresses, all because her daddy Michael claims that he chases us, catches us, and beats *me* because he loves *her*. That's a twisted kind of love if you ask me, but all the judges in the local courts around here seem to buy it hook, line, and sinker. Hopefully, Megan is young enough to be saved from the memories of the brutality we've had to suffer through, unlike Erica and me.

I looked up at Erica, who was talking a mile a minute.

"Daddy gave me breakfast. We're going swimming. Don't you want to come? It'll be fun."

I shook my head and motioned for her to bend down so I could give her a kiss. "Got too much to do around here sweety, you go ahead."

I got up, quickly dressed, and went downstairs. I searched through the boxes at the bottom of the stairs and found a carton marked "my room," but I knew it was kitchen stuff. I opened it carefully. I didn't want anything else broken. As I unpacked the glasses and put them on the shelf, I caught a satisfying sight out the kitchen window. There was my daughter Erica playing at the pool with her father Johnny. The sun glittered on the water and their similar features as they took turns splashing each other, giggling all the while. When we went to pick Johnny up the night before at his grandfather's house, Erica kept telling him all about the pool at the new apartment. You'd have thought that pool was an amusement park the way she'd gone on about it. He'd promised her he would teach her how to swim but she'd told him she already knew how. Johnny's face had darkened with sadness. I knew he was recalling the years of her life he'd missed.

"Then I'll teach you to dive," he'd told her, "and find a way to make up for the time we've missed."

By the way they were joking and playing at the pool, he seemed to be off to a good start.

Erica had been asking about seeing her daddy for months. Now finally her wish had come true. You could tell by the joyful look on her face that he didn't need to teach her a thing, if only she could sit and stare at him. Finally, she could be with her daddy, and the way he was carrying on, it looked like he was enjoying the visit as much as she was.

Johnny had begged me for the last few months to let him come and see us, but things were too dangerous. I'd talked to him on the phone when the girls and I were in the abuse shelter. He'd heard my marriage was going badly, and he said he wanted to help. I knew he still loved me, and I secretly felt the same toward him, but of course I didn't tell him this and discouraged his coming there. It always scared me how much I loved Johnny. But we had been too young when we married. He was an artist who couldn't find steady work, and it caused our marriage to come apart. Finally, I had to leave him to survive. Trickle down economics never got to us. People can't get welfare if they're married, so to keep Erica and me fed I had no choice but to leave him. As much as it hurt us both, I had to put Erica's needs first.

Sighing heavily, I folded my arms and leaned on the kitchen sink. Trying to rid my thoughts of past hurts, I focused on watching Johnny and Erica out the window. Johnny was now showing Erica his acrobatic skills. She seemed as caught up in his energy as I was the night I'd met him. Once again the past filled my thoughts and spun me backwards to that spring night in the city park. Johnny'd been with a friend of mine Dennis Ivans whose guitar playing was well known in the area. Johnny started showing off as soon as we were introduced. It was hard to believe that was over ten years ago. It had been like somebody cast a spell on me as I'd watched Johnny do back flips off that park bench. I'd never seen such energy and magnetism. His performance was hilarious. Not too many around like this one, I'd thought. In fact, though the years had passed, I had never met anyone like him, and I figured I probably never would.

Again I focused on the present. Erica sat on the side of the pool and cheered with laughter and satisfaction as Johnny completed a double back flip off the side of the pool and landed with a splash that soaked her. It was more than watching—she drank in his every move. It was good to see her smile after all she'd been through. She was so happy to see Johnny, and I had to admit he looked good.

At thirty-three he was more attractive than ever. Staring at his soft skin tanned by the summer sun reminded me of the years before Erica, when we'd play frisbee in the park and I'd sit in the grass and admire his agile movements.

I tried to keep myself from noticing his linebacker legs as he jumped off the side of the pool, but my eyes fixed on them. He hadn't changed much, that was for sure. And now he was charming his way into Erica's heart.

Lord knows she needed her daddy's attention. I knew how much Erica had suffered, although I'd done all I could to save her grief. She'd been moved from school to school, lost all her friends and the sense of security that children need. Watching Michael beat her mommy probably did her the most harm, but small things mean a lot to a child her age. She still cries about her "baby's first Christmas" ornament which was lost in our move last year. I had promised to get her another one, but she said it wouldn't be the same.

I'd already learned not to be sentimental about such things. I know how heartbreaking it is to lose everything and have to start again. But, as an adult, you get used to it. Erica was a small, lonely child.

I'd tried to remind Erica that she had me and Megan, and, now with Johnny back in the picture, hopefully things could get back to some form of normal. It hadn't been that way for a long time. I remembered one night when Erica came to me after the police had left because Michael had beaten me up so badly. She looked at me with her big slate-blue eyes, so much like Johnny's, and asked, "Mommy, why don't the policemen like us?"

"Why do you say that?" I'd asked.

"I thought when people got beat up the police would help them, but they don't do anything," she'd said sadly.

When she was young I'd taught her our phone number in case someone ever tried to snatch her. I explained to her she should run for help and call the police. But when we called the police time and again because of Michael's violence, she found it very confusing when they wouldn't do a thing to him or help us.

I heard the front door open and Erica running down the entry hall. As she rounded the corner and bounced into the kitchen, water landed everywhere. I didn't scold her.

"Come look what I can do, Mommy. Daddy taught me how to dive and I did it right on the first try." She was all smiles and her eyes sparkled behind the blond water-drenched curls that spilled onto her face. I hadn't had the chance to congratulate her when Johnny strode in from the pool.

"Janie, I think we have a superb little swimmer," he said, smiling. "She's something else. Everything I do she does right after me. I'm truly amazed. She's not afraid of a thing. A fearless Fraulein she is," he added in his German accent.

I smiled too. "I'm proud of ya, honey. Mommy saw ya from the kitchen window and I thought I was watchin' the Olympics the way you was jumpin' off the side of that pool."

"Mommy, why don't ya get your bathin' suit on and come out'n play with us? Me, you, and Daddy will have a lot of fun. And we can put Megan in her car seat by the pool. She loves to get splashed."

"I bet mommy still looks like Demi Moore in a bathing suit," Johnny added with a grin. I turned to my daughter. Erica hadn't caught the meaning of his comment. Knowing she wasn't looking, I flashed him a discreet smile.

"Baby, go on up 'n' get some dry clothes on. Maybe mommy can go swimmin' with ya tomorrow."

"But, Mommy, you have to work tomorrow," Erica said.

"Yeah, I wish I could stay here with you, baby, but we need the money so badly. I just have to work the waitress job. Afterward, though, it'll feel good to put my tired feet and worn out legs in the pool. Meanwhile, Mommy's gotta get this place shaped up."

Erica's good mood couldn't be dampened. She nodded, turned and headed out of the kitchen, down the hall, and skipped up the stairs to her room. We could hear her humming.

"What can I do to help?" Johnny asked. "I came here to lend ya a hand but I feel helpless when it comes to setting up house."

"That's all right. Just helpin' me out with the girls is enough."

"Yeah, but who takes care of you? When do you take time off?"

I shook my head sadly. Johnny leaned toward me. His hand smoothed my dark hair behind my ear and pushed the length of it over my shoulder. His touch was both comforting and disturbing, awakening sensations I hadn't felt in a long time. I knew he wanted to try to work things out between us. He had told me that the previous night as we watched the children sleep at his grandfather's house. But I was afraid, like a beaten dog who fears an unfamiliar hand. I told myself I knew Johnny. I knew the happiness we had once shared. We had so much in common, and he loved Erica so much. I wanted to respond to his longing look but quickly pulled away.

"Do you want some lunch? Erica hasn't eaten and it's gettin' late."

"Why don't we just have a big dinner? No sense in your having to fix both. We'll just snack now and eat something heavier later on," Johnny suggested.

"Mommy! Megan's awake!" Erica yelled down from her room. "Do ya want me to bring her to ya?"

"No, sweetheart, I'll come up 'n' get her."

I ran the length of the hallway, used the banister to swing to the first step, and took the steps two at a time to the top. Erica loved to take care of Megan, but I didn't want a child her size starting down the steps with a six-month-old, especially since Megan was already nearing twenty-five pounds.

At the top I walked down the hall and into the girls' room.

It seemed so bare compared to their old room. I need to get the curtains up, I thought. Megan smiled a big, wide toothless grin when I leaned over her.

"Hi, my precious little angel, did ya sleep good?" The cooing sound of my voice and my familiar face made her arms and legs wave as if to nod yes. She looked like a doll with ivory skin framed by coal-black hair that stuck up like fuzz on a baby bird. Her big brown eyes were the surest sign she'd take after me. As I patted Megan's belly lightly, Erica came into the room and walked to my side.

"Let me hold her," she begged.

"Let's take her downstairs so we can all enjoy her." I picked Megan up, put her on my shoulder and stooped over to take a blanket from the pallet I'd made for the baby to sleep in. Erica grabbed a few toys to play with and we started through the hall and down the stairs.

In the living room Johnny was sitting on my grandmother's old couch that we had covered with a blue flowered tapestry print shortly after we got married. His face looked a little tense, but against the plump cushions he looked familiar. I handed Megan to him. "I need to get back to fixing the kitchen," I said and stepped back to see how comfortable he was holding Megan, knowing it takes time to get back into the baby care routine. "Watch her head," I said, "she'll throw it back and get away from ya if ya ain't careful."

"'If ya ain't careful?'" Johnny said mockingly.

"Stop makin' fun of the way I talk or ya won't git no dinner."

"I'm merely pointing it out. You're in the city now, Janie. Lexington is three times the size of Ashland, ten times the size of Russell or Flatwoods, and more than a hundred miles away from the hills. You can't keep that hill talk or you'll never get a good job."

"I'm employed, thank ya just the same, Mr. Citified." I turned with a swift twist and marched to the kitchen. I knew my speech had slipped back into hill talk since Johnny and I had separated, but everyone around me talked that way. Except Johnny. Johnny was different. A city boy who'd gone away to make his fortune, he'd come back to town to help his blind grandfather and found me along the way. Or was it the other way around? I wondered.

I tried to stop thinking of the past, grabbed the refrigerator door, opened it, and got out the kielbasa. I thought I had some green beans and looked for them in the vegetable crisper. "Yep, there they are," I murmured. "I'll make one of my one-pot wonders. Johnny likes those little Irish potatoes, and Erica loves the whole dish." I opened the silverware drawer, reached for a knife, took it out, and started cutting open the sausage. Then my heart contracted as I heard the front door open and slam shut. I knew Johnny wouldn't slam it. I knew who would.

I was right.

"Where's Jane?" Michael demanded in a threatening voice which filled the house.

"Damn," I said only half under my breath and flashed a reassuring look toward Erica and Johnny as I stepped from the kitchen into the dining area where Michael stood.

He stood with his legs apart in a menacing manner.

"What are you doing here?" I asked dejectedly.

"I came to see my daughter." He spat each word out.

"You got no business here, Michael. There's warrants out for you. This is my home and you got no rights here. Your name's not on this lease. Now git on out."

"Who's he?" Michael demanded, pointing to Johnny. "What the fuck's he doin' here? I'll have these kids taken from ya, actin' a whore in front of 'em."

My temper rose. "This is Erica's father. You got some nerve callin' me names since you've been with everything in town that's got legs and wears a skirt now and then. Johnny came up to see his daughter. Now watch your language in front of my children and git on outta here."

"I'm not goin' anywhere. You can't make me. If he can stay 'n' visit his daughter, so can I." Michael stood staring me down. His eyes were in a narrowed mean squint as he chewed on his bottom lip. Here we go again, I thought. Michael will go to any extreme to get his way. I knew I had to cut him off quick. If his temper exploded, he could hurt someone. I stepped cautiously from the kitchen doorway to stand in front of him. I could tell he was leery of Johnny. His eyes shifted from Johnny to me, and then to the front door and back to me.

"I said you better git yourself outta here," I repeated. "You got no business here, and if I call the police, you're goin' away for a while."

"Bitch! I said I wasn't leavin'!" he swung his right fist and slammed it across my face. The blow sent me reeling across the dining area. I heard Erica start to cry as I landed on the floor. Johnny jumped up and handed Megan to Erica. With no time to check my own wounds, I fastened my eyes on Johnny and Michael to see what Michael would do next.

"You're not gonna do that to her as long as I'm here," Johnny warned. "I don't know you, but I know Jane doesn't deserve to be treated like this. Why don't you leave like she asked you?"

"Who the hell do you think you are?" Michael stormed. "I've been takin' care of your kid for a year. You got no room to talk."

Johnny flinched. Michael's cruel comment seemed to cut him deeply, but he tried to reason with Michael.

"Look. I came here to visit with Erica and help Jane get on her feet. Whatever's goin' on between you two, you'll have to work out. I know how bad it hurts to get divorced. I love Jane myself and my heart still aches that we broke up. But what you're doing to her she doesn't deserve. We should both be helping her."

I stood up and started over to the couch to comfort Erica who was still crying. The sight of Michael scared the daylights out of her. As I took another step toward the girls, Michael reached past Johnny and caught me by my hair with one hand and slapped me across the face with the other.

Johnny's face whitened. "You're forcing me to do this, mister," Johnny announced as he socked Michael who crashed into the wall and slid like the snake he was to the floor. The rest of us stared at him, waiting to see what brutal thing he would do next.

Michael checked his face and slowly got to his hands and knees. As his head started to lift, he propelled his body into Johnny's stomach. They both went down on the floor in a furious wrestling match. I ran over to the girls and carried them quickly upstairs to their room. "Erica, lock the door," I said, putting them down. When I got back downstairs, Michael and Johnny were facing off. I stood shaking, scared stiff. Johnny flashed me a compassionate look. Then, taking a deep breath, he turned to Michael.

"Michael," he said calmly, "we need to talk this over. Jane and the kids don't need this."

"Let's go to my place," Michael suggested with slithery friendliness. "I don't live far from here. We can walk."

Fear raced from my face to my feet. I was scared for Johnny to go off anywhere with Michael. I was also disturbed to learn that Michael had moved within walking distance of my new place. But more than anything I was frightened for my children. I ran upstairs and looked out the girls' bedroom window as Michael and Johnny walked out the door and marched up the street. Until they had stepped out of sight I was a nervous wreck. Erica's trembling body cuddled up under my shaking arm.

"Where's Daddy goin', Mommy?"

"He's gonna talk ta Michael and try ta settle him down," I said with some hesitation.

I thought about how quickly Michael had invited Johnny to leave with him, and it worried me. Michael was never one to cooperate or try to make peace unless the police had been called.

And, even then, he'd just lie to them and tell them the fights were all my fault. They believed him, too. I'd stand there with my face and hair a mess and he'd look like the neatly groomed, typical hard-working dad. I said to Erica, "Maybe I ought to get my hair combed and put some makeup on in case the police have to be called again." At least I'll have a shot at being believed if I look neat, I thought bitterly.

Meanwhile, any help was a long way off. I had to rely on myself and secure my family as best I could. I picked up Megan and with Erica at my side headed back downstairs. I locked the front door as we passed, closed the closet door, and checked the door to the basement. It was unlocked. Locking it, I thought of the garage door in the basement, but I didn't have the courage to go down and check it. I headed to the sliding glass doors in the living room. Here's an easy access for Michael, I thought. All he has to do is find a rock or a brick in the woods, and one forceful throw and he's in. "God, I wish we had a phone," I murmured.

Megan seemed to enjoy the way I was flying and zigzagging around the apartment. She giggled as I jerked the long blinds closed. God love her, she don't have a care in the world, I thought, my own fear rising. I tickled her stomach lightly to keep her laughing. As I'd hoped, it did. Erica flicked her fingers across the bottom of Megan's foot and her smiling face made Erica's brighten. I handed Megan to Erica and they sat on the floor playing with the toys that Erica had brought downstairs before Michael spoiled our evening.

Then I looked at my watch. I remembered the children hadn't eaten supper. The poor things must be hungry. What a life this was for them, I agonized. Tears rose to my eyes. As I walked into the kitchen I couldn't help but wonder what was going on between Johnny and Michael. I wished Johnny would come back. Damn, now I regretted Johnny coming up for the visit. Now look at what's happened, and he hasn't slept all night. He's going to be exhausted, I thought.

My mind ventured back to the night before when we'd sat outside his grandfather's place. It had been so long since Johnny and I had spent time together, and we had a lot of catching up to do. He showed me his new records, and we both found it amusing when I told him I'd bought the same ones. Our similarities were soothing. We'd lived in the country for several years after we got married, and last night had been like a homecoming.

Johnny treated me so gently. He took me up to the hill where we used to dream of building a house. We sat up there by ourselves while the girls were down at his cousins' trailer playing with their kids. We didn't talk about anything in particular. No bad memories. No plans for the future. We just lay on the grass and blew dandelion fuzz at each other, giggling as we did it. Once he blew some in my face by accident and white furry stems stuck to my eyelashes. He took them off with a few tender strokes using the back of his hand and stared deep into my eyes as he did. His fingers stayed gently on my cheek.

I pushed the memory away. I'd better concentrate while I chopped the sausage. I plopped it into the pot. I wasn't used to cooking on an electric stove, but I turned the heat up to high hoping the meat would cook quickly. While I stirred the pot, I kept seeing pictures of Johnny in my mind. I thought of his hair, with its thousands of soft brown baby curls with generous gold highlights that framed his face like dyed cotton. Images of Johnny playing guitar last night lingered, especially the way his hair swayed back and forth as his shoulders shook his head. Our eyes had fixed on each other when the rhythms slowed down. He swayed rhythmically back and forth, back and forth, his hands shifting swiftly while his fingers flew on the middle strings. His other hand moved skillfully up and down and around the neck of the guitar making me lightheaded as he did it. I smiled and nodded my head in time to his rhythm, my fingers tapping, a glow of satisfaction on my face. I didn't dare look away. I wanted to watch his every stroke and hear every chord change. I loved his music. "I could sit for hours listening to you play guitar," I told him.

Art and music had been the center of our world and the focus of our relationship. Our living room always held an easel and a box of oil paints with canvases, mostly unfinished, lining the bottom of every wall. Copies of posters and pictures by Seurat, Salvador Dali, M.C. Escher, and Monet's lilies were hung everywhere. Usually while Johnny painted we'd listen for hours to David Bowie, Robert Fripp, King Crimson, Brian Eno, Peter Hammill, The Furs, Gentle Giant, Peter Gabriel, and early Genesis. Not too many people enjoyed our kind of music. It was something we shared with only a few close friends. I'd missed that creative atmosphere. I was glad Erica would soon be learning all about it. It was a part of us she'd not gotten to know and part of my life that I would welcome back.

Johnny played some new songs he'd written. "They're mostly about you," he said, adding, "since we've been apart. Being back together will probably inspire me to write more." Smiling now, I reached for the plates and heard a knock at the door. God, let it be Johnny, I prayed.

I ran to the door, checked the peep hole. It was him. I let Johnny in, and quickly closed the door behind him.

"Is everything okay?" I motioned for Johnny to stay by the doorway and out of earshot of Erica. I didn't want her to think there was any trouble still.

"I think so. He said he just wants to see Megan. He said he didn't want any trouble with me."

My heart sank. "Johnny, I'm tellin' ya, he's lied ta ya. He may not want trouble with you, but that won't keep him from driving me and the girls crazy. He couldn't care less about Megan. He uses her as an excuse to keep his hooks in me. I'm tellin' ya what I know. He just wants to keep me under his control like a caged animal. Johnny, don't believe a word of what he says."

"Janie, honey," he shook my hand and told me we could work this out, "I think he's calmed down."

"He speaks with forked tongue, Johnny. He's a snake in the grass. They don't come any slipperier than he is. Go on upstairs in my bedroom closet and get that brown envelope that's on the floor. It's full of reports and warrants for his arrest. After each episode, quick as anything he straightens up and talks the talk to the cops. They eat it up. They even agree with him. Then he'll come back to me and beat the hell outta me for callin' them. Don't trust him, Johnny. I'm tellin' ya what I know he's like, a snake, cold-blooded."

"Well, I think he's calmed down for tonight anyway. How are the girls?"

"They're playing. Erica kept Megan amused while I got dinner ready. Do ya want some?"

"Sure. Are we gonna eat on the floor?"

"I guess we'll have to. We don't have a table other than that coffee table. Why don't ya git a blanket. We'll tell Erica it's a picnic."

I walked to the kitchen to fill the plates. As I spooned the food, I heard the front door crash open.

Michael!

"I demand to see my daughter and I ain't leavin' here till I do." He was yelling as he ran down the hall and found me in the kitchen. His face was contorted with rage.

"Michael, why do you keep coming here? Michael, you're destroyin' our life. Just leave us alone!" My heart was pounding fast in my chest.

"I ain't leavin' you bitch till I git my daughter." Michael spun around and saw Megan with Erica by the couch. He strode toward her. I jumped on Michael's back like a provoked bear protecting her cubs. He wasn't leaving with Megan! If I had to, I'd fight him to my death.

In a fury, Michael threw me off his back, slammed me to the floor, and drove his foot hard into my stomach. I felt the air leave my lungs and my head get hazy. Johnny came up from behind him as I tried to breathe normally and prayed the room would stop whirling.

"I thought we had this worked out," Johnny said in dismay.

"What did you come back for?"

I crawled over to the girls who were both screaming. I knew there was going to be a brawl. Johnny and Michael stood eyeing each other. I carried the girls upstairs to their room just as the fight broke out. I closed their door behind me and listened to them scream and yell as they clashed and knocked each other around and trashed the place. The noise rumbled through the ceiling. Erica stood next to me crying. We couldn't escape the racket. We couldn't escape at all. I knew I had to get the police, but I was afraid to leave the girls even to cross the street to dial 911 from the phone by the pool. I was afraid that instead of coming for Michael they'd arrest me for deserting my children. Mom had told me they had laws like that. But I had to get help. I'd seen Michael violent many times, but tonight he was in a fury. Somehow I knew he wasn't going to quit and someone could get seriously hurt.

"Erica," I said. "Mommy's got to use the nine-one-one phone over at the pool to call the police. You stay here with Megan and watch her while I go. Keep this door locked and don't let anybody in but me. If anybody knocks, just yell out the window and I'll come right back, okay?"

She looked confused and frightened, but she seemed to know what to do. I kissed her on the lips and locked her door behind me. As I ran down the stairs, out of the house, and over to the phone, I kept wishing my kids' lives were different. You try to teach them not to fight or hurt other people and then the police just look the other way and destroy what you taught your kids. "It ain't right," I cried as I ran.

Trying to open the pool house door, I was stymied. It was locked. There was no way to get in and use the phone. I didn't know any of my new neighbors. "What am I gonna do? God, I can't stay out here long. What if Michael knocks Johnny out and gets to one of the girls, or both of them? I'd never be able to live with myself."

I ran back to the front door, yanked it open, and went

straight to the living room to tell Johnny about the phone.

"I tried to call the police but the phone at the pool is locked up. You'd better call for help." I was nearly out of breath, but I managed to get to the kitchen as Johnny ran out the front door.

Michael came at me. I snatched the silverware drawer open and pulled out the biggest knife I could find just as he rushed through the doorway.

"Don't take another step," I cried. Then I screamed, "Get out of here. Don't take another step toward me." Michael had never seen me this furious. My wild eyes seemed to scare him enough for him to draw back to consider his options. For a few minutes he just stood there. He stepped out of the kitchen and eyed the front door as Johnny came back in.

"I called the police from the neighbors' house. They're on the way."

"They'll take you downtown when they get here," I reminded Michael. "There are warrants out for you. You've 'bout drove me and these kids crazy! I'm not playing, Michael. Git out!"

He took a few hesitant steps toward the door. He got there just as two policemen in a cruiser arrived. They ushered him outside. I watched as he walked calmly, just as he had so many times before, to the cruiser with Johnny right behind him. I raced upstairs taking three steps at a time. I flew to my closet, snatched up the warrant papers, rushed downstairs and out the door.

"Arrest him!" I called to the police. "I've got the papers right here! He's wanted in several counties for beating me up."

Michael didn't wait to give them an explanation. He took off running. One of the officers jumped from the car and ran down the street after him but, within seconds, Michael was out of sight. The other officer stepped out of the cruiser, holding his speaker phone and called for other cars to give chase. Johnny came up beside me and put a consoling arm around me as we explained to the officer what we'd been through all day.

"I have copies of two outstanding warrants from when he beat me before. He failed to appear and they issued warrants for his arrest. My attorney gave me these copies of the warrants. If ya check your city records, you'll find in spite of them Michael came to where I worked a few days ago and threatened me again. When my employers called the police, they said I had to get copies of these before they'll arrest him. Here they are. He's got two more in Greenup County for DUIs."

The officer looked over the warrants and seemed to take me seriously. "I'm worried about my partner," he said. "Wait here and I'll be right back."

Johnny and I went into the house to wait. "I'm going to check on the girls," I told him. Running upstairs, I pulled open their door. Erica sat scrunched up by the window with Megan on her lap. "Did they get Michael, Mommy?" she asked in a plaintive voice.

"Not yet, honey, but they're lookin'! Everything will be all right now. They'll git him. Me and your daddy are here, so don't you worry about nothin'. We'll be downstairs if ya need us."

"I love you, Mommy."

"I love you too, baby," I said, taking the baby from her and putting her down on the pallet. "Don't worry, everything will be fine now. Just try to git some sleep." Erica gave me a quick squeeze and ran back to her bed. This will be over soon, I thought. Tonight they'll get him. We'll be safe and he'll pay for wrecking our lives.

Johnny was at the bottom of the steps as I started down. He reached out his arms to me before I made it to the bottom, and I slipped comfortably between them. Thank God he's here. Thank God he still cares about us enough to deal with all of this. I looked into his eyes, but not a word was spoken. All the words in the world could not have said what his eyes revealed to me at that moment. Johnny was here and he was gonna stay.

As we held each other, I heard a car door open and footsteps approach the door. Prying myself from his arms, I rushed to the door. It was the two policemen. I threw the door open all the way.

"Did you find him?"

"I think so. We caught him just up the street. Could you come over to the cruiser and identify him for us?"

We walked down the path. I peered through the cruiser window. It was him. Michael stared at me silently, his eyes blazing. Finally, the police had him in custody. I turned my attention back to the officer. Meanwhile Johnny walked up to us and stood next to me. Just having him there gave me courage.

"Yes, officer, that's him," I said. "Thank God ya got him. Where are you gonna take him?"

"We're taking him downtown to book him."

"Do you need copies of these warrants?" I asked. "I want ya to keep him for a long while." Michael glared at me from inside the car, but taking a deep breath I went on. "He's wanted in two other counties."

"Let me tell you what to do," the officer began. "You get on the phone and call the jail. They need the numbers of those warrants to hold him. Call them and tell them we're on the way in with him."

"Yes sir. Thank you for your help. I'll sleep better tonight for it."

The officer returned to the car and drove away. As the distance between Michael and me grew, I felt only intense relief. Finally, after all this time, peace had come. I tilted my head back and let out a sigh. Up above I saw a blanket of stars and thanked the heavens for our release. Johnny turned to me and pulled me close to him.

"Let's go in."

"No. I need to go make the call to the jail and I need to do it right away. I don't want to take any chances, Johnny. Will you stay with the girls?"

"Of course. Where are your car keys?"

"I think they're in my purse. I'll git 'em." I rushed back

inside and got my keys, still clutching the warrant papers in my hands. Johnny met me at the door.

"Do you want me to make the call?"

"No. They're my warrants; this is my mess and I'm ready to git it cleaned up. I need to do this myself," I said. "I hope you understand."

He nodded.

"Will you check on the girls for me? Make sure they're covered up. Oh, and check the thermostat. The air-conditioning is probably more confused than I am the way we've been openin' and closin' the door all night. It might be too cold for the girls."

Johnny walked me to the car and started back to the apartment. As I got in I stared at the front door. Johnny was waving as I put on the headlights and shifted into gear. Just one more hurdle to clear, I thought. I'll get our lives back yet.

CHAPTER 2

Another
Place

A t the drugstore I telephoned the jail, just as the police had instructed me. I felt reassured when they informed me they were booking Michael. I hung up the phone, got back into my car, and drove back to my apartment to Johnny and the girls.

As I looked around surveying the wreckage, I felt discouraged. I had more work to do than I'd started with that morning. The place was thoroughly trashed from Michael's brawl. Even though it was late, I was determined to at least put Megan's crib together. I couldn't stand the thought of her sleeping on the floor again.

"Did you make the call?" Johnny asked before I reached the top of the stairs.

"Yeah. Are the girls okay?"

He nodded. "But you should look in on Erica. She was afraid Michael would hurt you while you went to use the phone. She's really scared."

I went directly to her room and opened the door. Erica, her eyes as wide as a frightened fawn, jumped and let out a startled squeak when I entered. She was clearly shaken by the events of the day. I knew she was trying to act like a big girl when she told me, "Don't worry about me and Megan. I'll sleep with one eye open in case Michael comes after us."

Despite my inner turmoil, I reassured her. "Don't worry, little one," I said. "He's in jail and they ain't going to let him go. We've both been waiting a long time to be safe, but now we will be."

Johnny started carrying in Erica's bed from the trunk of my car as I readied the girls for the night. I fed them and took extra time with them, speaking softly and caressing them gently as we went through the bedtime ritual. I knew that even the baby could sense the turmoil around her and they badly needed some sense of protection restored. I'd tried to explain to Michael how frightening it was for the children when he'd beat me, but the children's welfare was never his concern. Nor was mine for that matter. He'd beat me just because dinner was five minutes late or the kitchen floor had a smudge on it or I got the creases pressed wrong on his clothes. When I'd stand up to him and try to tell him how wrong he was, he'd just become more violent.

It didn't matter who was around either. Even the police looked away most of the time. But this time I'd collected my evidence and now they would punish him.

"Janie, do you have any tools? I'll start putting Megan's crib together for you," Johnny yelled from below. He was already a step ahead of me on the night's chores.

"No, I usually put her crib together with a butter knife and a hard-soled shoe," I laughed. "I'll bring 'em on up in a second." It was almost midnight as I helped him put the last nuts and bolts in our Megan's crib.

As we put the fitted sheet on the bed, Erica asked for a drink of water, which reminded me that I needed to put a fresh diaper on Megan. After I'd finished putting on their pajamas and giving them both one last kiss, Johnny and I said good night to them, closed the door, and walked quietly downstairs to the living room.

"We're lucky. Those girls are special," Johnny said as we reached the bottom of the stairs. I nodded, too tired to speak, and walked straight to the couch where I collapsed for a few minutes and tried to forget I still had a lot of work to do.

"What do you want, my Her, something to drink, a beer, coffee, tea?"

My Her. I hadn't heard that expression in years. It was a pet name Johnny called me after we got our first wedding present, a set of his and hers towels. After we opened them, he held them up and announced, "This is for my little 'Her,'" and it stuck. Whenever he felt affectionate, frisky or fretful, that's what he called me, Her.

"It's been years since you've called me Her. What brought that on?"

"I just feel comfortable. I feel like relaxing. Don't be so uptight, Janie. I want you to relax, baby."

"Johnny, how can I relax? Look at this place. The furniture is turned over, there's junk everywhere, and I still have to unpack the rest of our stuff."

"Janie, I'll help. Just relax, baby. My little Her has always been such a worrier." He put his head back on the couch and plumped the pillows for me. We were alone and there were many things we needed to talk about. I let my head fall back on the couch. While Johnny stroked my hair, some of the day's tensions seemed to fade.

"It's been a long, long time, my Her. How have you managed holding a job with two kids and a maniac like Michael around?"

"It's not been easy. I tried every way in the world to get away from him. He's been carryin' on like this for months. No matter what I do, it doesn't stop. Let's talk about somethin' else. I wanna put Michael out of my mind, at least for now."

Silence took over the room as I kicked my legs up on the coffee table. Johnny seemed absorbed in deep reflection for a few minutes but then he began speaking slowly.

"I feel a little timid right now. I hardly know what to say."

"You, timid?" I said with a laugh. Johnny being described as timid or anything close to it made me chuckle. "Mr. Rude and Aggressive is how you used to introduce yourself."

"But, I . . . well . . . it's because I'm with you again. I've been so far from you, so far from your arms. These years have been difficult. I've missed you, Janie. You've always meant the world to me, and I feel a little awkward."

"Is that why you never remarried, 'cause you still missed me?"

"How could I remarry? There isn't a woman in the world like you. You've always held my heart. You laughed at my jokes and supported my art and music. Most of all, you gave birth to our precious little girl and you've taken excellent care of her, Janie. You're such a good mother. I could never thank you enough for that."

"I hardly know how Erica's turned out the way she has after what Michael's put us through," I said wearily.

"Why did you stay with him?"

"I needed his money. It's hard to keep a house and two little ones on minimum wage or waitress's tips."

"I didn't mean that in a bad way, Janie. I know I've been away. I haven't sent you money like I should have. My family kept me up on how you were. I wanted to be with you. I wanted to stay in touch, but the longer I stayed away the harder it was to call, and what would I say? Call collect to tell you I hadn't made it yet? I had to get away to find work. I kept trying to find something decent and thinking I was going to send for you when I did."

"I been trying to get by," I told him. "And I did for a while. I bought those houses and had money in the bank. Had a few CDs for a rainy day. But when the rain came the law kept me from getting out of the storm."

"What do you mean, the law kept you in a storm?"

"Johnny, Michael started beating the hell out of me right after I got pregnant with Megan. I was determined not to live like that, so I called an attorney. I figured I had saved a little money and had some property from Grandma, so I could get by until after she was born. But the attorney said I couldn't get a divorce 'cause I was pregnant. It didn't make sense to me. I told the attorney that Michael was beating me, but he just kept repeating that I couldn't get a divorce until after the baby was born. Kentucky law, he said. Period, amen. What could I do? I was already pregnant, and I wasn't goin' to have an abortion. So I had to tough it out. What choice did I have?"

"Why couldn't you move away?"

"Because in Kentucky a man has a right to live with his wife, wherever she is. He can get a key to her house by court order."

"Why didn't you call me?"

"I really thought Michael would change back to how he was before we married. He treated me and Erica like princesses, flowers every Friday, and champagne bubble baths on the weekend. Damn, was I fooled!"

"How could you marry someone like him?"

"That's odd," I laughed, "my parents said the same thing when I married you."

Johnny slid back burrowing deep into the couch.

"I didn't mean for that to come out so harsh," I said. I searched for a way to explain my remark. "But life's been real hard for me and the kids."

I looked searchingly at him. "My parents didn't understand art or music. They just worked and existed. Mom lived for being Dad's keeper, and Dad worked to keep her. That was it. I wanted more. I still do. I wanted what we had, what you shared with me. I loved you so much, Johnny. I can't tell you the times I've fallen asleep cryin' and wishin' you were here. I thought you'd just left and forgot all about us."

Tears rose in my eyes. "I prayed all those years. I hoped you'd come back and things would change. I really didn't mind living poor. We had fun despite the hard times. But, when Erica came, I had to shift my concerns to her. I don't want to blame anyone for what happened to us. I . . ."

"It's okay, honey. Don't cry. I've shed enough tears for both of us, my Her."

I couldn't stop myself from saying it. "All these years I thought you were away because you were preoccupied with other things. I didn't know. It made me feel like maybe I should have tried harder, but I did what I had to do for Erica."

He nodded. "I know."

"I've spent my whole life trying to live up to everyone's expectations. First, my parents thought I was too young to marry you. Then, after our divorce, they said I should marry again so Erica would have a father figure. Then trouble came, violent trouble. Michael was as ruthless as they come. He'd beat me just to watch me beg him to stop. I thought I did the right thing getting another husband, but it turned out wrong, awfully wrong. I didn't want things to get like this. I've lived through hell, and I'm tired. I'm tired of living this way. I just want to get the children's lives and my own life together." I paused. The pain, anger and rage I'd held in for so long was starting to boil over, and I had to get it out. As embarrassing as it was for me to have Johnny see me this way, I knew it was okay. If there was ever a shoulder I could cry on, it was his. He knew I was strong for the children's sake, but I needed to tell him at what price my strength had come.

He looked at me compassionately. "Janie, I love you, you should know that. I know I'm not perfect. I know I haven't kept working, but hell, there's a recession out there. Maybe I can get something here. I'll get a job doing something. We'll start again. We'll try to make it work."

"Johnny, I need to find things out for myself and see what I can do on my own. I don't want to get into another relationship right now. I'm still trying to pay off this divorce. Michael hasn't given me a penny of child support or paid a dime to his attorney, so I got to pay that too before they'll make our divorce final. I'm bustin' my butt workin' two jobs and tryin' to find time to spend with the girls while he chases me down like a hunted animal!"

"I know, honey. I know you've had a difficult time."

"No, you don't know how hard it's been." I shook my head. "I have to take care of my kids and I've had to try to live with a violent jerk like Michael while everybody wants to judge me for things not workin' between us. They always blame it on me!"

I began to cry uncontrollably. Johnny went to the kitchen to get me some water. He held the glass to my trembling lips as I took a sip. I could hardly breathe, my chest felt so tight. I looked away as Johnny stroked my hair and tried to look into my swollen eyes, but I wouldn't let him. I felt needy, but I wanted to be independent and learn how to live on my own. I wanted to be alone to think things through.

"Janie, honey," he said gently, "I don't want to hurt you, I want to help. We don't have to rush things, we don't have to make plans, we don't need to go over everything that's ever hurt us, or how we've hurt each other for that matter. That's all behind us. We don't need any more pain. Let's just take it slow this time. I'll get a job, help you with the girls, and maybe you can go to school and take a class or two. It'll be different this time. We're not kids anymore. We've both grown."

"But, Johnny, I've never been a child. We were married when I was a teenager. I was just a baby. But, if Michael was to find out you were gonna stay here he'd have the kids taken from me. I can't take that risk."

"Yeah, but you can't run the risk of him coming around and beating on you all the time, either. I'll stay in your basement. We'll be housemates, and that way I'll get to see Erica."

I laughed. "Johnny, when have you and I ever been able to stay in the same house and not sleep together? You know how strong the passion is between us. Every time you touch me I tremble. You've always done that to me. Do you honestly think that we can stay here and keep our hands off each other?"

"I can sleep in the basement!" Johnny began to clown around then. His eyes widened excitedly and his tongue wagged. I knew he wanted me to loosen up and laugh.

"You idiot," I said. "I'm trying to be serious and you're actin' a fool. Johnny, I don't want any more trouble with the law. I want to get this horrible part of my life over with as soon as I can. I want you here with Erica. I hope you can stay around. But first I need to get on with things."

"And I'm going to help you, my Her. You know I won't ever hurt you or the girls."

"I want to take it slow," I said.

"I know I've been foolish sometimes, but I promise, Janie, it's not going to be that way this time. I'll go as slow as you need."

"I wish I could believe you, Johnny. It's so hard to believe anybody or anything anymore. I feel so broken and afraid."

"I know you must after what you've been through but, after this is over with Michael and your divorce is final, you got your whole life ahead of you. I'm not going to pressure you. I'm just here to help.

"Janie," he continued, serious now, "we can start over. I know the past is gone, but we can get on our feet and start again. You are the air I breathe. Won't you let me back in? Just to lay with you, just to hold you, run my fingers through your long silky hair, feel your skin against—"

"Johnny," I interrupted, "let's just take it slow. When I'm near you I'm weak. I want to hold you right now, but I'm afraid, afraid of touching you or anyone."

"Let me hold you," he said. "I want you so much. We have forever. I don't want to make you feel pressured or uncomfortable. We'll be together. Don't look away from me, honey. Don't turn my heart away."

My own heart felt tender. I knew if I cared for anyone and if anyone in this world cared for me, it was Johnny. I cried on his shoulder for some time as he rubbed my back and ran his fingers through my hair. His gentleness chased away my apprehension. Delicately, Johnny drew back and looked into my eyes.

"I love you, my Her," he said. "I'm going to help. We'll get through this. We just have to take our time."

CHAPTER 3

Gunfire

It was late when Johnny and I parted for the night. He bedded down on the sofa. With Michael finally behind bars, I slipped into a dreamless sleep and felt a release I hadn't had in months. It seemed like I'd hardly dozed off when Erica came into my room and called me.

"Mommy, Daddy wants your car keys so we can go to the store and get something for breakfast." Erica was so excited to be with her daddy again. Johnny probably hadn't slept but an hour and already she had him up and going. Before I could even sit up or wipe my sleepy eyes, Johnny poked his head into the room.

"Good morning, my little sleepyhead." It had been years since he had awakened me with that playful and catering voice. "What do you want for breakfast, doughnuts or sweet rolls?" he asked, remembering that I craved sugar in the morning.

"Raspberry crullers," I said as I pulled myself up carefully so as not to wake Megan. I rolled over from the pallet I'd been using as a bed for me and Megan and began the search for my purse. She stirred slightly as I slipped my arm out from under her head. I was careful not to wake her.

Thoughts of last night flooded my mind as I searched for my purse which held my car keys. Finally I found it under the mixture of clothes, sheets, shoes, pictures, and baby items lying tangled in a heap. Sifting through the wreckage, I found the keys and handed them to Johnny.

"Do you have money?" I asked him as I grabbed for a shirt and pushed some other things back into the pile.

"Yeah, I still have a couple of dollars. Is there food for supper?"

"I think there's somethin' down there I can whip up. I gotta work tonight, so I'll have some tip money and with any luck I can grab the leftovers from the restaurant before they throw 'em out." I thought for a moment, then added, "But maybe ya oughta get some soup for Erica. Oh, and Megan needs some formula. Can you get some?"

"Sure. What kind?"

"Similac with Iron. Ya want me ta write it down?"

"No, honey, you take it easy. I'll get the name off the can in the fridge." He pushed back the hair from my eyes as he gazed deeply at me. "You get some rest. I'll take care of everything. Do you want me to take Megan and give you a break?"

"No, she'll be fine."

Johnny stooped beside the baby and covered her as she slept. I was touched by the way he was calling me honey again and felt even more comforted when I saw how gently he treated Megan.

"She looks so much like you, Janie, it's incredible," he said as he brushed the back of his hands across her chubby cheeks and onto her coal black hair. He stared for a minute and kissed her on the cheek. "Sleep well, little one."

"Are you ready, Daddy?" Erica was anxious to go.

"Yeah, let's be off, baby," Johnny said as he put the keys in his pocket and placed her hand in his. He turned toward me and smiled. "We'll be back soon."

"Be careful. I don't have insurance. That car's been on fire a few times and some of the controls have a mind of their own."

As they left, Megan started to fuss, wanting a feeding. Cradling her in my arms, I walked down the stairs and into the kitchen to warm a fresh bottle. As I stood there, my whole body ached. I have to work today no matter what, I thought. I should probably call my attorney and tell him the police have Michael. At least I don't have to worry about Michael showing up at my job.

When the bottle was ready, I returned to my room carrying the baby and sat on the floor cuddling Megan as I fed her. Watching her, I wished I could've kept breast-feeding her as I had Erica, but there was no way it was possible when I had to work two jobs.

As I held her, I felt my eyes getting heavy. For the first time in too long I felt at peace. I looked at Megan whose eyes were closing and saw she too was drifting off to sleep. I touched her soft cheek. She was beautiful, and I was happy that Johnny had taken to her. After the feeding, lying back on the pallet next to her, I slept again.

Sometime later Erica came in, said something softly, shook me, whispered in my ear again, shook me again, but, exhausted, I was in far too deep a sleep to hear what she said.

I said, "In a minute, honey. Mommy will get up in a minute. I promise." But in my exhaustion I rolled away from her and fell back into unconsciousness.

Only a short time seemed to elapse when, suddenly, loud exploding noises and terrifying shrieks broke into my unconscious state. I bolted straight up on the pallet. It sounded like Johnny screaming. "Oh my God! Oh my God!" he cried out. I looked over at Megan who was still fast asleep.

Jumping up, I jerked open my bedroom door. The sight which greeted me made my heart stop for a second, then pound furiously. Johnny lay sprawled on his back across the stairwell in front of my bedroom. Blood gushed from his mouth. My ex-husband stood on the second step down from the top, his face twisted with hate and rage. He was pointing a gun at Johnny. I stood there in shock and tried to think, but my mind and body seemed paralyzed. From a distance, I could hear the fire of Michael's gun as he pulled the trigger, again and again and again, taking deadly aim at Johnny as he lay there flinching with each pull of the trigger, like he was convulsing. When Michael's wild eyes saw me, he shifted his gun to aim at me. His eyes said I would be next.

Then instinctual self-preservation kicked in.

"Oh God!" I cried. "Oh Jesus! What the hell am I gonna do?" I slammed my door frantically, locked it, and tried to think of a possible way out. Somebody help us, I prayed. I realized I had to get my girls. I grabbed Megan and eyed the window. I thought about jumping out the window with Megan, figuring we'd probably survive the two-story drop. But where was Erica? How? What? Even if Megan and I could get out through the window, I'd be leaving Erica behind. There was no way I could leave her to face Michael with a gun in his hand. I had to get her out, too.

Suddenly I heard her voice outside my bedroom door. "Please," she was crying, "don't kill my mommy! Don't kill my mommy! Please! Don't! Don't do it! Don't kill my mommy!" Erica was shrieking in terror. I could hear her fragile limbs stomping fiercely against the floor as Michael tried to bash his way in.

In all the terror and confusion I hadn't seen that Erica was still out there with Michael.

By now he was kicking his way through the thin plywood of my bedroom door. If it meant my death, I knew I had to get to Erica. I had to try to save her or there'd be no reason for me to live.

An instant later, Michael's foot busted though the door. I realized nothing was going to keep him out. I had to confront him. Grabbing the doorknob, I flung open the door.

Instantly, I felt a cold swift wind sweep across my face as he whipped his gun into firing position at my forehead. As I stood staring down the barrel of his gun he had cocked and aimed at me, I was convinced I was about to die.

"Please, just let me git the girls out," I pleaded, holding Megan tightly against my body. "Just let me git 'em out, Michael. They don't need to see this. Don't make 'em watch me die."

Near my feet where Johnny lay, I heard a gurgling sound. I wanted to look, I wanted to reach down and touch Johnny to see how badly he was hurt, but I didn't dare take my eyes off Michael's gun. Oh God, help me, I prayed. Suddenly, a knock at the front door distracted Michael for a second.

Michael recoiled, pressing his body to the wall and out of sight from whoever was knocking. The distraction gave me a chance to lean over slightly and peer down the stairwell. I could dimly see a figure through the beveled glass, but I couldn't tell who it was.

"Whoever it is, they're not going away," I said, trying to rattle Michael.

"It don't make any difference. I'm going to kill you, and then I'm going to kill myself," he hissed as he pointed the gun toward my face. I knew this was not just posturing. He'd just shot Johnny, a virtual stranger, and I was the one he really wanted to kill. Michael looked me straight in the eyes, his gun still shoved in my face, ready to end my life while the bangs on the door continued.

Quickly, I searched my mind for a way the girls and I could get out of there and survive this nightmare. Through my mind raced questions. How many bullets had he fired? How many does his gun hold? What do I know about guns? I've never even held one. Is it a six-shooter? How many bullets are left? Is there one bullet for me and one for him? Can I possibly talk him into letting us go, or at least the girls? Or if I provoke him more will he kill us all? Oh God, how could he do this. Why hadn't the police kept him behind bars? Would he torture me by forcing me to watch him kill the girls? Would I be the last one killed?

Just then an especially ferocious banging at the door

seemed to really throw Michael off. He looked agitated and desperate as the sound persisted. I took advantage of his distraction and began to inch my way toward the landing in hopes of reaching the steps where I could be seen by whoever was knocking, but he caught me.

"Don't take another step or I'll waste you," Michael snarled.

"I ain't leavin'," I said. "I swear. I just want to git the girls out." I knew he wanted me dead, he had told me that so many times before. I thought if I could convince him I was moving toward the door to let the girls out, then he could have his way with me.

"Oh, Mommy, please git us out! I want ya to come, too! Please, please, don't kill my mommy," Erica begged as she ran from the doorway of her room. I hoped he wouldn't fire at her or me. She slid her small, slight body by Michael, stepped over Johnny, and ran to my side. Michael didn't look at her; his focus was clearly on me. She clung to my leg and I could feel her body quiver as we started to cross over Johnny's body. I was desperate to hold him, while he took what might be his last dying breath. My heart was pulling me toward his body, but my mind pushed me on step by step with the girls clutched in my arms. I had to get them out. My weakened legs could hardly carry the load as I stepped over him. Here he lay mortally wounded and I couldn't even take a minute to caress him, to tell him that I loved him. To feel his soft curls in my hands. To make his hurt go away. To lay with him on what might be his deathbed. To tell him that I had always loved him and always would. God, give me just another minute. Don't take Johnny away. Don't take him. I'll get out. I'll get help. Just be still, Johnny, I'll get help. My voice wasn't working. I wasn't even sure if I was breathing. My heart was all I could feel and I thought it was going to break. I forced myself to think. I had to concentrate on getting the girls out alive.

The knocking at the door pounded on as I shifted my way down the stairs trying hard not to provoke Michael. With both girls fixed to my body and my arms wrapped around them, I couldn't use my hands to shield my face from the gun Michael still pointed at me. He watched my every move. I felt my blood run cold. With each step I took I wondered when he would kill me. Just a few more steps. I've got to get there. Don't move too quick, Jane, or he'll shoot. Erica dug her nails deep into my thigh as we stepped down another stair.

Reaching the bottom, I took small, hesitant steps toward the front door hoping the police and safety were on the other side. With Megan fastened to my right hip and Erica fused to my left side, I grabbed the knob with my right hand and opened the door slightly, intending to slip through. Suddenly, I felt a sharp jab of Michael's gun in my right side as I stretched my left hand over my head in a failed attempt to pry open the door.

"I said you're not leaving!" he snarled, exposing his glistening teeth as his left foot slammed the door on my fingertips. He pressed his body against me, trapping me between him and the closed door.

"Just let me git the girls out," I begged. My left hand throbbed painfully.

"We've got things to talk about, and no one's leaving here until we do."

Talking to him was the last thing I wanted. I had been married to him for one violent year, and I knew it was always his way or none at all. I had to somehow get away and bolt out of there with the girls. Again I jiggled the doorknob.

"I promise. I'm just gonna set 'em outside. You can kill me then." I'd grant his wish, I thought as I continued to struggle with the door. Michael shoved his gun deeper into my ribs and I heard the trigger click. No explosion. I felt no pain, but I could feel Michael's body relax slightly, as if his mission was complete. Thinking he had shot me and my body was beyond feeling pain, I shoved him back with all the force my 115-pound frame could muster. He stumbled over some unpacked boxes, then fell to the floor. Quickly looking over my shoulder, I yanked open the door and saw him thrashing in a wild and savage struggle to regain his footing. It was my chance. I burst out the door, both children in tow.

The thrust caused me to lose my balance. I fell to the pavement and felt the skin on my elbows and knees peel back. As hard as I tried to protect her, Megan's head hit the pavement with a bang. I lifted my head and caught sight of a woman police officer. Her gun was pointed at the door I had just come through.

"Get away from the door!" she shouted.

I snatched up Megan, who was crying but otherwise unhurt, and ran. I looked back over my shoulder and saw Erica panic-stricken, unable to move. Our fall through the door had separated us. She was frozen on the doorstep directly in the line of Michael's fire.

I had to convince her to follow us.

"Erica, honey, we're okay now. Come this way. Come over here with me and Megan." She didn't hear me. Her blank face looked directly at a male police officer. God, what if Michael shoots her?

"Erica, look at Mommy. I'm right here, come on. I'm right here, baby." I noticed her head seemed to turn in my direction and I had to get to her before Michael did. I inched closer to her.

"Get back there," the woman officer warned me.

"Erica, look at Mommy. Come with me. We're safe now." This time I got through. Her eyes caught mine and I motioned for her to come. She started easing off the step. She stumbled and looked at me. "Erica, come," I begged. Finally, she ran over to where we stood and collapsed in my arms.

"What about Daddy?" she asked. "We've gotta git him out. I know he's still alive, Mommy. His eyes were open! Tell 'em ta git him out, Mommy!" I too wanted to believe that somehow Johnny was still alive. I clung to that hope as we waited for the ordeal to end.

Suddenly, absolute strangers appeared, offering to take my girls to safety. I held them tight until Carol Portecelli, a neighbor we'd met when moving in, said she would keep them. A dark-haired police officer approached us as the blond, woman officer remained in front of the door with her gun cocked and aimed. The girls and I huddled together trying to comfort each other, but this new officer told me the children would be safer indoors. I kissed them goodbye and tried to assure Erica we would be safe now that the police were here. But she had seen police officers before. They had been called to help last night and they let Michael out of jail to kill us. Erica knew. She was not going away from my side. I handed Megan to the neighbor and convinced Erica she had to go. I pried her fingers from my arm and squeezed her hands tight and looked into her eyes.

"Honey, you have to go. It's safe there. I have to help the police get your daddy out." Reluctantly, she let go of my hand and went with the neighbor, her eyes glued in my direction as they walked to the woman's apartment.

The dark-haired officer grabbed my arm and moved me to the upper level of the parking lot. "More shots could be fired at you from the window," he explained. He told me that Michael had an accomplice he's met in jail who had been apprehended. I later learned that Michael's plan was to flee the crime scene in the accomplice's truck. Why would this man, a stranger to all of us, be so willing, even eager, to help Michael murder his estranged wife, another man, and maybe even two kids?

As I stood talking to the officer, I became self-conscious about wearing only the T-shirt and panties I had been sleeping in. I was grateful when a considerate neighbor handed me a pair of sweat pants. As I slipped them on, I couldn't contain my curiosity about the man who had so casually agreed to help Michael destroy lives.

"What's his name?" I asked the officer.

"Eric Carlyle. Do you know him?"

"Never heard of him," I said.

"He and Michael were released at the same time and, according to Carlyle, Michael asked him to drive him around, find a gun, and bring him here," he explained.

"My God, why didn't you keep Michael last night? I gave the arresting officer copies of two outstanding warrants, both from him beatin' me up back in Ashland. Plus I gave him the ID numbers for two warrants that were DUIs."

"He was booked for public intoxication," the officer replied, as if that were sufficient explanation. What about him beating the hell out of us all in my house?

"Public intoxication? After everything he did last night? After he ran from the police? After he beat me? Let alone the fight with Johnny, and how he trashed my apartment. The arresting officer even brought him to my front door and asked me to identify him before they carted him off. They told me to call the jail to make sure they wouldn't release him. I did everything I was told. Why didn't you keep him away from us? With four outstanding warrants, why did you let him out?"

In my fury, I continued to rattle off questions that remained unanswered as tears streamed down my face and burned my skin. I needed answers, but they never came.

Meanwhile, dozens of armored vehicles began surrounding us. A SWAT team, ambulances, and television camera crews assembled as the officer steered me to a cruiser, almost out of sight of my building. I got in the car and he introduced me to a ruddy-faced officer who needed information on the layout of my apartment. Since I hadn't yet had a phone installed, there was no way for the commander of the SWAT team to talk with Michael holed up inside.

"We need you to calm down, ma'am. We've got to have your cooperation if we're going to get that guy out of there."

I was on the verge of collapsing, but I tried to do as he asked. I described the floor plan of my apartment. "Inside, just to the right of the front door, is a staircase with wrought iron railing. At the top is my room and the hallway where Johnny is lying."

Suddenly, a picture of him lying there flashed through my mind. "Please, ya gotta hurry up and git in there! Johnny may still be alive!"

The ruddy-faced officer looked grim.

"He may very well be alive, ma'am, but we don't know if the gunman will try to kill one of our men. We need to proceed with caution so no one else is injured."

Another officer approached the car and leaned his head in.

"You probably saved you and your children's lives," he said to me.

His praise did little to relieve my stress. If they'd only helped me the night before, or the week before, or the month before, or all the other times Michael beat me or threatened to kill me, none of this would have happened. Pictures started to flash in my mind of the times Michael had humiliated me, the rejection, all the affairs I'd caught him in, and the endless beatings. The sun relentlessly poured through the windshield of the police car. I felt my concentration weaken as I tried to cooperate with the officers and answer their questions. My emotions were a grab bag of anger, resentment, fear, and grief. I kept thinking that even if Johnny were still alive, they'd have to get in soon or he'd bleed to death.

After over an hour of questioning, One policeman in combat dress said "We're moving in." Their plan was to shoot tear gas through the windows. If Michael didn't surrender, the SWAT team, outfitted in combat gear, would storm my apartment. As they stood ready for their commander's signal, I sat in the car, praying Johnny was still alive. Boom! Boom! Boom! I nearly jumped out of the car as each grenade of tear gas was blasted through my apartment windows. Even at this distance, I thought I was being shot at. I stretched my neck to see if Michael came out.

Within minutes, he was brought out in handcuffs and flanked by several policemen. They shoved him toward a police cruiser and loaded him into the back seat and drove off. Then the rudy-faced officer guarding me said I could get out of the car. I stepped out and within what seemed like seconds I was approached by a petite woman with blond-brown hair who introduced herself as

Kathleen Donovan, a crisis counselor with a local agency the police had called in for assistance.

"I know you've been through a great deal today," she said. "But I need to tell you about Johnny. He's dead. It appears he went fast. There was very little blood, which means his heart probably stopped right away. He suffered very little."

The woman telling me of Johnny's death was the bullet that Michael's gun had failed to fire. Nothing could have prepared me for what she said. I collapsed to the ground. Kneeling beside me, Donovan tried to console me as I sobbed. Then, helping me to my feet, she pulled me aside trying to shield my view from Johnny being removed in a bright blue body bag. But she couldn't. As I watched, I couldn't help thinking again that Johnny's death wouldn't have happened if the police had kept Michael in jail. I shed bitter tears. But there was little time to grieve or agonize with so many other immediate concerns to deal with. The most pressing one was, how was I going to break the news to Erica?

"Would you like me to go with you?" Donovan kindly offered. "I will help in any way I can."

I nodded yes.

"I need ya ta help me tell Johnny's daughter. She's at Carol Portecelli's, a neighbor just across the parking lot."

"Do you have a family doctor?"

"No, not here anyway. I got one back home."

"You should go see a doctor. Try to make arrangements for Erica to be looked at. She'll need help dealing with her father's death."

As we walked close to the building where the girls were, I thought of how difficult that suggestion might be. I didn't tell the woman we didn't have insurance. God knows how, where, or when we'd get to see a doctor.

"There is something else you should be aware of."

"What's that?"

"The officer mentioned that your children have different fathers."

I nodded.

"Well, since one father killed the other, you may want to observe them closely as they get older. They could have emotional difficulties. One could blame the other. Just keep an eye out."

Donovan tenderly supported my arm as we approached the neighbor's door, and I was grateful for her compassion about future problems. I just wanted to be with my kids so that I could comfort them now and worry about other such things later.

Erica had been anxiously waiting for my return. As soon as she saw me, she ran to me and hugged my neck with all her might.

"Are you all right, Mommy?" she asked as she looked at my tear-stained face.

I couldn't think of a way to soften the news. "I have something to tell you, honey. Your daddy didn't make it." Painfully, I watched her lower lip begin to quiver. Her tear-filled eyes looked pitifully into mine as she fought to talk.

"What do ya mean? Where is he? His eyes were still open when we left, Mommy. I know he's still alive!" The tenor of her disbelief was more pleading than angry as she buried her face into my shoulder and cried a cry no mother should ever have to hear from her child. At that moment, I felt utterly powerless to protect my child from pain. I pressed her close and we cried together. I had to let it out myself, but I had to keep enough strength within to support us both.

"I know it's hard for you to understand, honey, but Daddy has gone to heaven."

"You mean Michael killed him?" In her child's mind and, aware that Michael was Megan's father, suddenly her role as "big sister" took hold of her. Running across the room, she covered Megan's ears and whispered to me.

"Does Megan have to go with her daddy?"

"No, baby. The police have taken him away for a long, long time. He won't bother us again," I said, believing my words.

A beefy, dark-haired officer came to the door. "I'm Tim Moran," he said, "we need you to go downtown to police headquarters for questioning."

Erica began crying. "I'm afraid *he'll* be there and try to kill you, Mommy."

The officer assured her that nothing else would happen.

I hugged both my children as tightly as I could. "I love you both, and I'll be back soon ta git ya. Everything is gonna be all right," I told them. I looked long into Erica's eyes. Partly because I wanted her to be calm, and partly because I was afraid of the same fate she feared. What if they let Michael out again?

As I walked away with the officer, I turned my head and looked back. Erica was holding Megan in her arms so both of them faced me. She lifted Megan's baby hand in her own and moved it back and forth in a goodbye wave to Mommy. These girls loved each other so much, I thought as I moved toward the police cruiser. How could I possibly explain to them what had happened today, particularly to Megan, who would probably have no memory of it. What lay ahead of us, I wondered. How would Erica recover from this nightmare? How would she react to her half-sister, whose father had just killed her father? How could I tell Megan when she got older that her father was in jail for killing her sister's father? I dreaded the future I envisioned. As I was led to the cruiser and taken downtown for questioning thoughts of the past engulfed me.

CHAPTER 4

Hill Girl

Living in Appalachia without a husband made you a pariah and aroused suspicion among every other female in our radius. I had married my childhood love at seventeen, but youth and poverty had caused us to part. My family wanted me to remarry, if only to provide a father for my daughter.

My grandmother had a rental house she no longer could handle, so she sold the house to me for the mortgage. I loved my paradise and felt sure I could give Erica a good life, but my family and relatives made me feel guilty for not having a man around. Eligible bachelors were not easy to come by in the hill country since I had a child and was older than twenty-one. The good ones always seemed to be taken, or they wanted younger women without children.

Then I met Michael. A few weeks after our first date he began sending me roses, taking my laundry to the cleaners, and sending a woman to clean my house. When he took me to dinner, it started with a bottle of Dom Perignon and ended with a long night of dancing.

Michael was a fashion plate. He dressed in finely tailored suits, and his shirts were starched to perfection. He bought me silk dresses, insisting I should match his attire if I was going to be attached to his arm. Michael was a connoisseur of French cuisine, wines, and the good life; a very sophisticated man for a hillbilly from Appalachia. In no time Michael swept me off my feet with his charm and manners. And there were other benefits. With a man secured, I was no longer a threat to my married girlfriends, who worried I'd steal their husbands. Moreover, my family was relieved that their daughter was spoken for again.

Michael wasted no time explaining to me how hard he'd taken what he called his "awful second divorce." He said the marriage was short lived, but he didn't say much else. Michael did tell me about his first wife. They'd been married while in high school and had two children before they were twenty-one. Michael cried when he told me she had remarried shortly after their divorce and he was never allowed to see his children again. "It's been more than ten years since then, and I vow my next marriage will be different."

I wanted to believe that he would love me and Erica, but at times I was suspicious of his past. At his age, I thought there would have been other relationships, but he brushed my questions aside. He didn't explain why his marriages had fallen apart. I reasoned they grew apart at a young age, or maybe money was the problem. I never gave other possibilities much thought.

I didn't have time to think about it with my schedule of long working hours, taking care of Erica, and trying to keep up with Michael's social plans. Michael and I did everything together. We rarely left each other's side. Within months after we started seeing each other, Michael moved into my house.

I was surprised when all he brought was a shaving kit and two suitcases of clothes. I thought a man his age and with his love of fine things would've acquired more, a few pieces of furniture or some antiques or something. When I questioned his lack of possessions, Michael told me he didn't want to clutter my house with his belongings, so he'd left them at his sister's house. He said she needed them more than we did anyway.

After living a near honeymoon existence for almost a year, we decided to get married. We agreed that since Michael was ten years older than me and badly wanted another family, we should waste little time having a child together. Erica had begged me for years to give her a brother or sister. She was already five, and the puppy, kitten, rabbit, and stuffed animal collection I'd bought to pacify her sibling needs hadn't worked. Within weeks of our marriage, the pregnancy test turned positively pink and our little bundle of joy was on its way. We were both thrilled by the news but at times Michael seemed overwhelmed with becoming a father again.

As the weeks of pregnancy went on, his fuse grew shorter and shorter. The least little thing ticked him off. When I mentioned us attending childbirth classes, he didn't think he'd be comfortable. I asked him about his participation in his other children's births, and he said, "I wasn't around when they were born. That chore should be left to women."

I developed gestational diabetes followed by debilitating bouts of morning sickness. I grew increasingly weak and had difficulty holding down food. Despite this, one day Michael came to me with great urgency and announced, "Jane, pack your things. We're goin' on a trip."

"Where are we goin'?" I asked.

"Just do as I say," Michael snapped. "I just got off the phone with my other children. I've asked 'em to come live with us. Get busy packing."

I was shocked speechless. He'd never told me about any children and had never spoken to me with such disrespect. Within hours we were sitting in front of his ex-wife's house.

Michael wouldn't let me go into the house. He ran inside by himself, and moments later our trunk was loaded with his sons' luggage. After a short introduction, the boys scrambled into the car and we drove away. That quickly, I became the step-mother of a fifteen and a sixteen-year-old son.

I worked hard to adjust to the sudden change, but soon I

was witnessing a side of Michael I'd never seen before.

"I want you to be at home," he said. "Quit your job."

I needed more rest during my pregnancy and with the added housework brought on by our expanded family, I agreed. But money got tight. After a few attempts to talk things out, I tried not to bring up money matters because Michael would fly into a tantrum. He blamed me for our lack of funds. "Look at you sitting around all the time."

As the weeks passed and my stomach grew larger, keeping quiet grew more difficult. There were late notices from the utility companies in our mail followed by gas and electricity disconnects. I couldn't understand it. I'd written checks to pay these bills, so I was confused when the overdue statements arrived.

Finally, I asked Michael to look things over with me, but he stomped out of the house and did not come back until late. When bank statements came, I noticed that many of my checks had bounced because money had been withdrawn from a twenty-four-hour teller without my knowing it. By this time I was a nervous wreck. When I tried to confront Michael, he said he didn't know what was going on. He blamed the bank. He blamed me, insisting I couldn't handle money. I knew the salary he was making on his job, and I used my rental proceeds to help pay the bills. Still, the late notices kept coming.

I noticed Michael buying more and more new clothing, but when I outgrew my sweatpants and asked for maternity clothes, Michael told me to quit eating, disregarding my prenatal needs. "Cut strips in your pants to allow for your growing belly," he ordered.

Our debts made me increasingly alarmed. I began watching the mail more closely for signs of disappearing money. It wasn't unusual for Michael to come home for lunch, and he began working later and later at night. Gradually I began to notice a pattern. Most of my credit card statements (Michael didn't have credit cards; he said they were too much hassle) came on a certain day, as did the mortgage notices on my rental property. One day I saw Michael go to the mailbox, sort through the delivery, and stuff several envelopes into his pocket. I was becoming increasingly fearful. I said not a word when he walked in the door, but after he left for lunch I went to the post office and put a hold on our mail.

A few days later I discovered the horrific extent of the financial mess we were in. Not only had my credit cars been run up beyond their limit; they hadn't been paid in months. The payments on my rental property hadn't been made either, and the bank was threatening foreclosure. There were countless bounced check notices. After only a few days, I had amassed an enormous pile of evidence and presented it to Michael.

"What the hell are you goin' to do about it?" Michael snarled.

"Michael, I'm just tryin' to find out what's goin' on. I'm goin' to lose my property. Where'd this money go?"

"*Your* property?" Michael shouted. "What happened to *our* property? When we got married half of this became mine."

"All right. Then where's my half of the money from the rental property? Besides, the bank gets their payment first and *then* we spli—"

Smack! Michael hit me across the face with the back of his hand. I lifted my hand to my burning face. I couldn't move fast enough to escape the flying fist that smacked the other side of my face and created a room swirling before my eyes. When I fell to the floor, I tried to cover my pregnant belly as I lay there fearful of what would happen next.

"Stay there." Michael spit on me as he left the room. I didn't dare move for a few minutes, not until I heard the front door slam and the family car pull out of the drive.

After collecting myself, I searched the phone book for a divorce attorney. I made an appointment for the next afternoon. I made sure I could get Erica from school, stop the hold on our mail at the post office, and be back in time to get supper on the table.

At attorney Don Hayes's office, I sat in a numbed state as he explained, "You'll have to wait until after your baby is born to file for divorce." Hustling me out, he slapped me on the back and chuckled in amusement. "I don't know of a judge around here who would grant a divorce with one in the oven."

I didn't argue or question why. I didn't say anything. I was so shocked by his information. I just left. I drove home in a catatonic state.

"Where in the fuck have you been?" Michael yelled when I walked in the front door. "I've been waiting for two damn hours to go out. I was supposed to meet some people at the bar an hour ago, and I need a shirt ironed."

As I pulled out the ironing board, added water to the iron and turned it on high, I was counting my blessings that Erica hadn't blurted out where I'd been. I had left her a number to call if she needed me.

Since the law would not help me out of my hazardous home, I had to find another way to escape. After Michael fell asleep at night, I began sneaking a few dollars out of his pants pockets. I'd wait until he came home really drunk so he would have little recollection of how much he'd spent the night before. He wouldn't notice a few dollars here and there had disappeared.

My problem was where to hide it. He went through my purse daily, looking for money or pieces of paper with any kind of numbers written on them. If he found numbers scribbled anywhere, he'd go to the phone and dial them forwards and backwards. If that didn't go through, he tried to unscramble the numbers, thinking they were in code.

He'd come home every evening from work and go to the phone and press redial. I was now six months pregnant with his child and he screamed at me that I had another lover. It was very embarrassing explaining to the person he'd dialed what was going on. I'd try to cover his controlling behavior by telling the people he called that we were experiencing problems with our phone and were just trying to work them out. Other times I told the people at the other end that we had a new phone with automatic dialing and I was programming in their numbers.

After each call I made during the day, I dialed Time and Weather or rang up Dial-a-Prayer. Of course it didn't take long for Michael to realize I'd gotten the better of him temporarily. After catching on, he gave me a more vicious beating, reminded me what a disobedient wife I was, and disconnected the phones and took them with him every time he left the house.

When I wasn't "fetching" for Michael and his boys, I was in tears, worried senseless about Erica, my unborn child, and myself. The only rest I got was after Michael beat me and he stormed out the door and left for the night. Afterward he'd apologize for his abusive actions, but he expected me to respond to his generosity by having sex with him or rubbing his feet or both.

"Give your old man a good foot rub, will you, darlin'?" he'd command. I believe he thought I should feel privileged to serve him. During this endless upheaval, I tried desperately to take care of myself during pregnancy, sustain the family needs, and keep Erica shielded from Michael's aberrant behavior. I was trapped. I had to focus and maintain my senses until we could get away. Unfortunately, when a follow-up letter from the attorney came indicating he'd be glad to handle my divorce after delivery, Michael intercepted it and went berserk.

"You think you're going to leave, do ya?" he yelled. "Who'd want a bitch like you?" Slap, bang, thud! My body landed on the floor just as the kids were coming in from school. They stood in the doorway with wide eyes as Michael tore my clothes off.

"Look at this!" he screamed at his sons, pointing at my near naked body. "See why I screw other women! Who would want to sleep with a fat bitch like this!" I tucked my head between my knees trying to cover myself and protect my protruding abdomen. Michael kicked me in the back, then charged past the kids out the front door to the car. He didn't return that night.

When he came in the next morning, he quickly removed his shirt and handed it to me with lipstick stains facing me like a trophy he had won. He told me, "Go wash it before it dries." I did as I was told. For the rest of the day Erica and I kept out of his path. Hours later, he tried to make up with me, or at least talk to me. But he didn't apologize for what he'd done, and I didn't confront him with it. I'd already learned what would happen to me if I pressed the wrong button.

I waited for days before I'd get the nerve to ask him anything. Sometimes, when his blatant wrongdoing was more than I could handle, I would take my chances. Once I asked him why he insisted on taking his sons, both under age, to bars. He smiled and answered, "I teach them how to pick up women. They won't have to work hard if they can charm a woman with money."

I lowered my eyes to the floor subserviently, but inside I seethed. The rage in me grew, but fear and good sense told me to bide my time. Just don't get hurt. Just don't let him hurt the children, I told myself. Then you can run.

Meanwhile, Michael's sons told me about Michael's secret past. I'd already grown leery to the point where I wouldn't confide in or question Michael about private matters. His sons told me that their father had several other children and that he had been married at least three other times. I agonized for days and nights when I realized how much I'd been deceived. During our courtship Michael had acted like a total gentleman, but once we married I became his slave. Married, everything I was and everything I possessed became his to do with as he pleased.

Panic set in. I wanted to get out while Erica was young and was hopefully unscarred by Michael's brutality. But with the laws as they were, all I could do was work to preserve peace.

When Michael came home, he continued to walk straight to the phone and push redial and wait for the call to be answered, trying to spy on who I'd been talking to. Once I'd been talking with my mom, and when he dialed it back and my younger brother answered, all hell broke loose.

"Who was the guy you were just talkin' to?" Michael demanded.

"I was talkin' to my mom, not some—"

Smack! He knocked me down. Each time I tried to get up he hit me again. After awhile I learned how to survive.

I learned to keep my mouth shut, the house spotless, the clothes pressed, and dinner appetizing and timely. But no matter how perfect I kept things, Michael found fault. I didn't mind the nights he went out, probably to be with other women, but I no longer cared. I'd rest and be out of harm's way. On the nights Michael stayed home, his moods varied. Occasionally he was affectionate, but increasingly he was violent and hateful. Often he tried to pick fights so he could brutalize me. I had little control over these violent outbursts. I had to ride them out, protect my unborn child, and hope that I'd live long enough to get Erica, the baby and I away from him.

Michael's merciless beatings increased perversely. Knocking me to the floor wasn't enough for him anymore. He chased me through the house, pulling my hair, dragging me up and down the stairs by my feet. Bald spots appeared on my scalp. I had to experiment constantly with new hair styles to camouflage the hideous signs of abuse.

Meanwhile, I had to put on a happy face when we went out or when people stopped by for visits. If his mom came by, she'd usually call first. If my face was bruised or I walked with a limp, Michael made me hide in our bedroom until she left. When his brothers came over it was different. If one dared ask what had happened to my face or noticed swollen ankles or bruises shaped like hands around my throat, Michael would brag about them.

"Somebody's got to keep her in line," he'd tell them, as if his brutal work was a great deed. "It's my duty to show these sons o' mine how to handle women. What's a father for?"

None of them asked if I was okay. They'd shake their heads up and down as if they understood the necessity of a man's duty.

As my pregnancy advanced, my trips to the doctor became more frequent. If I was badly bruised before a visit, Michael would call and reschedule my appointment. He explained to the receptionist that he had an important business meeting he couldn't miss. Acting as if he was concerned, he'd tell her how much he wanted to be included in the birthing experience.

More often than not, Michael stayed out all night when he went out drinking. When he did come home the next day, he'd be broke and would have to wait on another paycheck or for one of my rent checks to come in. Several times, when he was really broke, he'd look in the paper in the Merchandise Wanted ads. He'd call and see what the people would give for whatever he found of value around the house, which was all my previous marital property. He'd have the people come to the house, pick up the item, and he'd make a deal with me. As long as I didn't cry or tell them what he was up to, Michael promised he wouldn't beat me.

Strangely, he kept his promise, and the worry of injuring my unborn child kept me silent while all I'd ever worked for was hocked or sold to finance Michael's pleasures. It was a sick trade off, but it worked.

As I watched my possessions disappear, I worried how I'd finance the children's and my getaway. With Michael selling most everything of value, I knew there would be little left for Erica, the baby and I.

Every chance I got, I gave my sister Beth some keepsake to hide. When Michael came home drunk, I'd continue to snatch a few dollars from the pocket of his pants left on the floor for me to pick up. Since I couldn't put the money in my purse or in my bra for safekeeping, I had to find a place that only I knew, where he'd never think of looking.

I rolled the bills tight and slipped them under the draw string of my ironing board cover. I'd never seen a man touch that woman's tool. I knew the money would be safe.

I was nervous and embarrassed every time I went to my doctor. I knew if she noticed the bruises across my body she would want an explanation. Michael went with me and waited until after my exam with Dr. Collins. Then he was ushered into her office, seated next to me, and informed of the progress of my pregnancy. Michael acted so interested. His Jekyll and Hyde act amazed me and made me sick. He pretended to be a good husband instead of our family's resident terrorist.

The first time Dr. Collins spotted several obvious bruises on my face and body, I felt humiliated when she asked me why.

"Jane, has someone been hurting you?" Dr. Collins asked calmly as she measured my belly and listened for the baby's heartbeat.

"Well, I've had trouble with my husband," I said shamefully. "I tried to leave him and get a divorce, but the lawyer said I couldn't until after the baby's born. I'm doin' the best I can till then."

"Have you tried the local abuse shelter?" she asked.

"No, well, I can't. Ya see, Michael's cousin works there and he said he knows where it is. Plus, I could only stay there thirty days, and I've got that much more to go until I have this baby. Michael reminds me of his shelter connection every time he hits me. He said I shouldn't think of runnin' off there. He says he'll find us if we try. I don't believe his cousin would tell him, but Michael knows where it is and I'm sure he'd trace me there."

"Have you considered the risks you're taking?"

It's a risk either way, I thought. I constantly feared that Michael's beatings would hurt my unborn child, but I couldn't tell the doctor. Overcome with pain, I bolted up from the exam table and cried. Dr. Collins hugged me and told me to relax. I tensed up when I thought what might happen if she interceded with Michael.

"You can't say anything to him, please, Dr. Collins. It'll only make him angrier and somethin' worse might happen," I pleaded.

"Jane, I'm concerned that you're going to get seriously hurt," Dr. Collins admitted. "I won't breach your confidentiality, but we need to get you out of this abuse."

"I know. I'm workin' on it, but if you say anything to him it won't get no better."

"I understand, but I wish you'd find a way to get out," Dr. Collins said. "It's nearly Christmas, a time when I'm trying to keep my patients away from cookies and urge them to exercise away the turkey, stuffing, and pumpkin pie they ate for Thanksgiving. I'm very concerned about you. You haven't gained one pound since September."

I cringed, realizing I'd been so miserable that I'd forgotten I had to nourish the baby. My only comfort was knowing my due date was just around the corner. For me, this delivery took on great meaning. Not only would I give life to a child, but I could get myself and another innocent child out of a war zone, out of enemy territory. My chance for freedom was not far off. Although the date of a baby's arrival is guesswork, I was sure if I didn't give birth by the first of the year then it would be some time in January, less than a month away, which meant I could start making serious plans to get away from Michael.

Dr. Collins kept her promise. She didn't tell Michael, but she must have communicated her dislike to him, because he quit going with me to her office. During December I had to see her every week. Dr. Collins was amazed I had the strength to walk into her office, because my blood pressure was seriously low. She gave me strong vitamins to help keep me healthy, but they upset my stomach and I had to stop taking them. During every visit she'd take a few extra minutes to talk to me. She ordered tests to be certain the baby was unharmed.

Meanwhile, I had the other children to care for. One afternoon when the children came home from school, Erica ran to me with pitiful tears running down her face.

"Mommy, it's not fair! The boys get spending money for candy, and I don't." She was so broken hearted. Michael controlled the money and wouldn't give me an allowance. I knew the boys were older and should get spending money, but it was unfair that we should watch them eat their treats in front of us. At times I wanted to treat myself to cake or candy while I was pregnant, but Michael wouldn't give us money. He insisted it was simply an older child's privilege to get an allowance.

I was furious. I'd taken so much of his abuse, but when it came to hurting my daughter I was livid. I decided to go on strike, despite the consequences.

"If they get allowances, so should I," I insisted. "I'll give Erica my earnings for her spending money."

"I'm your allowance, honey," Michael replied. "What do you need money for when you've got a fine husband like me. You couldn't buy a husband more handsome. Ol' Dad can still turn all the ladies' heads!"

"Well, you don't turn mine," I said bitterly. "The sight of you turns my stomach." As I completed my sentence, a lamp whizzed by my head and crashed into the living room wall. I turned and saw Michael running at me with his hands stretched out. Grabbed by the neck, I could feel my air supply being squeezed off. I looked around the room for help.

Face on fire, I saw Michael's older son look at me sheepishly and usher Erica out the front door. I thought I was going to die and was comforted Erica wouldn't have to watch.

My body went limp as I fell to the floor. I heard nothing. I wasn't sure if I was still alive, but I could feel my baby inside me thrashing, spinning in circles. I heard Michael speaking to someone at the door. I pulled myself up and crawled over to see if help had arrived. It was a muscular police officer. This was my chance.

"Officer, please, you've got to help me," I said as I revealed my belly nearly nine months gone. "He almost killed me. Choked me unconscious. Arrest him."

Michael closed the door slightly as the officer peered in.

"She's been like this almost her entire pregnancy," Michael said smoothly. "It must be those hormones." He grinned as he waited for the police officer's reaction as blood trickled from my mouth.

"Yeah, buddy, I know just how they are," the officer said to Michael. "I've got a wife myself, and I just a'soon send 'em away when they git pregnant. I finally got mine fixed. Don't have to worry with it no more."

I was speechless. I tried to tell the officer about Michael's life-threatening attack, but he ignored me as Michael pushed me away from the door. As the officer went away, I knew there would be hell to pay. I tried to walk to my room hoping the whole nightmare would end. But Michael wasn't finished.

"What the hell did you say that for? Are you trying to get me arrested? Why did you call the police?"

"I didn't call them," I said, shifting the blame where it belonged. "Maybe the neighbors did."

When Erica and Michael's older son walked in from outside, they were shivering from the cold December temperature. Neither of them had taken the time to put their coats on. Erica, probably trying to change the mood of the room, said, "Mommy, Michael, can we get a Christmas tree tonight? They look so pretty with lights on them."

Michael spun around, stuck his finger in Erica's face and screamed, "We're not havin' a tree this year! Now get to your room and go to bed!"

Without a whimper, Erica climbed the stairs to her room as I followed behind.

"Where do you think you're goin'?" Michael barked.

"I'm goin' up to tuck her in." I figured as long as I was doing something, he wouldn't try to stop me. I curled up with Erica and held her while we both cried. We drifted off to sleep huddled in fear.

At Christmas, I had to act like my old happy self whenever family came by or we went out for visits. By now most of my friends had stopped seeing us because they got uncomfortable with the distrustful looks Michael gave them. He always sat within earshot, intimidated them, and acted jumpy and nervous like he was afraid they might ask me to leave with them and I'd accept.

I couldn't leave the house for anything other than a doctor's appointment. Erica and I were caged like zoo animals. I was anxious for school to start up again, so Erica would have something to do. It was hard to entertain her during these grim days and my increasing waistline prevented me from active play. The stress left me quietly disconnected. Climbing stairs was a strain, especially if I was wounded from one of Michael's attacks.

Michael continued to take the phones with him whenever he left the house. I tried to remain calm. I didn't want to throw myself into labor without being able to call for help, especially with Erica right beside me. Thankfully, Erica's school vacation was over on the third of January. Five days later, I started labor.

When the first tinge of pain signaled the onset of labor, I walked cautiously through the ice and snow piled outside to a neighbor's house to call my sister. Aware of Michael's violent behavior, Beth sent her husband to get Erica. I thanked him for relieving me of that worry. I knew Erica'd be comfortable and safe with my sister. I promised to call her as soon as the baby was born, but explained it would probably be the next morning.

I was packing my suitcase for the hospital when Michael came home and asked why supper wasn't on the table.

"Michael, I'm in the early stages of labor," I said calmly. "I sent Erica to my sister's, and now I'm getting a few things ready."

"We need to go now!" Michael yelled. "Don't you know if that baby stays in there too long it could be deformed!"

"Look, Michael, I've done this before. My pains are far apart. We live less than a mile from the hospital. I'd rather relax here and save my energy for delivery."

"'Relax!' I'm not letting you ruin my child," Michael insisted. "I'm not gonna have it! Get your ass in the car before I put you there myself!"

I grabbed a few things and was out in the car before Michael had finished styling his hair and drenching himself with expensive cologne.

When we came through the emergency room doors, a nurse noticed Michael's mood and tried to calm him.

"Sir, everything will be fine. Is this your first child?" she asked.

"No, it's his fifth, maybe sixth," I answered. "He always acts like this."

"Who told you that?" he growled.

"I have my sources." I realized I was safe within the hospital walls. I acted on an urge to put Michael in his place and reveal the secrets that he'd tried to keep from me. As an attendant wheeled me to the labor room, Michael screamed obscenities at the hospital staff stationed along the hall.

"Get up!" Michael yelled at them. "My child is about to be born and you all are sitting on your ass! I'm not a welfare client! I've got insurance and I expect you all to treat me with respect!"

I rolled my eyes at the nurse who patted my arm to comfort me as Michael continued to curse out every member of the maternity ward. He insisted on knowing how much it cost, how often each one failed, and when was my doctor coming.

"She's downstairs taking a nap," a nurse informed us ill-advisedly. "She'll be up after a while."

"A nap!" Michael screamed. "My child is on the way and the doctor is sleeping?"

"Michael," I pleaded as tears streamed down my face. "I'm in early labor. The baby might not get here till morning."

"Better not wait," Michael snapped. "They better get that kid out of you before it's deformed or I'll file a lawsuit! I'm going to the bar."

"Then why don't you go now," I begged. "Let me and these nurses have some peace!"

"Yeah, right, and leave you to handle these incompetents?"

"Michael, they're trained professionals. Babies are born every day. We don't need you here."

The nurse was rubbing my shoulder, trying to relax me, when Michael shoved the silver bedpan to the floor in a rage.

"You're not goin' to talk to me like this, you understand!"

The nurse stepped away, inched toward the door, and asked Michael to leave. "Sir, you need to leave her alone," she said.

"You stay out of this," Michael yelled. "Get the doctor or do something useful, but stay out of my business. This is *my* child and *my* wife, and I'll do what I please. Do you hear me?"

The nurse retreated, and a sharp contraction stole my breath. I held my abdomen and tried to take slow, deep breaths.

"Great acting job, Jane," Michael sneered as he moved closer to my face. "I guess you think 'cause you got one coming you can cry your way out of it," he said as he rolled up his sleeves. I looked around for a button to press for help.

"Please, Michael," I begged. "Just go to the bar. This will be over with in the morning."

Michael continued his snarl, contemplating his next move as two orderlies ran into the room.

"Sir, you're going to have to leave this room," one said as the other stood closer to Michael in a ready-to-leap posture.

"Who says I have to leave?" Michael asked as he put his hands in his pockets and regained his best gentlemanly manners.

"Doctor Collins and the hospital officials. If you prefer, we can call the police," the orderly said.

"I think I'll go out for a smoke. This baby business is hard on fathers," Michael said as he walked toward the door. "Excuse me," he said as he passed the orderlies.

With Michael gone, I tried to relax as much as possible. My doctor came in sometime after Michael left. She explained that with all the stress I'd been under, they wanted to keep a closer eye on me. Dr. Collins made sure I had plenty of care and medication to relax me as my pains grew stronger and closer together. Hours later, Michael reappeared as I was taken down the hall to delivery.

I ignored him for the most part. He'd calmed down after his eviction warning, not saying a word as I delivered. The room seemed empty to me. The beep of the monitors blended into background noises as my doctor gently coached me to push. I could see the birth through mirrors on the walls and squealed with excitement when I saw the black mop of hair come out, followed by the healthy, beautiful body of a baby girl.

Dr. Collins placed the baby on my stomach for my inspection. I checked every detail, thankful she was not injured. I pulled Megan close and whispered to her a promise that life would get better for us now that she was here. I cried as I put her to my breast for her first meal, relieved that all was well. Erica was a sister, I thought, and now we'd be free to leave.

Michael stood away from us. I glanced over at him. He looked away. He could probably sense being unwanted. After hanging around for an hour and watching me as I started the bonding process with my daughter, he left.

The next evening I stayed calm as Michael paraded his family into the hospital. Smiling pictures were taken. Inside I knew this facade was only temporary. It was only a matter of time till Michael became violent again. I tried not to think about it. I tried to enjoy the moments with our new baby Megan.

When I brought Megan home from the hospital, snow and ice covered our uncleared sidewalk. I could hardly walk on the ice without feeling the pull and the sting of my stitches. Dr. Collins said I had more lacerations than normal because of my poor health. Before I was dismissed from the hospital, I was told to abstain from sex for six weeks, but Michael wouldn't obey the doctor's orders. Forced intercourse was excruciatingly painful.

In between caring for the baby I slept as often as Michael would allow. Fortunately, Megan was a very content baby. She nursed well and often, so I had to get up several times a night. I wanted to give her a good start, so I didn't mind. Michael stayed away a lot during our first few weeks home, which helped.

I wanted to heal and get Megan out of the newborn stage before I left Michael. Moving would be easier for Erica if we waited until spring break or even summer vacation, if Michael would behave. I'd saved over one hundred dollars, but I needed more. The expense of setting up a new home, diapers, and day care would be high.

I'd only been home from the hospital a few weeks when I asked Michael if I could take the car to the store and get some things the baby needed. He said okay, as long as I left the girls with him. I felt my face redden. So he knew I wanted to leave and was taking out insurance. He knew I wouldn't leave without my girls, but I was more than a little surprised when he let me go out.

It felt good to get away, even for a short time. But then I realized I couldn't trust him with Erica and Megan. I grabbed baby clothes, lotions, and a candy bar for Erica at the mall and wasted no time getting home. But when I pulled back into our parking space, my concern changed to panic. I couldn't believe what I saw.

In the front yard sat all of my antique living room furniture. When I knocked on the door, it opened slightly. Michael peered out.

"What's happening?" I asked, not hiding how upset I was.

"I figured you'd do anything to get back in," Michael said with a smirk. "So here's the deal. Take this money and go to the doctor written on this paper. It's where my girlfriends go for prescription speed. Tell the doctor you want to lose weight. If you do and come home with some goodies, I'll let you back in. And maybe I'll bring the furniture in, too."

"Michael, you're crazy!" I screamed. "I need to feed Megan in less than an hour. She'll be hungry."

"No, she won't," Michael answered. "Dad's got a bottle ready for her."

"Formula might make her sick! She's not used to it! Michael, please, I'll swell up with milk!"

"Then you better hurry," he said with the smirk still on his face, and slammed the door.

I couldn't believe what was happening. I stood outside, sat

in one of my chairs ten inches deep in snow, and cried. Erica waved at me through the window. I blew her a sad kiss, wiped my face, and went to the car. I felt my milk let down in the warmth of the car. I stared blankly out the frosty windshield and wondered what to do next. I decided to try getting into the house again.

I walked through the snow and pounded on our door. I heard Erica run to the door to answer, followed by Michael's voice.

"If you touch that door, I'll bust your ass!" he yelled at her.

"Don't you touch her, Michael!" I screamed. "Let me in!" I knocked for several minutes, but he didn't answer. I tried my key but the deadbolt was locked, and I didn't have the key to it.

I ran out into the yard and looked up. I saw Erica staring out her window. Her expression, sad and confused, gave me my answer. I'd have to do what he said in order to get back in. Calling the police might get me arrested and would leave Erica and Megan in danger.

It wasn't enough that I'd just given birth, took care of the children, and starched his shirts for his dates with other women. I was worn out by the living hell Michael had made for me. I wanted out, and I wanted my children with me. It was so unfair that I had to bear humiliation and pain and the police didn't offer me any protection. Worse still, my children were caught in the crossfire. I couldn't wait any longer, I decided. I'd leave when I finished his one last dirty deed.

When I reached the address on the paper and went into the doctor's office, I was weighed by a nurse and quickly handed a prescription by a doctor who barely introduced himself. Then I left. Michael must have known how easy it was. I stopped at the pharmacy to fill the prescription and headed home.

When I got there, some of the furniture had been brought back inside. I stood away from the door and dangled the bottle of pills in front of me and out of Michael's reach. I was capable of playing games, too. He was going to have to open the door and come out if he was going to get them.

As the door opened, I sat the bottle down on the sidewalk and ran by Michael as he scrambled to get the pills. Megan was fussing in her carrier seat, but appeared unharmed. I snatched her up and ran to Erica's room.

"Are you okay, Mommy?" she asked when I opened her bedroom door.

"Yes, honey, I'm fine. Are you okay?" I asked as she ran to my side. I looked in her eyes and brushed her hair with my ice cold hands. Megan squirmed and rooted around my neck. She needed to eat. I took them to my room and laid them both on the bed with me while I fed Megan.

"Mommy, can we go away?" Erica asked.

"Yes, we'll go somewhere, baby," I answered. "I need to find a place, but we have to keep it a secret. Do you understand?"

"I'll keep a secret, Mommy. I promise. We'll run away together. Can we take Megan?"

"Of course," I whispered. "But we have to wait until the time is right. Not much longer, but you may have to go to school for a couple more days before we go. And you can't tell anybody."

"Pinky swear, Mommy. No-o-bo-dy."

I stayed in the room for several hours until Michael came in and told me to get downstairs, which meant it was time for me to do something for him. After I tucked Megan in, Michael yelled again from downstairs. I went straightaway.

"I guess you're thinking about leaving," Michael said like a father disciplining a child. "I don't think that's a good idea. You should forget about taking Megan. She's stayin' with me," he said as he laid down his law.

"Now that you're taking drugs," he grinned, "or should I say it sure looks like you're doin' them. The bottle's got your name on it. If you try to leave with Megan I'll call the child welfare people. They won't think highly of a woman using drugs while she's breast-feeding a baby."

I sat quietly in the stifled room, but inside my chest and stomach seemed to burst. Michael had woven me deeply into his web of control. I sat quietly as he preached to me, knowing he was trying to pick a fight. I kept my cool, knowing it would take all my strength and energy to get me and two small children away from him.

Over the next few days the fights continued. More threatened than ever that I'd try to leave him, Michael watched my every move. The speed prescription kept him up all hours day and night, which made it harder for me to sneak change from his pockets.

Cold weather made the cops who came to our house a little cranky. They weren't as inclined to side with Michael when the neighbors called them because of the racket resulting from him assaulting me. The police would get out of the cruiser and slip and slide their way to our front door. They warned him to keep it down when they arrived. Once they threatened to take us both downtown if they had to come back that night.

Nevertheless, Michael's irrational behavior increased. He would stand guard when I had both of the girls with me in the living room. He wouldn't leave me for a second. He moved my entire wardrobe to the trunk of the car. I had to ask for a clean change of clothes when he let me take a shower.

As spring approached, I told Michael I wanted to take Megan out for some fresh air. He disapproved. I was never allowed to take her out alone. As flowers bloomed, I wondered how or when we could get away. At times I felt my mind slipping from the stress of living in a prison policed by a madman.

The night Erica needed eggs boiled for a project at school, all hell broke loose again.

"Jane, what are you doin'?" Michael yelled from the living room.

"I'm boilin' some eggs for Erica to color at school tomorrow. They're havin' an Easter party."

"Fix me a sandwich," Michael said.

"I will in a minute," I answered. The steam rose from the boiling water on the stove as I felt Michael grab my arm, then yank my hair and jerk my head until my eyes saw the ceiling.

"I said now!" he growled.

Something snapped in me. I ignored him. He picked up the hot sauce pan and dumped the eggs and boiling water onto my head. I heard Erica cry out. When I turned toward her, Michael followed. She flew upstairs to avoid his fury.

"I said I will in a minute, Michael," I growled back. I couldn't stop. I opened the refrigerator and got out more eggs.

"Now!" Michael screamed as he wrenched the eggs from my hands. He smashed them over my head. Still I couldn't stop. I kept getting more eggs and he kept smashing them over my head until two dozen eggs had been fractured and were flowing over my hair. My head was spinning from the repetition of Michael's pounding fists and cracking eggs. When all the eggs were gone and the steaming water had burnt my skin and soaked my clothes, Michael threw me across the table. As dishes and glasses crashed to the floor around me, Michael smiled.

"You think you can outdo me, don't ya?" he sneered.

"Please leave me alone," I pleaded as I tried to crawl around him and get to the stairs. I got to my feet and saw Michael pulling an extension cord from the wall socket. He ran toward me, fashioning a noose with the cord. I fled up the steps. He chased me and caught me.

Erica stood in the upstairs hall and screamed, "Mommy! Don't hurt my mommy!"

Michael ignored her. He pushed me back down the stairs. I rolled and tried to keep my balance. He clinched both my ankles and wrists in his hands, anchored his foot on my ribs, and tightly wrapped the extension cord around my limbs. He rolled me down the rest of the stairs, and laughed as I screamed for help.

For hours he taunted me. He made fun of the way I looked and said that he was the master and I his slave. When Megan began to wimper from upstairs, then cry, I asked if I could feed her.

"I'll take care of her," Michael insisted. "She doesn't need you for anything," he snarled.

When he brought Megan downstairs, I begged him to let me feed her. He ignored me. I laid on the floor, my breasts swollen and burning with unused milk. I felt ill watching him coo and google over Megan. Then I thought of a way to get him to stop the game.

"Michael, she needs her diaper changed," I said. "Her skin is very sensitive. If she breaks out, she could get an infection, bleed, maybe die. Child welfare would take us both into custody if that happened."

He'd never changed her diaper. Not once. And he wasn't about to start now.

He untied my hands. "Hop over and get her a diaper," he said. He laid Megan on the couch in the living room and stood watching me, a sardonic grin on his face. I hopped into the room. I picked up Megan. She smiled at me and nearly broke my heart. I didn't want her life to be like this.

"Soon," I whispered. "Somehow we'll break free." I looked into her eyes and tried to relay to her my thoughts. *We're getting out, baby, don't worry.*

Michael left my feet tied but let me hold Megan until Erica came down. He insisted we stay apart. He sent Erica to her room again. "You can tuck her in," he said to me, "but leave Megan with me."

The isolation lasted all night. He made me get up when milk poured from my breast and soaked my shirt. "It's disgusting. Go wash up," he'd scream and hit me. All night he ranted. For over ten hours the beating, the screaming, the begging, pleading, and separation continued.

When morning came he allowed Erica to watch television after Megan became fussy. "Take her upstairs," he said, "and nurse her to sleep and stay there." I could hear most of what was going on downstairs throughout the day. I wondered what else might happen and feared night would come again and I'd be hurt too bad to leave. Every once in a while, Michael came upstairs to smack me or yell at me. I could tell he was preoccupied with something on television by the comments he made. I began to plot our escape.

The main thing was to catch him off guard. I kept blankets close to Megan in case our chance to flee came. I waited until I heard him go into the bathroom. When I heard the bathroom door close and the toilet seat lid clank against the tank, I made my move.

I walked as quietly as I could and tiptoed down the stairs. The toilet flushed as I reached the bottom. Erica was in a chair next to the front door.

"Run, Erica!" I shouted. "Run, honey! Go next door and call the police! Mommy's right behind you!" When the bathroom door opened and Michael emerged, the chase began. I sprang out the front door and into the parking lot gripping Megan to my torn shirt. Erica was several steps ahead of me and out of harm's way when Michael began catching up with me and Megan.

"Where in the fuck do you think you're goin'?" he yelled from behind me.

"I'm getting outta here before you kill me," I said calmly.

"I say when you can leave." Michael picked me up by the waist with Megan's foot trapped in the middle of his grip, and slung us onto the hood of a car. I tried to keep Megan's head from hard impact by wrapping my arm around her head. Unable to catch myself, I hit the hood hard and lost my breath as the street lights dimmed.

I didn't see Erica. I could only pray that she was safe and getting help, or we were in terrible trouble. I worried someone would kidnap or hurt her.

Michael picked us up and slammed us on the hood of the car repeatedly. I worried I'd lose consciousness and drop Megan. I could hear her squeak and whimper every time we hit the hood.

She was only six weeks old and I didn't think she would survive this attack. I saw headlights coming and Erica running beside the vehicle. It took me a second to recognize the police car.

I heard Erica telling the officers what had happened. Michael continued to pull and throw us on and off the car until the red and blue lights flashed from atop the cruiser.

I heard the police radio squelch and announce that a back-up cruiser was on the way. The sounds around me were faint as I tried to stay conscious.

An officer yelled at Michael, "Get away from them or I'll shoot." I felt a hand touch my shoulder.

"Are you okay, ma'am?" the voice asked.

"Yes, I think so. I hurt real bad," I answered. "My body's throbbing but I think my baby is okay."

"Well, that's good," the officer answered. "Are you numb anywhere?"

"I, I don't think I am, but I'm shakin'," I sobbed.

"Don't worry, ma'am. We're gonna get you to the hospital."

"No! I, I can't go to the hospital! Who'll take care of my other girl?"

"We'll call Children's Social Services," the officer said, as I thought of the speed prescription Michael had made me get. "They'll take care of both children until you get out of the hospital."

I had to convince the police I could take care of us. I knew Michael would do anything to get Megan taken from me.

My body was covered with blood and dried egg from the night before. Bruises were scattered all over me. My shirt was ripped off my body, and I didn't have shoes on. Slowly, I sat up on the hood of the car as both officers talked to Michael. Erica ran to my side.

"Are you okay, Mommy? I got the police. Can we go now? Please, Mommy?"

"In a minute, baby," I assured her. "I need to talk to the police. Then we'll get outta here."

One of the officers came over to us and asked what we wanted to do. He asked if I wanted to go with Michael and try to work things out, or did I want to leave.

"I want to go to the abuse shelter as soon as possible," I said. "And I want to press charges. This has gone on for too long. I want Michael arrested."

"We can't arrest him, ma'am. Not without a warrant," the officer answered. "You need to go to the courthouse tomorrow and try and get one."

"Why can't you arrest him?" I asked, dumbfounded. "Look at me!"

"Well, ma'am, we didn't see it happen. You need to convince the judge he did this to you and then see what the judge wants to do."

This explanation of justice made me queasy, but I held my tongue as the officer helped us into the cruiser and drove us to the abuse shelter four blocks away.

The intake counselor at the shelter listened to my history and recommended that I go to the hospital. Fortunately, Megan didn't have a scratch on her and was smiling throughout the interview. I told the counselor my fear of leaving the children, but she assured me they'd take care of them while I was gone. She had children of her own and emphasized no one would take them unless I gave my permission. She took a picture of my injuries before I left and reminded me that my bruises would hurt worse the next day. I put the girls to sleep in the quarters they gave us, then called a cab and went to the hospital.

The doctor said I was lucky I wasn't killed. He said my injuries were consistent with an assault. He prescribed several anti-inflammatory drugs and recommended ice packs and bed rest. I chuckled for the first time in weeks when he said bed rest. "With a newborn, there's no such word, doctor, and tomorrow I have to go to the courthouse." And who knew what the following day would bring.

The next morning at the shelter a volunteer introduced

herself to me. "I'm Michelle Green," she said. "I'll take care of the girls while you go to the courthouse." We spent a few minutes discussing the girls' habits while she got to know them. She had grown children and enjoyed holding a newborn for the first time in years.

Gayle Ryan, an advocate from the shelter, went with me to the courthouse to help me through the legal labyrinth. We detailed the history of my case to the court clerk. Gayle and the clerk knew each other and chatted as they filled out my paperwork. I glanced to my right and was nearly struck dead with horror. There stood Michael. "He's over there," I warned Gayle.

Briefcase in hand and wearing a stylish suit of clothes all charged on my credit cards, Michael stood in the next line filing a domestic abuse charge against me. Gayle tried to calm me. "Most abusers try to blame their victims," she said. "Most men are wounded in fights, and their battles with their spouses are no exception." She patted my arm. "It's one of the oldest tricks in the book to blame their injuries on their wives or some other silly excuse."

Michael advanced to the front of his line. We stood at the counter at the same time, but spoke to different clerks. They realized we were the same "incident" and scheduled us for court the next day.

The next morning the judge shuffled papers as he listened to each of our stories. Gayle Ryan had guessed correctly. Michael said on his complaint that I became violent with him and broke all the dishes that were on our kitchen table.

"Did you break those glasses?" the judge asked me.

"Well, sir," I began. "When Michael threw me across the kitchen table, the glasses fell off the table and broke."

"So you did break things," the judge answered and smacked his gavel before I could correct him. He dismissed our case until the next week. Before we left the courtroom, he ordered both of us to stay out of our house until after our hearing.

Later that night at the shelter, an officer arrived with a notice that our order had been changed earlier that day. The officer said that the judge had reversed his order after Michael went to his chambers and pleaded to let him go back home. The order stated that since I was in protective custody and Michael could not physically harm me there, Michael was permitted to return to the house. When I read the notice, I knew I'd lost everything I owned.

I couldn't get the money I'd hidden in the ironing board, so we had nothing. I desperately needed to find a job. The shelter provided us with diapers and food, but Erica needed school supplies and my legal fees were costly. I signed a promissory note to repay the shelter the court costs they'd advanced me. Despite my injuries and frazzled mind, I had to look for work immediately.

The shelter paid for taxi fares for urgent business and work, but they didn't provide child care. Volunteers weren't available daily. There were more than thirty women and children in our shelter and we were encouraged to help each other out. Megan was so young and adorable people asked if they could keep her. I had to adjust to not breast-feeding her while I was away. I arranged transportation for Erica to school and started my search for a job.

I applied heavy makeup and practiced walking without a limp, and it paid off. I found a job the second day at a bridal shop downtown. I would do alterations.

During that first day at work, my boss complimented me on my concentration and speed with the needle. He couldn't know how bad I needed the job. But on the second day Michael, who knew we were at the shelter, followed me. After my thirty minute break my boss called on the intercom.

"Jane, you have a phone call on line one."

It was Michael.

"What do you think you're doin'?" Michael asked over the phone. "You're never gonna get away from me," he threatened.

"You may try to leave, but I'll make your life miserable, I promise!" Click. Michael kept calling every few minutes. In each call he made similar threats and hung up.

During my fifteen minute break, my boss came over and reminded me that I could only receive emergency calls. I nodded okay, but didn't elaborate on the source of my problem. I didn't tell him I lived in the shelter, either.

When I went back to work, the phone continued to ring. After the fifth call in less than thirty minutes, my boss came upstairs with a warning.

"You need to tell the man who's calling you to stop," he said.

"It's my ex-husband," I confessed. "He won't leave me alone."

"Jane, we like your work. You do a very fine job here and we'd hate to lose you, but this is a business and we can't tolerate this."

"I understand, and I'm sorry he's doing this. I'll try to get him to stop."

After work I told the advocate at the shelter about Michael's persistent phone calls. She told me we could file harassment charges, but the judge probably wouldn't hear it until our hearing later next week. She recommended I get an attorney and handed me a list of lawyers that were sensitive toward battered women complaints.

Don Hayes, the first lawyer I called, took my case after I explained the circumstances. I learned that Don served on the board of the shelter. He volunteered to help me build my case by retracing the violence.

We spent a Saturday afternoon walking my neighborhood knocking on doors, asking people if they had seen Michael hit me. Most of them told Don they'd heard fighting. They remembered the furniture outside and recounted most of the things I had told him. But none of them were willing to testify in court. They didn't want to get involved.

Since bad luck usually runs in streaks, I wasn't surprised when I was fired from my job on Monday. Michael started calling first thing in the morning and after fifteen minutes of work, my boss let me go.

I went back to the shelter feeling defeated, but determined to win. I called my sister Beth, and we decided after my hearing I should get the furniture she was storing for me and have a yard sale. I needed to raise money somehow. She ran an ad for me and began pricing the things I'd hid at her house when Michael started hocking everything.

When my court day arrived, Michael didn't appear. We held up the court docket waiting for him. The same judge that had reversed the order and let him back in the house issued two warrants for Michael's arrest for contempt of court. He said I was free to go since Michael had failed to appear. He said I could go back to my home, but I knew all I wanted to do was get my things and leave.

We asked for police protection but didn't get it. Don volunteered to go with me after work. I took him up on his offer. Don picked me up in his car and we drove to the apartment. We found the door unlocked. I opened it. The place was empty. Not a stick of furniture remained.

I walked through the rooms and found a few of the girls' things in their closet. I found a shirt and some socks of mine on the floor of my closet. In the kitchen pantry I found my ironing board, money still in place. I'd lost a two-story house full of furniture but at least I'd recovered my small nest egg.

Still, the pain of losing my property on top of everything else was overwhelming. I'd fought hard to follow the rules but it had done me no good. The rules were made for other people. Michael was a swindler and a wife-beater. I tried not to think of my losses. I tried not to think about anything that had happened over the last year. I craved a fresh start. I knew it was time for a change. I decided to move after my yard sale. I'd go to a city a hundred miles away where I'd once lived with Erica's father,

Johnny. Thinking of him made me want to call him. Although it had been some time since we'd seen each other, I decided to let him know as soon as possible where I was taking Erica.

When we got off the Greyhound bus in the city, I bought a Sunday paper and rented a hotel room not far from the bus station. The room was clean and on the city bus line. I had to bargain with the desk clerk to get a cheap price. He rented me a room with a funky television set. Only one channel came in— sometimes. I only had around three hundred dollars left from the yard sale after buying the bus tickets. We didn't have much other than our clothes.

I called my mom, my sister, and my attorney after we settled in. Later that night, I called Johnny. "Let me help," he offered. I couldn't accept. He was glad to hear we'd made it safely to the city, and promised to call regularly.

Living at a hotel was not easy, especially with no friends or family around. It was hard not having a crib for Megan and only a few toys for Erica, but it was not having a car that crippled us. I tried to keep my hopes up. After what Michael had put me through, I didn't think our lives could get worse.

I found a sitter. The day care took over half of my money; so I needed another job fast. Potential employers raised their eyebrows when I listed a hotel as my address. The temporary service wasn't as discriminating, and they put me to work the next day.

I was exhausted after my first day of shuffling the girls by bus, then to work and back again at the end of the day. We fell asleep after eating some peanut butter sandwiches we made in the room. It wasn't great, but it was a refuge.

The second night, I added up my hotel costs and child care bill and figured we'd be broke and living in the street in two weeks. I bit my nails as I read the paper, scanned the ads for a waitress job, and found one. I didn't know how my war torn body would hold up, but waitressing was fast money, and I had kids to feed.

I limited my phone calls to one or two a week. My sister called me regularly and would relay messages from Mom or Johnny. When I called my attorney, I was surprised when Don told me he'd been in touch with Michael.

"Jane, Michael has offered to pay child support if we won't arrest him," my attorney said. "I'm sure you could use the money."

"Yeah, I could," I admitted. "I need to pay you, too. But I really don't want his money. I just want my furniture, albums, and clothes back."

"Maybe he'll give those back later. Meanwhile, I think you should take the money. What's it gonna hurt? He's living out of state and sounds very remorseful. When he calls back, I can give him your address and number."

"I can do this on my own. I don't want anything from him," I maintained.

"But you and your children *need* this, Jane," he emphasized. "You shouldn't turn down help. Hopefully, Michael will keep his promise. It can't hurt to try."

I didn't like it but I guessed he was right. My waitress job helped but the children and I had so little and saw each other less. I worked Monday through Friday in offices the temp service sent me to, and worked Thursday through Sunday at the restaurant.

Megan changed so much during those first months. She was now five months old, and I couldn't think of one tranquil day since she was conceived. Erica was depressed and withdrawn, which disturbed me. I wanted to get her in counseling, but I had to think of our primary needs first. I had two months to get us settled before school started.

When Johnny called, he again offered to help us. But I couldn't trust anyone, not even Johnny. I was afraid he'd want something from me. "After my ordeal with Michael, I have to stay focused on trying to survive," I said.

"But," Johnny pleaded, "Janie, I still love you. I swear I

won't ask anything of you. I only want to help you and the girls."

He sounded so sincere and our need was so great, I agreed.

I took the bus back home. When I went to see my parents they gave me an old car that my brother didn't need anymore. After they gave me the keys, I wasted no time driving to get Johnny.

CHAPTER **5**

Further Interrogation

In the cruiser, the lump in my throat thickened as I fought back tears. I wanted the girls with me. They needed me as much as I needed them. I wanted to scream, to cry out over the unfairness of life. I wanted Johnny. I just wanted to hold him. Oh God. My thoughts turned once again to my children. I hardly knew the woman who was minding the girls. Why did the police expect me to leave my kids with a stranger at a time when the children needed me the most? Why couldn't they just ask me the questions at her place instead of downtown? Why did I have to go anywhere?

My head ached as I tried to remember whether I had left adequate instructions about caring for the children. Did I give her formula for Megan? I don't think I did. When did she eat last? I bet she's starving. The woman probably doesn't have clean diapers in the house. Yeah, she does, or she should have. She has a baby. Hopefully she has the same formula and an extra bottle for Megan.

Officer Moran wasn't saying much. He was just driving down the road on a hot, sunny Sunday afternoon in July. Another day another dollar. Not a care in the world while my

78

head exploded with gruesome images of Johnny's murder. I felt like I was slipping in and out of consciousness. As hard as I tried, I couldn't stop thinking about it.

Finally I spoke. "Where will the police take Michael?" Fear that I might have another confrontation with him became my main concern. The officer mumbled a reply. It was indiscernible.

Police headquarters was only a few miles away. We drove past beautiful stately homes that appeared vacant. Without signs of life they seemed surreal, far removed from the real life nightmare I was living. It occurred to me that the girls and I couldn't go back to the apartment in which we'd been living even if we wanted to. I worried about who I could call to come get me. Where would we stay? I thought about calling home but I couldn't bear to tell my folks what had happened. Who else could I call? My marriage to Michael had left me with very few friends. Most were afraid of the scenes Michael caused. I didn't blame them, but I needed help.

I thought of my sister Beth. Would she be at church? She never missed a Sunday. I didn't even know what time of day it was. Maybe I should call my attorney. I remembered the movies I'd seen where a person being questioned by the police would always say, "I have the right to one phone call. I want to call my attorney." But my attorney was in Catlettsburg, two hours away. I doubted they'd let me call him long distance. Maybe collect. My temples throbbed. I rubbed them as my thoughts ricocheted. "God, I hope the girls are doing okay," I murmured.

When we arrived at the police station, I was led into the building and somebody offered me something to drink. I took some water and asked to use their phone. I had decided that I had to get in touch with my family. I called my parents' house but the line was busy. I thought about calling an old friend, Allan Collins. I knew he was at his mother's house. I had stopped by to say hello to him when I picked up Johnny and the warrant papers just two days before. The thought of Allan relieved my anxiety a little. I had grown up with him and he was like a big brother to me.

As I dialed Allan's number, I prayed that he'd answer. I almost cried with relief when after only two rings I heard his voice.

"Allan, it's Jane Wells. I need some help." My voice quivered but I managed to blurt out the news.

"Michael killed Johnny and I'm at the police station. I tried to call Mom and Dad but their line's busy. I hate to ask, but I need ya to run up to their house and tell 'em to get off the phone, that I have to get through and talk to 'em. We need a ride home."

Allan seemed to understand and didn't press me for details, assuring me he'd go right away. I hung up the phone and walked over to the gray-haired officer on duty and asked if I could have an attorney present while I was being questioned.

"You don't need an attorney," he said. "You aren't a suspect. You're only a witness to a murder."

I thought I should have a lawyer but I didn't insist. Feeling scared and apprehensive, I went back to the phone on the desk of one of the officers and called my parents' home to get my sister Beth's help. At the sound of my anxious voice, Dad's own anxieties rose. He screamed into the phone.

"Janie! What 'n the hell is wrong now?" His reproach stung but I tried to calmly explain the situation.

"I need someone to come get me, Dad. Can you try to call Beth for me? I can't drive and we don't have nowhere else to stay. Tell her I'll call her when I'm through being questioned."

"Call back after you get through," he said. I hung up the phone and an officer led me to a semi-dark room, furnished with only a table, a few chairs, and some recording equipment. The starkness of the room intimidated me.

"This is Detective Andrews from the Crimes Against Children Unit of the Police Department," the gray-haired officer said.

Andrews greeted me and again assured me that I didn't need an attorney present. "I'll make my questions brief," he said.

"I'd be grateful. I'm still in shock and quite rattled, but I'll do the best I can to answer your questions," I told him.

Slowly, I sat down on one of the cold metal chairs across the table from the youngish blond detective. Overhead, a ceiling lamp swayed and stirred the stale air. When I looked up at Detective Andrews, his green eyes seemed to narrow underneath the bright light as he shuffled his papers. I was still suffering from the shocking vision of Johnny's dead body and feeling the terror of being held hostage by Michael. Again and again, the scene played out in my head.

I worried about the girls, especially Erica, who no doubt was experiencing the same emotions I was, but without Mom there to ease her pain. If I couldn't understand or cope with all of this, how could she, a six-year-old child, possibly deal with such a traumatic ordeal? And Megan must be wondering why everyone was crying and where was Mommy. She must be confused. At least Erica is there with her, I told myself. Suddenly, the detective cleared his throat, turned on his recorder, and began to speak.

Thoughts swirling through my head, I tried to focus on what he was saying.

"This is Detective Keith Andrews." The tall gangly man nodded to himself. "I'm in the Crimes Against Children Unit of the Detective Bureau with the Police Department. Today's date is July 10, and the time is, uh, 2:12 in the afternoon. I'm conducting an interview with Mrs. Jane Haney, a witness to an incident that occurred on Plainview Drive on this date. Ms. Haney, I understand that you were a witness to a shooting that occurred earlier today."

"Yes."

"Okay. I also understand this incident began last evening, uh, with some type of altercation that gave the police cause to be at your apartment."

"Yes," I murmured.

Andrews leaned toward me. "Okay. Can you tell me why the police had occasion to be there last night?"

I frowned. "It wasn't the first time they'd been there."

"Okay," Andrews said and gestured for me to go on.

"Because of Michael, they had been there before."

"Okay. Now who is Michael?"

"Michael is my ex-husband." I felt exasperated. "Well, it's not final yet. We filed in February or March."

"Okay." Andrews nodded. "So, basically, he is your husband right now?"

I bit my lip. "Technically, I guess he is."

"What is Michael's last name?"

"Haney."

"Okay."

"His real name at birth was Jerry Michael Haney."

"Okay."

I brushed away some of the hair which had fallen over my eyes. If he said okay once more, I thought, I might jump out of my skin. "Last night," I explained, "Erica's father was there to see her, and Michael just walked into my apartment. He just slammed. . . ."

Andrews broke in. "Okay. Now Erica's your. . . ."

"First child."

"First child," he repeated. "How old is she?"

"She's six years old."

"Now, would that be Michael's daughter?"

I shook my head. "No. It's Johnny's daughter."

It was his turn to look exasperated. "Johnny's daughter. Now, who is John?"

"John is my first husband."

"Okay. What's John's last name?"

"Eidson."

"John Eidson."

"He has two middle names. John Thomas Robert Eidson."

"So you have a child by each of these men?" He seemed to be chiding me. I wondered if he was aware just how many marriages ended in divorce.

"Yes."

"Okay. One of 'em's an ex-husband. One of 'em's a current husband. Have they had trouble before?"

"No, they'd never met."

"They'd never met. Okay."

"They'd never met. As a matter of fact, when Michael stormed the apartment last night, Johnny and him went out and talked."

Andrews's eyebrows went up. "Okay."

I nodded. "And appeared to have worked things out. I mean, you know, Michael just said, 'Hey, I'm here to see my daughter.' You know, nothin's wrong here, whatever, you know, he just, that's what Johnny told me, and Michael had, he'd walked down to uh, walked down the street with him."

"Okay. Why did the police have occasion to be there?"

I felt like this was going to go on forever. "Because he came back."

"Okay. A second time."

"See, we thought it was straightened out."

"I see."

"Johnny went out and talked to him and said, 'Look, I'm just here to see Erica, you know, it's no big problem or anything like that,' and you know that's what Johnny had told me. He said that they'd gotten along, there hadn't been any . . ."

Andrews's patience seemed to be wearing thin. He broke in. "What happened when he came back?" he said so sharply it unnerved me.

"When he came back, he, he came back in and he just started, he just started arguin' and accusin' me and callin' me names."

Andrews leaned toward me. "Now, who was arguing?"

"Michael . . ."

"Okay." He was nodding to himself again.

I stiffened. ". . . was yellin' at, at me primarily."

"Okay."

"He was primarily yellin' at me, and I told him to git out of the apartment. He said no. Uh, he just said he's not leavin' and he, he had every right to be there because his daughter was there. . . ."

"Uh huh."

"And I kept tellin' him, 'Your name's not on the lease.' I even told him ahead of time. I said, 'Michael, you know there are so many warrants for your arrest,' and I said, and I'm scared of this man. I mean, this man will not leave me alone."

"Was he drunk last night?"

I nodded my head affirmatively. "He had been drinkin' last night."

"Okay."

"Okay? And I," I hesitated, then went on, "and I know when he drinks you can talk to him some times to get him to, you know, and he'll start cryin' or somethin'."

Andrews cut to the point. "You told me earlier in a conversation that you thought he was uh, just very, very jealous."

"Yes, extremely," I said, my voice low.

"Extremely jealous," he repeated. "That's the term you used."

"Extremely jealous," I said.

"Do you feel like that's why he was there last night?"

"Yeah," I said, shuddering. "I felt like that."

"Because Johnny was there?"

"Right."

"Basically?"

"Well," I was stuttering again, wondering how I could communicate the terror of it all to this man who seemed so matter-of-fact. "But see, it, you know . . ."

"But, does he usually do this even if Johnny's not there?"

"Yes." I nodded. "See, like, he calls, he would call me at

work, and he would, he called at both of my jobs and he would start askin' me who I was, you know, sleepin' with or this that and the other, and I kept sayin', 'You know, Michael, I work two jobs, I don't have time for this stuff.' You know. He was callin' harrassin' me at work constantly, and it was constant. The police even came out to the hotel where I worked one time."

"Okay, what, what was the," he stumbled over the word, obviously trying to further upset me; but he didn't succeed. "How did it end last night? Did the? . . ." He paused.

"There was a . . ." I began to cry. "He came at me and started swingin' at me, and was comin' at me and I was tryin' to fight back with him, and then, Johnny pulled him off me."

"Okay."

"And then, uh, then, I don't have a phone, and I had to run, the girls were upstairs in bed."

"Uh huh."

"And what scares me," I paused, trying to stop trembling, trying to sound coherent. "I was afraid he's gonna take off with one of the girls, you know, or harm us."

"So you left John and Michael in the apartment together?"

"Right."

"What happened then? You have any idea?"

"I don't know. I ran across the street. There's a nine-one-one emergency phone by the pool that the security guard at our pool complex had told me to use if I needed it. Well, it was locked up."

"What was the situation when you got back?"

"He, he was . . ." I paused trying to collect my thoughts. "I told Johnny when I came back in, I told Johnny they're. . . ." I stopped again, thinking I'd misjudged what he'd asked. "What do you mean, situation?"

"Well, were they both still there?"

"Yeah, they were both still there."

"Were they arguin' or what?"

"No, not really. Michael was arguin' more with me."

"Okay. Did the . . . ?"

I broke in. "You see I'm sayin', I mean, he was . . ."

"Now, Michael got put in jail last night."

"Right, 'cause, see . . ."

"Did they arrest him at your apartment?"

I gave a heavy sigh. All these questions. What was the difference now? When was he going to talk about today and the real reason we were here? It was too late to help us. What I had been afraid of all along had happened. Michael had done more than beat on me. He had killed someone. Still the detective kept asking, and I tried to answer as best I could.

"No. He, see, when, so Johnny left and called the police. I told Johnny that the phone was locked up over there and I couldn't call."

"Okay."

"So Johnny left and called the police. Okay?"

"Okay."

"So then when the police came, I'd had these papers hid 'cause I'd gone to Ashland to get copies of the warrants."

"Okay."

"Because the warrants were misdemeanors, they don't show up on the police file."

"Right. Right."

"Okay? So I'd gone to Ashland to get copies of the warrants, and so I had 'em in an envelope hidden, 'cause I was afraid if Michael saw 'em, he'd tear 'em up, you know. If he knew the police were on their way, and so, when he came out, when I went and got the envelope and ran back downstairs, Michael was standin' out there sayin' somethin' to the police, and I started sayin', 'This man has warrants for him,' you know. I started explainin' to 'em as quickly as I could. Well, he starts takin' off. . . ."

"Uh huh."

"Up the street. So he takes off up the street and I show these stack of papers I have. I explained to the police officers . . ."

"To the police officers that were there?"

"Right, to the police officers. I showed 'em a copy of the warrant that was not gonna show up, and the only thing that shows up when they run a check on him is that his license is revoked."

"Okay."

"And so I explained what I had and why they weren't comin' up on the computer 'cause they were misdemeanors."

"But by this time, he had already left."

"He ran."

"Okay. So he got arrested later that night?"

"Well, just a matter of a few minutes later because the police came back by and told me that they had arrested him for public intoxication."

"Okay."

"And for me to call the jail and tell them about. . . ."

"About the misdemeanor warrants."

"About the misdemeanor warrants."

"Okay."

"And I did that. I went to a pay phone, and I called the jail and I told them, 'There's a man that is on his way down there or already there,' and I gave 'em his name and they checked for me and they said he was there and they were bookin' him in then."

"Okay."

"And I said, 'Now listen to me,' I said, 'There's warrants for his arrest and I want him held.' That's what I was tryin' to do was get him held." If only they had. If only they had. The phrase repeated itself in the back of my mind like a chorus while I spoke.

"Okay. Uh, when was the next occasion you had to see Michael?"

I took a deep breath. My frustration was rising. "The next time I saw him, he was shootin' Johnny."

"Okay," he said, so matter-of-factly I wanted to shake him. "That was about what time today?"

Upset, I shook my head vehemently. "I have no idea. I have no idea. I was upstairs with the baby."

"Okay. Where was, uh, John at the time?"

"He and Erica were downstairs. They were downstairs playing and talking."

"So this morning just prior to all this happening today, uh, John and his daughter were downstairs?"

"Right, exactly. They were downstairs, just visiting."

"My understanding, he hadn't seen this girl for a long time."

"Exactly. He had been begging to see her and Erica had been questioning me about her father."

"I understand that. How did John have occasion to be in Fayette County?"

"I brought him here."

"Okay."

"He asked to come. He said that he wanted to come down. He wanted to visit Erica."

"So you went to Ashland yesterday?"

"Well, I went down there to get my copies of all the warrants. I went to see my attorney."

"Johnny came back with you."

I nodded. "Right. Since I was there, and I knew I didn't have to work the next day, I took Erica to see him. We were with his other family members, and they all visited and had a good time."

Andrews asked questions about Johnny getting to Ashland. Stop, I wanted to yell. Stop all this nonsense. Why do you care whether he came by car or foot? Is it so important? Finally he said, as if hearing my unspoken words, "Okay, let's get back to the events of this morning. You were in an upstairs bedroom?"

"Yes, in my bedroom."

"With one of your children?"

"With Michael's child, the baby."

"Okay. Uh, do you recall hearing Michael come into the apartment this morning?"

"No, I don't."

"Not at all?"

"Not at all," I said definitively.

"Uh, what's the first thing that you remember hearing, seeing or whatever?"

"One of two things. There's . . . there, I can't place in my mind which happened first, but I heard a gunshot and, and Erica screaming."

"Okay, that's fine. In your bedroom, was your bedroom door closed?"

"No, I think," I paused, trying to remember, "seems like it was cracked. I had brought Megan upstairs and I think I shut it but not tight."

"And you heard a scream and/or a gunshot. You don't know which one was first?"

"Uh huh."

"What did you do at that time?"

"Well, I looked . . ." His bloodied face flashed in my mind. I shuddered. "I saw Johnny layin' there and I saw Michael pull the trigger again."

"So the door must have been open?"

"Yes, well, it wasn't locked because I don't remember doin' anything."

"You looked out the door."

"I looked out the door."

"Okay."

My voice was growing hoarse. I sipped a little lukewarm water from the glass in front of me and took a deep breath. "Right, and saw Michael shootin' Johnny."

"You actually saw him pull the trigger?"

"Yes. At least one shot. I don't remember, I know I heard a shot and I don't remember if I saw that first shot or it was the second shot and I'm not really sure how many shots there were."

Andrews was nodding rhythmically now. "Okay. That's fine. That's fine. Then what?"

"Then I turned around. He says, 'I'm gonna kill you, too.'"

"Okay."

I tried to go back to that awful moment. "Well, now I have one daughter at the bottom of the stairs, the oldest one. The baby is in my arms."

"So the oldest daughter never came up the stairs?"

"She did eventually."

"Oh! She did."

"She did eventually. The baby was in my arms and I shut the door and locked it. There was a thousand things runnin' through my mind right then: How do I get outta here? How do I get the kids out?"

"Okay, let me get—"

I interrupted. "How many shots were there?"

He didn't answer my question. "Let me get this in my mind now. You were back in the bedroom at this time with your youngest daughter."

"With my baby, right."

"Okay, and Michael and John, John was down at this time."

"Yeah."

"And had been shot?"

"Right," I said so softly I was afraid he hadn't heard.

But he had, and interrupted, "And your daughter was also in the hallway with them out there."

"Right," I said, looking off in the distance.

"Go ahead. I'm just trying to get in my mind . . ."

"So then, he kicked the door."

"Okay."

My heart was beating furiously. The words tumbled out. "He kicked the door open and I went, he started talkin' to me, you know. I'm kinda dazed."

"I can understand that," he said in a monotone.

"And my main worry was gettin' both the kids out, and I was tryin' to think of a way to get by him without gettin' me shot and getting' both the girls out, and so, I start pleadin' with him. He says, 'You drove me to this,' and 'I was not gonna let this man be around my daughter.' And I don't even remember exactly what all he said to me."

"Okay."

"I was just tryin' to appease him."

"I understand."

I didn't think he did. I went on. "How I could try to get downstairs and out the door?"

"How did you manage that?"

"We were standin' at the top of the stairs, and there was a knock on the door. So Erica had run up the stairs. She said, 'Mommy, somebody's at the door.' And she was hangin' onto me, and I kept Megan up like this around my face 'cause I was afraid he's gonna blow my brains out."

"Okay."

A shudder shook me. I tried to still the trembling going through my body. "I really thought he was just gonna blow my brains out. Well, I remember kinda backin' down the stairs. Well, he come down and got in front of the door. I mean, he just shoved me away."

"The downstairs door."

"The downstairs door goin' outside."

"Okay. Who was at the door?"

"I don't know." I shook my head numbly. "See, from what I understand, this is what I kinda heard. The neighbors heard somethin'. I don't know if they heard the gunfire or what, and I think it was a neighbor that came to the door, and knocked on it, or a police officer. I'm not sure. I have no idea who knocked at the door. But all I know was by the time I got there it wasn't very long."

"From the time the shooting occurred until you got out, it wasn't that long?"

I wasn't going to be able to make sense much longer. The words were sticking in my mouth. "Right," I said hoarsely.

"Just long enough for you to go in the bedroom and him to kick the door in."

"Right." I was starting to cry again. I couldn't help it.

"You pleaded?" the officer asked.

"Right." I nodded slowly.

"And then managed to get down."

I nodded again and tried to speak. "And," I took a breath, "and managed to get downstairs, and there was a struggle downstairs, and he put the gun in my side." It was then I had seen my daughter. Oh my God. "I said 'Erica,' and I looked at him, and I said, 'Michael, just please let Erica out. Just let Erica out.'"

"Okay."

The memory stuck in my throat. The memory of seeing my child in danger. I tried to tell Andrews. "I said, 'Please let her out,' and so the door came open. I'd stuck my, see, I'd got my fingers smashed a little bit where he . . .'"

"Uh huh."

He had to know how horrible it had been. I went on, my voice rising now in anguish. "He slammed the door once, and I said, 'Please, Michael, let Erica out,' and he'd had the gun in my side then and we were leanin' over against the door and when I had to open the door wide enough for Erica to come around, and when he did, I just kinda kicked him back, and fell forward. I fell on the concrete, that's how this happened, and I had the baby with me, and I just fell on the concrete to the ground and I got out."

"You didn't see him after that?" Andrews said disinterestedly, glancing at his watch.

"No," I replied softly. "I didn't see him anymore, and there was a lady police officer standin' right there."

"When you fell out the door, there was a policewoman standing right there?"

"Right. Right."

"Was she aware of what was going on?"

"I don't know. I mean, I didn't call the police."

"Let me rephrase that. I was, my question was more like, did she seem to be appreciating what was happening or did she stumble upon this?"

"She was like . . ."

"She had a gun out?"

"Yes."

"Oh. I see."

"Uh, I think. I mean, it seemed like she was very prepared, and I 'member Erica kinda froze."

"I see."

"Erica just didn't know what to do."

"Okay. I understand."

But he didn't. I could see he didn't. How could he? He hadn't seen it or felt it. We were no one to him. Crazy nameless people. Our agony wasn't his. It was our own.

Nevertheless, I went on. "So, when I fell, and I 'membered the baby kinda fell on top of me, and I was so scared he was gonna shoot me when I walked out the door."

"You never looked back at the door, then?" he asked, as if berating me.

"Erica just stood there frozen. I cried out, 'Erica, run.'"

"Okay."

"And she did. She ran right behind me."

"Okay. Let me just ask you a few more questions about the actual event at the top of the stairs." My God, more questions. "Okay? When you got to the door of your bedroom, you say you think maybe it was ajar at that time, or at least it wasn't closed. Earlier in our conversation you said that someone had told you it was three shots that . . ."

"Right."

"But you thought maybe there were four."

"I don't know. I didn't know for sure. That's what I'm tryin' to put together in my mind."

"We discussed that and I also told you I didn't really expect anyone to start counting."

"Right. Exactly, but I was tryin' to think in my head, how many did he shoot? Because I wondered, did he have a bullet for me, a bullet for Erica and a bullet for Megan, a bullet for himself? And I don't . . ."

"So, basically, this took a few seconds for you to do this, right?"

"Well . . ."

"I mean, what happened at the top of the stairs wasn't necessarily a quick thing. It took a while to unfold?"

Or a lifetime, I thought, wincing. "Yes, well, a minute, two minutes?"

"Possibly, I don't know. I'm asking you."

"Yes. I mean to me it seemed less than a minute. Less than a minute. It was so fast."

"Because they were already at the top of the stairs?"

"Right. Now, see, what I'm sayin' is I don't know if there had been words outside. I don't know how Michael got in. See what I'm sayin'? I don't know any of that."

"You didn't know either one of them was even at the top of the stairs until the shooting occurred?"

"Right. Exactly."

"And, and the scream."

"Right."

"Okay."

"Right. See, I mean, are you followin' me?"

"Yes, yes."

"You know."

"Yes, I am."

I sighed heavily trying to think, trying to calm myself.

Andrews said, "Is there anything that I haven't covered?"

There was something, something I had to know. "Who is the guy that brought him there? Who is that guy?"

"Uh," he said, looking uncomfortable, "they were in jail

together last night."

"Okay." I nodded. "They told me that."

"They were incarcerated together."

"The police told me that."

"I guess maybe they just became friends in jail or something."

"And so . . ." Through my mind passed unspoken words. A stranger. Why would a stranger aid Michael in ruining so many lives? "Okay," I said wearily.

"Uh, I spoke with this guy, and he said he didn't know Michael prior to last night. So, I don't think there's a connection at all between the two."

"Yes. I mean you have to understand, you know."

"Before last night?"

"Right. 'Cause I didn't ever know for Michael to own a gun either."

"Okay."

"I've never known him to own a gun 'cause he always told me. He said, 'It wouldn't be safe for me to have a gun 'cause of my temper.' He always told me that."

"Okay. Anything else?"

"I just wish that it all hadn't happened," I said, trying to say something, something that would express my own pain.

He gave me no sign that he understood. "Okay, we'll conclude the interview," he said and got up, dismissing me with a wave of his hand.

After the interview was over, I felt like I'd been raped, beaten, and left for dead. After living through Johnny's death, I'd had to suffer through Detective Andrews's probing, inane questioning. He couldn't possibly understand what my life had been like during the violent time since I'd been married to Michael. He didn't understand the hell that Michael had put me and the girls through and Andrews was in the Crimes Against Children Unit? Why didn't they have somebody that thought about children first instead of men? He didn't seem to care that I had tried to do everything the right way, through the courts and the police, to escape Michael's abuse. Why did it have to take Johnny's death before the police took Michael away?

I wasn't even sure if they were really listening to me now. It hadn't seemed to matter to any of the police that Michael had tried to kill me, too. But I'd never forget how he'd jammed that gun hard into my side. Thank God I managed to find a way out with the girls. Otherwise, we might not be alive either. Michael might have murdered us all.

I began to tremble all over as I started to realize how close we'd come to dying. Suddenly I went limp in mind and body. I could hardly understand what the officers were saying to me. My body felt like a limp rag and my legs were becoming as unstable as my terrorized mind.

"I have to get back to the apartment complex and get the girls," I said hoarsely. Someone must have volunteered to drive me. They must have noticed my condition.

"We'll take you," one of the young officers said. "But I think you should call someone to stay with."

I nodded. I knew we couldn't stay in that bloodied apartment. They led me to the phone and I called my sister. "Beth," I cried when I heard her voice. "Could you get me and the girls and take us over to Mom and Dad? We've got nowhere to stay." And I poured out to her the story of Johnny's death. "It'll take over two hours if you meet me at Jerry's restaurant near the interstate."

I asked the helpful officer with the sandy hair, and he agreed to give the girls and I a ride there. It took only a few minutes to go first to the apartment but seemed as if time stood still. When we arrived at the complex, television crews and cameras were milling around outside my apartment.

As I got out of the car, I heard people yelling, "There she is!" Reporters clamored for an interview but I was in no condition to talk to anybody. Bright yellow police tape was wrapped around the front door of my place. My legs seemed to turn to jelly as we approached that door. The door I sprang from with my girls so Michael wouldn't kill us. The door I just moved into to get away from Michael. The door where I hugged Johnny last night under the stars. Oh, Jesus.

"I don't think I can go in," I murmured. "I need some help. Tell me this isn't happening."

Assisted by the sandy-haired policeman who told me this was his first murder case, I entered the apartment that just hours before had become my worst nightmare. I needed to gather a few things and get out as fast as I could. What do we need? I tried to think, my head throbbing. Clothes, Megan's bottles, some diapers. In order to get clothes for the girls and myself, I had to go upstairs. I forced my legs to move. Slowly one foot, then the other. When I reached the top of the stairs, my eyes fastened on the blood stains on the hall carpeting. I couldn't look away. I couldn't stop the pain. Johnny's blood, blood that had trickled out of him as he lay dying. Johnny took my bullets. I couldn't help but cry out. By now I was barely functioning. My head clouded. I had to get out. I've got to get to my girls. They need me now more than ever.

I fished through the clutter on the floor of my bedroom and managed to get some things together that the girls and I would need. Somehow, I got back downstairs.

As I got ready to leave the apartment, I looked back into the living room and saw the food on the coffee table. Automatically, I stepped toward the table to clear the food away. Then my heart clutched. On the coffee table, artistically arranged in a triangle pattern on a plate, were three raspberry crullers. The sudden realization that Johnny had set my breakfast table with the sweets I had asked for that morning, the last time we spoke, flooded over me. I sunk to my knees as grief finally overwhelmed me. Clutching the clothes I had gathered for the girls, I rocked back and forth on my knees, sobbing uncontrollably.

"Johnny, Johnny, Johnny." I repeated his name as though

calling it out might somehow bring him back and put an end to my misery. I don't know how long I cried or how I got out of the apartment. The young officer who was with me must have somehow guided me outside. Once there, the cool air brought a measure of control. I had children to care for. Erica and Megan needed me. I had to find strength. I had to find them a place to stay. I had to think of them first. I didn't have time to grieve. And once the children's basic needs were taken care of I had to plan a funeral. I didn't know how. My fractured thoughts jumped from one problem to another. Oh God. I prayed for strength. I can't bury Johnny. I may as well die myself. But who would keep the girls? What am I thinking? Just let me get my girls. Please. Somebody. Just let me get my girls.

CHAPTER 6

Going Home Again

I hardly felt the young officer's hand as he guided me across the parking lot to my neighbor's apartment where the girls waited and left me at the door. Inside, Megan, her face as serene as a cherub, was snuggled up fast asleep on the sofa, but Erica, dazed and stony-faced, grabbed my leg as soon as she saw me and held onto it just as she had this morning when her father died.

With Erica fastened to me, I made my way over to the baby, picked her up, thanked my neighbor and her children, and went out to the waiting cruiser. Opening the car door, I untangled Erica. We got in and sat huddled together with the baby in the back seat.

At Jerry's on New Circle Street and Broadway we all got out, and I thanked the policeman who looked pale and shaken up. I had no money to buy food so we sat at the counter under the glaring eye of the waitress sipping ice water and eating crackers.

Almost an hour passed before Beth picked us up. With her was my younger brother, Gary. Gary hadn't married and still lived at home with my older brother, James, who had returned after his divorce. I truly felt sorry for Beth and Gary having to come pick me up under such horrible circumstances. Gary swore to me most of the way home he'd do Michael in some day, but I knew that was just brotherly protection talk. Beth was more quiet and solemn about it all. She took me gently by the arm before we got in the car and tearfully reminded me we'd lost a special person and a great artist when we lost Johnny. "I loved him like a brother," she assured me. "Jane, you have a guardian angel now that Johnny is in heaven." She'd always relied on God during a crisis. Though my faith was not nearly as strong as hers, thinking of Johnny being in heaven comforted me. But my own life had become even more of a hell. Had it not been for my two girls I would have wished it ended.

On the ride back to Russell my mind was vague and confused. At times it felt like my head would burst or my heart might quit. I dreaded going home. I'd left home just months before with great hope and expectations of getting a job and settling my family. Michael had dashed these hopes. Now, here I was, going home again, with nothing but stories of death and destruction.

The drive turned into a crying session. Beth tried to ease my mind, but she seemed as unhinged as I was as I repeated the grisly story of Johnny's demise and the children's and my near-death struggle with Michael. Each time I looked into Beth's rearview mirror, I saw tears running down her face and her hands trembling on the steering wheel. I knew it took all the strength she could muster to get us home fast and safely in order to put an end to our agonizing journey. She sent the car full throttle a few times when I'd burst into a tortured wail. I did the best I could to keep it together and not talk so much about Johnny's murder, but it was all I could think of. Memories tormented me, whirling through my mind until we got close to the exit, and the dread of going home and facing my family overcame me.

As our car passed through downtown Russell, I envisioned some of the neighbors grabbing their phones and calling one another to announce my arrival. When Beth and I were teenagers, they'd always kept track of the girls who'd stayed out past curfew, got pregnant without marrying right away, or had run-ins with the law. In Appalachia, little went unnoticed when it came to a girl's honor; some felt it was their duty as good citizens to keep an eye on us so they could inform our parents of the possibility of us ruining our reputations. Not that our parents weren't forever reminding us of the consequences. Any time Beth or I left the house, Mom was quick to remind us of the dangers outside. "People will think you're white trash if ya git in any kind of trouble," she'd warn. I hadn't been considered a wild child or anything, but I did have a streak of independence in me and that, in our neighborhood, was not something to brag about in a girl. If I'd slipped the minds of the few excessively curious neighbors over the years, being away and all, I knew the news of this day was bound to put me at the center of the town's scuttlebutt. I couldn't remember a murder ever happening around our parts, and I knew my second husband killing my first husband was bound to make me the talk of the town. I shrunk back tighter into the corner of the back seat and shuddered thinking of my predicament and how it would seem to others. I said a silent prayer that I could save my children from the tongue wagging, hide them from the whispers and the shameful feelings the gossip might bring. Now was a time we needed nothing but comfort and understanding, not reproach and ridicule.

As we turned onto the street where Mom and Dad lived, I could see by all the cars out front that the children and I'd have plenty of probing we didn't need. It was the custom when anybody died for the neighbors and relatives to gather from all over, bringing covered dishes of food and commence to tell stories which began "I remember when" and "I wish I could have said this or that before he died." I sighed heavily. It was obvious this time was going to be no different.

Beth pulled the car into the driveway and parked. I noticed straightaway my aunts Louise and Tara Lynn's cars were already there, and I felt sure one of them was bound to have brought Granny with them. My aunts were a welcome sight and always good to talk to at such trying times, but I hated more than anything to put Granny through my wretched story. She was getting up in years and didn't need to be involved in our nightmare. My mom's family was a tight-knit bunch, and every attempt was made to keep Granny from turmoil. There were six girls in the family to help keep her in good care in her older years. Not a son was sired, and Mom never failed to remind us of how Paw Nolan bragged about his exceptionally beautiful girls with their ivory skin, dark hair, and high cheekbones. "Bragged about his girls more than anyone with a house full of boys," she'd say. But we all knew, despite her words, that Appalachian families coveted sons.

My grandfather died when I was only twelve, and his daughter, Jenny, the second oldest daughter in their family, died from breast cancer that same sorrowful year. Another sister, Aunt Betty Ann, was the only one who'd moved away after marrying. She and Uncle Jed, who came from Candy Holler, made it big, first selling pantihose and then insurance, and settled in the suburbs of Atlanta. They lived in a house the other sisters could only dream of. There was little chance Uncle Jed and Aunt Betty Ann would've had time to get here.

Mom was waiting at the side of the driveway. She peered in the car's open window.

"God, I'm glad ya'll made it all right. Beth, did ya have any trouble findin' 'em? Give me that baby. Ain't she a doll? I bet ya'll are about starved ta death." Mom winced when she said death, realizing the inappropriateness of her metaphor. She opened the car door with trembling arms.

I handed Megan to her, slid Erica out, and hoisted myself from the back seat. In my nervousness, one of my knees buckled as I stepped out. Fortunately, a breath of air revived me at least enough to keep me moving toward the house.

As we stepped onto the porch, opened the front door, and went in, I was too upset to recognize the people who were saying hello and offering me food. They must have noticed my disorientation and the room became quieter, more subdued. It was all I could do to concentrate on Erica and her needs. She refused food and conversation and clung to me as the unfamiliar visitors approached her.

The clove sweet smell of honey-baked ham and potato salad drifted into my nostrils, but I refused the inviting scents. I had no appetite and could not help the tears which kept falling from my bloodshot eyes. I blurted out my recollections like a child awakened by a nightmare when my dad asked what had happened. Mom had begun showing Megan off to some of the neighbors. Then she walked over to us saying something about how pretty everybody thought Megan was until she noticed my pathetic condition and obvious instability. Megan began crying from hunger, and Mom handed her right over and I gave her a bottle. Then Mom took her back.

Erica and I sunk into the couch and tried to comfort each other while everybody around us made small talk. Poor little Erica was trying so hard to be a big girl and hold her tears and heartaches inside while the company was around. But as she snuggled up closer I could feel her shaking and I knew she was about to let go. I stroked her moistened bangs back from her eyes and whispered quietly to her. "It's best to try to think of the good memories of your daddy," I said softly, but I knew my words were spoken in vain. Johnny and the image of his violent death overpowered us both. I leaned my head against hers and from the corner of my eye caught a glimpse of Megan, clasping a cookie in each hand while Aunt Tara Lynn tried to feed her Jell-O. Megan gorged like a happy baby and I was relieved that at least one of us had escaped the trauma seemingly unscathed.

Since my aunts were there helping Mom with Megan and she seemed content, I knew they could do without me for a while. Rest would do Erica and me some good, I thought, and the seclusion of a private room would allow us the perfect place to cry out our nightmare. I quietly took Erica's small hand in mine, eased us off the couch, and led her upstairs.

At the top of the stairs on the right was the room Beth and I had shared beginning in the fifth grade. Dad bought the house and all its contents from his parents after they retired and left for Florida. Beth and I slept in the bed they had left behind until my senior year when I ran away with Johnny to get married. I hadn't slept in the room since.

As I opened the door, I noticed that the padlock my sister had put on to keep out our brothers was still dangling from the door. Dad hadn't worked since his injury at the railroad and nobody knew when the cash settlement would come. Mom had no choice but to go out and work more than before and no longer had time to do the minor repairs on the house like she used to.

Very few of the objects in the room belonged to me. It had been cleared out after Beth married and our bed replaced long before Dad's mishap. But despite the absence of my past, looking out the seven windows overlooking the Ohio River instantly conjured up memories of my childhood and growing up. Looking out, I remembered that the river had frozen nearly solid the year I met Johnny. I could still hear the sounds of barges crashing through the ice as they carried coal from the mountains and oil products from the nearby refineries. The vessels had large intrusive searchlights that wandered the banks and the waters and occasionally threw their wide beams into our windows: a sleep-awakening invasion that continued to a lesser extent year round. The huge boughs of the hundred-year-old tree outside the window were the only obstacle that interrupted the bright flash of light once the barges drifted far enough downriver in search of the Mississippi. I examined the tree's massive summer-bloom shape, appreciating the protective duties it had attempted to fulfill during my childhood. For years people had speculated that the magnificent maple would be struck by wind or lightning when the next big storm hit and take the street and the front yard into the river as it tumbled, but so far it had proved them all wrong and I was glad of it. The green, graceful branches stirred slightly as I admired the tree and the gray marbled river water that flowed beneath the Ironton bridge.

I turned to my daughter, trying to cheer her up.

"Erica, this used to be your momma's bedroom. Look at what a pretty view this is. Ain't it beautiful?"

The sound of a thud interrupted my reminiscing as Erica threw herself on the bed and started to cry. I stood painfully silent for a second, then leaned over the bed to hold her as she wept. I hadn't had time to prepare for this. I didn't even know how to begin to ease my child's pain. Her slight frame shook violently as she sobbed harder and harder. I sat on the bed holding her and watching the river flow down its banks as I patted her petite back in search of the words to cure her wounded soul. Nothing had prepared me for such a miserable moment. This was not like a scratched knee that I could wash off, cover with a Band-Aid, kiss, and make all better. It wasn't like a goldfish who died or a puppy struck by a car. I became so caught up in my child's pain I didn't have time to think of my own. The sight of her crumpled body made my spirit wither as tears spilled from both our eyes. I thought of how hard I'd tried to shield my child from the beatings, the humiliation, and the thievery Michael had put us through. I'd moved us many times and in each place secured the best home that I could and tried to be strong in front of her. I'd kept promising her life would be better once we got away. Now I was afraid she'd never believe another word I said, that she'd think I was filled with lies, but God knows I'd tried to protect her. I sat helplessly, wordlessly at the moment she needed me most. All I could do was hold her. I leaned closer to Erica, laid my head on hers, and a low bleating moan escaped my lips, a mourning sound that could be heard throughout the house.

As I watched her, Erica's labored breathing began to worry me. As tenderly as I could, I turned her frail body toward mine and caressed her petal-soft, tear-drenched face as she rubbed her hands over her red, runny nose. I wanted to tell her how beautiful I thought she was, and so much like her father, but

I was afraid the mention of his name might further wound her fragile mind. Her swollen, soulful eyes looked long into mine as if she wanted to speak but couldn't.

We huddled together silently for a long time. Finally I said softly, "It's okay, baby, cry it out. We'll git through this. Momma's right here with ya and nobody's gonna hurt us here."

Even as I spoke I feared I wasn't telling the whole truth. She seemed to know what I was thinking and spoke between sobs. "But what if they let Michael out again? He'll know ta come here. He knows where Mamaw and Papaw live. He'll git us, Mommy!"

"Erica, you just let that thought go. Clear it from your mind. He ain't gonna git out."

"But they took him last night, after he hurt you and Daddy and they let him out this morning. I'm afraid he'll git out 'n' kill us."

"Yeah, but, honey, killing somebody is real serious. They don't let 'em out for life. He'll be in there forever. Before, he was just a thief, a drunk driver and a wife beater, and they don't usually keep people in jail for stuff like that. Just close your eyes, baby, and try to rest. Everything's gonna be okay. I promise, honey."

"But, Mommy, I can't sleep. When I close my eyes, I see Daddy on the floor with blood comin' out of his mouth. His eyes was open. Mommy, I think he's still alive."

"No, sweetheart, as much as I'd like to believe that too, he's gone from us. Gone to heaven to be with Jesus. I miss him, too, honey, but he's gone from this world now."

"I want to go there, Mommy."

I couldn't hold back the tears as I looked away from her and thought of Johnny and how Erica would suffer over this. I felt that crushed spirit inside myself. I knew she'd miss him as much as I would. I thought of how funny he was, how handsome, his talents, their likeness and all the things Erica would never get to see him do. Those beautiful images shifted to gruesome ones as I pulled her into my weakened arms and rocked her like a suckling infant until her eyes grew heavy and I laid her back to rest. I watched her face turn gray as I stroked it. I felt she was dying in front of me, not in the physical sense, but her childhood innocence was gone forever.

I took a deep breath between my quivering lips as I began to dwell on all I had lost on this dreadful hot summer day and wondered if I could ever repair our fractured lives.

"Janie! Come quick!" Dad yelled from his living room recliner downstairs.

Erica sprang up as if another shot had been fired and threw the covers off her. We both ran for the stairs. Erica raced down the stairs ahead of me. I followed her as fast as my feet would carry me.

"What's this?"

"We tuned in the Lexington channel on the cable TV. They got coverage from the murder," Dad said excitedly.

Before I could finish a sip from the glass of cool water somebody sat in front of me, I glanced up and saw the end of the whole nightmare replayed before my eyes. The building where I'd lived and Johnny's life was taken flashed before me on the screen. The yellow police tape that was wrapped around the crime scene blew in the hot breeze as I tried to keep from being overcome with grief about the events that had happened there just hours before.

"Mommy! There it is! That's our house! Daddy's still in there!" Shaking my head, I reached out to pull Erica to me.

"Honey, hush," Dad yelled from the recliner. "We can't hear what they're asayin'."

I knew this wasn't anything we needed to relive. I quickly led Erica back upstairs while they watched the remnants of our nightmare. I had seen enough and didn't think watching it would help our state of mind.

Looking out the window when as we got back in the room, I noticed the moon had begun to creep up from behind the mountains and would soon replace the evening light with darkness. Erica hesitantly changed her clothes into the nightshirt that someone had placed at the end of our bed. I folded back the covers as she climbed in and laid on her back facing me. She continued to search my eyes as if I'd have some miracle cure for her agony. I stroked her gray, flushed skin as she squinted hard to keep her eyes closed. Watching her, I was haunted by her resemblance to her father. The more she relaxed, the more she appeared to lie lifeless on the bed, almost anxious for burial. The realization of how lucky we were that the gun had jammed sent chills up my spine. God, Michael could have killed us all or taken her or any one of us had I not managed to get us out. All the possible combinations of death or maiming we could have suffered swam in my mind and mingled with the image of my daughter's agonized face.

The funeral I knew would be further torture for us both. I'd lost my best friend Kim when I was ten years old. She'd died on the operating table from open heart surgery and certain things still caused me to cry over her passing. I'd lost my friend Bunny in a car accident our junior year, and my junior high sweetheart, Robbie, took his own life just weeks after we graduated from high school. But this death was different and this funeral would be the most difficult. I didn't have to watch the others die. My memories of them were playful and happy ones, not blood-spattering and horrifying like the ones of Johnny's death.

I continued to stroke Erica as I wept silently, thankful that, at least, we had escaped with our lives.

CHAPTER 7

The Funeral

Unable to sleep, I watched night turn to day and hadn't once thought of anything but Johnny's murder. There was much to be done, but numbed by grief, I couldn't seem to begin. I had to call Johnny's family and discuss the funeral arrangements. I'd paced the floor for hours wondering what to say and how to say it. I knew they'd have questions and expect answers. Calling my attorney was important because our safety was in jeopardy. I was afraid the police might let Michael out as they had before without even giving us a call. Michael would know we'd have no other place to go but Mom and Dad's house. The detectives who questioned me at the police department said I had to report back to them right after the funeral and make arrangements to testify at the murder trial, but I didn't know where to go or who to talk to. The idea of having to figure out who was on my side scared me. I didn't trust any of them since they'd done nothing for me but turn Michael loose time and again. Look where that got us.

And then there was work. I knew I'd better call my boss and explain everything to him in hopes of salvaging my job. As a waitress at the Morley Hotel, the tips were better than most other places. I'd been a reliable employee since I was hired and hadn't caused any trouble except the couple of times Michael stormed into the dining room and demanded the manager release me early so I could leave with him. I'm just glad the owner Leona Helmsly wasn't there or I might have lost my job on the spot. I'd heard stories of how ruthlessly she'd treated her employees, but I'd never met her in the short time I'd worked there. I was thankful my food and beverage manager had a sense of reality and compassion. He knew how badly I needed the work, and I needed it more now than ever since I was Megan's and Erica's sole support. I had to find a new apartment and start over again.

Mom came into the kitchen as I started looking up phone numbers and she asked, a worried look on her face, "What can I get you for breakfast, dear?"

"Nothing. Maybe some black coffee," I said wearily.

"Oh, Janie, please let me fix ya some sausage gravy and biscuits. You know nobody fixes 'em better than your ol' Mom does—no lumps and plenty of sausage chunks. The secret is the little touch of morning coffee I add, but don't give that secret away. How long's it been since ya had somethin' to eat?"

"I couldn't eat a bite, Mom, I just couldn't."

Her face held a look of disappointment, but she didn't press me.

"Janie, did you sleep any?" she asked, already knowing the answer.

I shook my head and then, looking at the dark circles under her eyes, which mirrored my own, I asked, "Did you?"

"Not much. Dreams of y'all dyin' woke me every few minutes. It's hard to believe how close you and the girls come to gettin' killed and I can't help but think about Johnny, and how pitiful he was that time your dad and I run him off after you were divorced. It's not easy for us, either, Janie. I realize now that Johnny loved you more than anything, and I guess I somehow feel responsible and guilty that we didn't help y'all more when hard times hit." Her shoulders shuddered, heaving out her regrets.

"We always thought you could marry better, Janie. That's all it was. It wasn't like we didn't like Johnny. But you were our brightest child. We just hated to see you marry some ol' musician or artist with no future. Every mother wants to see her daughter marry money so life will be easier. We just didn't realize how much Johnny really loved you and Erica, and I guess sometimes that matters more than money. Maybe if we had treated him better you two would have still been together."

"Mom, you couldn't have done anything. We loved each other but we were just too young."

She couldn't seem to stop her own regrets. "And then, when you were divorced, your brother needed us to help him. And you always acted so strong, like nothin' was wrong. I just figured you'd find a way."

I sighed heavily. "I got that from you. You always endured when life got crazy; I guess ya had no choice. I didn't know how to take care of a baby but I learned. That's just how it is for women."

She nodded. "Ain't it the truth. Women have to be strong to endure all the shit men put us through, but I guess you know that more than ever. Janie, I guess you're just a chip off the old block," she added, giving me a tired smile.

I looked at her closely for the first time in a long while and realized that she must have once been beautiful. Like most all the women in Appalachia, Mom was too old before her time. After she poured my coffee into one of her good china tea cups, which I knew she'd used to make me feel special, I took a sip, sat it in the matching saucer, and began to make my phone calls.

When I spoke to Johnny's dad, John Sr., he said Johnny's body was still at the coroner's office in Lexington. "It's being delayed because they have to perform an autopsy, but I'll call you and let you know when the visitation will be."

"I don't have a thing for the girls to wear to the funeral home," I told Mom. "Do you have any of Erica's baby clothes put away in the basement that Megan might be able to wear?"

"You're not thinkin' of takin' Megan with you to the funeral home around Johnny's people, are ya?" Her large brown eyes flashed. She stared me square in the eye, waiting for my answer and I knew it'd better be the right one.

"I thought all of our family should go."

"Janie, ya better not take Megan with ya. Ya never know how somebody in his family might react to her. You don't want nothin' to happen to that baby."

"To Megan?"

"It was her father that killed Johnny and ya don't know that his people might take it out on her."

I couldn't imagine somebody acting that way toward a baby, but Mom's remark did make me question my plans. Why would they blame a baby, I wondered. I couldn't think of an answer, which only confirmed I had better let Mom lead me through this. I didn't think my mind was capable of making a sound decision at that moment. My body was weak, and my reasoning confused. It was all I could do to finish the couple of calls I had to make. My head felt dizzy and my fingers had an uncertain shake with every spin as I fumbled to dial.

My boss, Andy, wasn't in the office when I called. Luckily, Harry, one of the cooks that I'd become friends with, answered and said everybody there knew about the murder and Andy had already filled my shifts for a couple of days. I told Harry I'd be back Monday to work my regular shift after the funeral. "I badly need the money," I said. He understood my financial predicament. Harry had a child to support and said he couldn't imagine losing a week's worth of pay, let alone dealing with everything I was going through.

When I called Don, my attorney, and explained what had happened, I asked him to check if Michael was still behind bars. He assured me he was and began to explain the proceedings. I tried to keep track of which court appearance came before or after what hearing, preliminary or otherwise, but it was all very confusing to me. I'd never been in court before other than for a divorce and those were usually cut and dried. No one I knew had ever committed a felony, and even if they had I certainly couldn't call to ask what it was like! How had this all happened to me, and why? I buried my head in my hands, cried quietly, and pondered the unknown.

Mom quietly left the room when she saw me crying. Maybe she wasn't sure what to say or was trying not to break down herself. Like me, she didn't know the first thing about criminal proceedings and she knew that I'd have to face yet another crisis on my own.

As Dad came in for his morning coffee, I lifted my head, brushed the tears from my face, and tried to pull myself together. He hated to see anybody cry.

"Did you sleep last night?" he asked.

"A little," I lied, thinking the truth might upset him.

"It didn't sound like it to me. Your nightwalking woke me up several times. What were you doin' down in the basement?"

"Looking for pictures."

"Of what?"

"Of Johnny. I found an old box of stuff stuck back in the fruit cellar. It had canceled checks from when we was married, but none of them had his signature on it, just our names and address."

"What do ya need those for?"

"Just to have, Dad. I wanna look at anything that belonged to Johnny. I can't even find a picture of him, and I don't want to remember him with blood spewin' out of his mouth as he was reachin' up for me."

Shaking his head sadly, Dad walked out of the room. He mumbled something under his breath. I didn't question what it was. I had no answers, only endless questions revolving through my confused mind. Why did Michael kill Johnny? How had my life gotten so out of hand? What was I going to do next?

As I continued to sip the coffee, I couldn't help but search for something in the back of my mind that would help answer the never ending questions rumbling through my head. How could I have married somebody that was capable of killing? I hadn't noticed Michael's evil side until after we got married and I'd become pregnant with Megan, but then it was too late. Why wouldn't anyone help us once the beatings began? People all around these parts were always screaming and protesting about the rights of the unborn child, yet when Michael was battering me, everybody acted like it was just my lot in life to take that kind of mistreatment. God knows I tried to get away, and lost about everything I had while doing it, and the only person who'd stepped in to help me took my bullets.

I could never let go of him. Johnny'd guided me from child to womanhood and encouraged me to expand my mind in search of peace and truth. He explained to me how painting and creating music could ease personal pain. He was at times help-less, and had had a tumultuous childhood, but he was the strongest person I knew when it came to standing up for his beliefs. Johnny never gave in when questions were thrown at him about his choice in life to be an artist and a musician. I knew he could be nothing else. It was just what he was and nobody could change that.

My muddled mind searched for the words for one of his songs, just a verse or a line of comfort, but all I could come up with was more unanswered questions. I spent the rest of that day trying to chase away those questions and the images of all the possible ways the girls and I could have been harmed or worse yet killed had Michael's gun not jammed.

It was all I could do to kiss the girls good morning with-out crying. I couldn't eat and, with no appetite, my limbs grew weaker as the day took its time ending. The sight of Erica made me thankful and sick to my stomach, knowing how lucky I was she was with me but how horrible the rest of her life might be. She'd seen it all, every punch, fight and flight to find safe shelter. Now I didn't know what to say to her, nor did I want to ask her more questions, though I kept wondering what had happened in those moments before I was awakened by gunfire. How did Michael get in? Did he hunt Johnny down, or was there a fight that led to his death? Damn, why didn't I wake up? I remember Erica coming into the room and trying to wake me. It was probably better I stayed down or I might be dead, I thought. I was just so damn tired that morning, and I thought for sure Michael was locked up until we could have a hearing. Why didn't I wake up? Maybe I could have talked Michael out of killing.

By the time John Sr. called back with the funeral arrangements, grief and pain had overcome me. I couldn't have taken Megan to the funeral if I'd wanted to because I was too weak to carry her. I found something for Erica to put on and borrowed one of Mom's outfits to make myself look at least presentable. I called Johnny's cousin Sammy and his wife, Nancy, and they told me everybody would be meeting at Aunt Harriet's trailer before the funeral and we were welcome to come with them.

Aunt Harriet was my favorite of all Johnny's aunts. When Aunt Dotty would come in from Dayton, I loved to go over to Harriet's place. They were always so nice to me, making special treats.

I was glad I could ride along with them to the funeral home. I didn't want to go in alone. I couldn't stand the thoughts of seeing Johnny laid out in a casket after seeing him so alive and filled with love the day before. All I could think of was the bloody image of him dying as I pulled open my bedroom door that morning. I wanted to remember him alive. I wanted to hold him. I wanted to be consoled by his arms. It had been so good to have him back after so many years away. I had felt like this time we could work things out, but now the only new arrangements to be made were for his funeral.

I'd called Sue Collins, the doctor that had delivered Megan and Erica, and explained to her the circumstances. "Will you call in a prescription for me?"

"I'll call in two," she said. "One for your nerves and another to help you sleep." She reminded me of how Michael had carried on in the delivery room when I was in labor with Megan. He'd screamed at all the nurses and orderlies and demanded they get his child out of there before it had brain damage. He threatened to sue them all if something was wrong with the baby. I figured he carried on that way to ease his own conscience, in case his punches had harmed her. He could blame them for his wrongdoing. Dr. Collins had Michael removed from the delivery room so I could concentrate on my labor. "Call me if you need me again," she said now. She was a good woman, loving and compassionate. I picked up the pills on my way to the funeral.

I'd attended other funerals at the place Johnny's was being held. So, the place wasn't strange. The one-story building was red brick with colonial columns. Short immaculately trimmed shrubs mulched at the bottom lined the front. From the outside it resembled a three-bedroom ranch, gutted and reconditioned for grieving. The large, white double doors opened slowly as I stepped to the entrance. The usher at the door handed me a memorial card as I walked in.

I was glad to see that Johnny's and my friend Allan Harris who I'd called from jail and his wife, Candy, had come. Allan was an architect and had shared many an animated conversation and argument with Johnny over art and how it was ruined when corporations got involved. Allan told Johnny he had to make a living, but Johnny didn't think creativity should ever be compromised. They had great respect and love for one another. They wrote letters and exchanged countless drawings throughout the years.

Allan bent over and hugged Erica, put his arm around her, grabbed my hand and helped us to the next room for the last viewing of Johnny. The bittersweet smell of flowers that lined the walls seemed to lead the way, growing stronger with each step. My chest tightened, my heart pounded against my ribs and lungs till I reached Johnny's mahogany coffin, trembling at the sight.

Looking down, I couldn't believe it was him, and Erica seemed equally as bewildered. Crying, she grabbed the sides of his taffeta-lined casket with both her hands, stared at her daddy, and tried to make sure he was really dead. I waited in vain for this to be over somehow, wishing that Johnny would spring up and laugh like it was one of his best jokes yet. But that wouldn't happen. His face reflected the pain he left this life with. I leaned over the top of his coffin and wrapped his curly hair around my fingers. I pulled Erica close, knowing she was all I had left of him, but I couldn't take my hand off his lifeless locks. This would be the last time I could caress his soft curls, that had just days before bounced with life, laughter, and enthusiasm, but mostly hope, hope that we could spend the rest of our lives together.

Eventually someone led me back to a chair. I noticed Erica was now sitting in the front row, but there wasn't a seat for me. I wanted to be close to him, but I also needed to be with Erica. I pulled a chair from another row and sat beside her as the organ whined out songs Johnny would never have picked to be played. Nothing in the room personified him. This was a ceremony and a ritual for everyone but him.

Erica had cried and sniffled throughout the visitation, but I broke down hard as they closed the casket. The minister's scripture readings and assurances did nothing for my broken heart. Johnny had been the love of my life, and had given his life for mine.

As the pallbearers lifted the box of his remains, the organist played another unfamiliar tune. I softly sang *Indigo*, one of our favorite songs by Peter Gabriel, as they carried him out of sight.

"I'm going away, I'm going away, see you again someday. Darling, I'm going away. This time I'm going away."

Right after the funeral, Allan and Candy came toward me. "Would you like to see where Johnny lived?" Allan asked softly.

I nodded, unable to trust my voice to speak.

"I'll bring Erica to your folks," Candy said and, taking Erica's hand, she guided her away.

During the drive to Johnny's house Allan and I were silent, lost in our sad thoughts.

When we got to the place, I was amazed at how much it looked like the living room of the house Johnny and I had lived in after we were married. Art and music were Johnny's passions. His only explanation for having easels in the living room had been, "Janie, honey, why do you think they call it a living room?"

Choked with agony, I gazed at his paintings, many of them unfinished. I walked over to the window to quiet my pain. The window looked out on the holler he loved and had lived much of his life in. Tree-covered hills with houses of his relations scattered in must have provided the serenity for him to paint. I neared the area where his paintbox sat, filled with hundreds of brightly colored tubes of oil paint, in front of his easel and favorite stool. Beside his stool and easel sat his favorite oak desk, and behind it, a bookcase containing his books on art and music. I strained my eyes to see the titles. On the top shelf set apart was the music theory book I'd given him as a gift a few months after we had started dating. Remembering I had signed its back cover, I lifted the paperbound text and recognized my handwriting. "You have so much natural talent I thought this might be helpful. If you ever need help with your theory, give me a call. You know I'll be glad to help. Love, Janie."

I closed the book quickly and looked away. Those words had meant so much when I wrote them and Johnny must have felt the same for he had kept them near. Tears rolled down my face as I stood there helplessly.

Allan must have sensed I was at misery's edge. He put his arm around my shoulder and guided me to the door.

"I just wanted you to see it," he said. "It'll never be the same. Do you want anything?" I shook my head miserably. I would never dare take anything. To me, it is a sacred monument and should remain undisturbed. I wish that some day I could bring Erica back and let her see her father's best artistic works.

Back in the car, Allan tucked his and Candy's phone number in my pocketbook. "If you need help with moving or anything, please call," he said, and dropped me off at my parents' home where, despite taking the sleeping pills the doctor had given me, I spent another sleepless night.

CHAPTER 8

Memories
and Confrontations

The hot, midmorning sun burned stronger and brighter than my swollen, red eyes could stand. I'd managed to lay down with a pillow over my head for a few hours, but the recurring images of the last couple of days continued to keep sleep out of my reach. The memories of Johnny's funeral were permanently implanted in my brain: the eerie sounding organ, the blur of people mourning, and the cemetery workers lowering Johnny's remains into the grave on the hillside. These thoughts clashed with my memory of Johnny's softly curled hair wrapped around my fingers while the lingering aroma of the flowers stacked by his casket filled my head. I wanted to hold onto any pleasant sensation, however small.

The phone ringing by the bed woke me from my reverie and provided me with a momentary escape. I peeled back the covers, tossed the pillows off the bed, and reached for the receiver.

"Hello."

"Where's the deeds? You got 'em, didn't ya?" The thunderous voice on the other end of the line sounded familiar but the preposterous accusation left me tongue-tied and confused. "I want ya to know right now. You're not gonna keep it. That's my property and, by God, you're not takin' it from me."

By now I'd recognized the irate voice. It was Johnny's dad.

"I don't know what you're talkin' about," I said. "What do ya mean the deeds are gone? To what property? I don't know what you're talkin' about," I insisted.

I replaced the phone on its stand. Stunned and feeling like a brick wall had landed on me, I pulled myself off the bed. Standing on shocked and weary legs, I managed to go down the stairs in search of Mom. She was in the kitchen when I told her about my conversation with Johnny's dad. I broke into tears before I could finish telling her of his accusation.

"Sit down, honey," Mom said. "Johnny's dad was probably just awful upset from burying his son and unable to find the deed and you shouldn't let it worry you. He can git another copy of the deed at the court house," she assured me. "They'll take care of it when his estate's settled. Now don't you let it worry ya. It's just his way of grievin'. I know it hurts, but try to understand. Some people do foolish things when they're in pain. Now try to straighten yourself up before somebody comes in. Ya don't want Erica comin' in here and seeing you tore up. You'll just upset her more."

But Johnny's father's charges cut me deeply and shoved me further into a state of despair. I wanted Johnny to return, but I knew I couldn't wish him back from the dead. More than anything, I wanted to somehow wake from the whole nightmare, but my shaking hands, pounding chest, and throbbing head reminded me that I was not only awake, but still alive. At that moment, I wished Michael's gun hadn't stopped working and he had taken me out of this world instead of leaving me to face this tormented existence. But what would happen to Erica and Megan if I were dead? As bumpy and inconsistent as Erica's young life had been, I knew that at least she'd had me to lean on. I had to find a way to stay strong and pull through this for her and the baby, but it was all starting to collapse on me. I'd always managed to get through the hard times and make the best of bad situations, but this was beyond bad. Maybe if I called Johnny's dad back and talked to him more he'd understand my grief and we could comfort each other.

Finally, I decided to call Allan. He'd given me his number and told me to call him and Candy if I needed any help. I had to move my remaining furniture from the apartment where Johnny had been killed, and I couldn't do it alone. I plucked his number from my purse at the foot of the bed and dialed it. The phone rang and rang, and he didn't have an answering machine. I hung up. The only other person to call was Johnny's cousin Sammy.

Sammy had grown up in the holler with Johnny and the rest of his cousins. He stayed there in a trailer with his wife and their two sons. His mother lived next door, where she had raised four of the finest boys in the world after her husband deserted them. When it came to respecting other people, Sammy was the best. His warm eyes and gentle laugh were his most endearing features, but if trouble was stirred, his husky build would step from the back of the crowd to quiet a conflict before harm came. He'd always treated me like one of the family, even after Johnny and I'd divorced. And of all his good qualities, you could always count on his honesty being foremost.

"Sammy, I just got a terrible call from Big John. He thinks I took the deed to some property of Johnny's. I didn't even know he had any property. What should I do? He says he's goin' to town to git a warrant for me."

"Janie, don't worry about it. He came down here and asked me to go into town with him and swear out a warrant, but I told him he was crazy. He's just upset. I knew you wouldn't do anything like that. He's just thinkin' of himself right now."

"Sammy, look. I wouldn't take anything."

"Don't worry about it, Janie. He'll get over it. You know how John is. He's probably feeling guilty because he didn't raise Johnny. Think of all those years Big John was at the racetrack and playing guitar in honky-tonks while Mamaw and Papaw raised Johnny and Patty. I'll go into town and tell the sheriff he's misplaced the deed and ask 'em not to let him take out a warrant. This'll pass."

"Thanks, Sammy. I appreciate your help."

"Just don't worry and take care of that little Erica. You're gonna bring her around to see us again soon, aren't you? Now don't be a stranger, she needs to know her people."

"I'll come by before I go back to Lexington."

"When are you goin' back?"

"I think in two days. Don Hayes, my attorney, said he'll drive me back and introduce me to the people I need to talk to before the murder trial, but I'll stop in before then. Thanks, Sammy. None of this is easy and none of us needs to have it made worse."

"I know. Just take care of yourself and those babies. I can't wait to see that little one again. She looks just like you."

I knew he'd handle it or let me know if he couldn't. But that didn't stop me from worrying. I spent the rest of the day crying "why" and throwing up every bite of food I tried to eat. The pills the doctor gave me didn't settle my nerves. They made me confused and thirsty. I knew I needed sleep, but I couldn't figure out how to get it. Every sound I heard made me bolt out of bed or off the couch. Finally, I tried to sleep with the television on, but that didn't work either. I was afraid Michael would be released again, and I wanted to be wide awake if he came back to get me and the girls.

The next days passed slowly.

To fill my sleepless nights, I continued my search of Mom and Dad's house for old pictures of Johnny. I became desperate for a picture of him, especially after Erica woke up screaming and said she was afraid.

"Afraid of what, honey?"

"I'm afraid Michael is gonna git us."

"I promise this time he won't. They've got him locked up tight and for good this time, honey."

She was quiet for a time. Then her face grew worried again. "Mommy, I'm afraid."

"Of what, Erica?" I asked gently.

"I'm afraid I won't remember my daddy. I try to see his face in my dreams, but it looks so ugly with all that blood on it. Mommy, I don't want to remember him like that. I can't remember his smile, just the blood comin' out of his mouth and his eyes wide open starin' at the ceiling."

I held her till she cried herself back to sleep. I knew I had to find a picture of Johnny. I didn't dare call up Johnny's dad and ask him for one after his words to me. The search at Mom and Dad's was futile. My last chance would be that a picture might be tucked away back at my apartment, but who knew when they'd let us back in. Michael had pretty much ripped up everything that had Johnny's name on it during our marriage. I'd managed to hold onto one of Johnny's best paintings he'd completed years before, and I had to lie to keep it. I told Michael my sister Beth had painted it and might want it back one day. As much as I dreaded going back to that bloody apartment, I had to look for some pictures and I prayed hard I could find one.

The next morning at dawn, Johnny's dad showed up. "Please forgive me," he begged. "I was just out of my mind with grief."

"I forgive you," I said. "I understand because at times I too seem to be losing my mind."

He'd always been a nervous person, and had had several bypass surgeries and was in line for his second pacemaker. It scared me when he began talking about Johnny, shaking as he cried.

"Why him?" he cried and took deep struggling breaths. He rambled on as I tried to comfort him. Suddenly he asked, "Why did you have him killed?"

"I didn't!" I tried to explain again how it all happened. But he kept babbling, rambling one minute that I had Johnny killed and the next minute trying to make me promise that I'd bring Erica to see him. I was afraid to bring Erica to him, but at the same time I felt sorry for him and knew that she was all he had left of Johnny. So I went to get her. I didn't want to upset him any more than he was, and I was scared that at any minute he'd slump over with a fatal heart attack and then I'd have to live with the image and regret of Johnny's father as well as Johnny dying in front of me.

Mom and Dad had both stayed within earshot of the entire conversation, but, after Big John started getting more overcome with grief and raising his voice at me, Dad came in.

"We have to leave, Jane, and go see your sick granny."

I was thankful when Dad lied about Grandmother being sick. Mom had kept Megan out of sight upstairs while Johnny's dad was there, and I knew the children were both probably getting restless being cooped up. Thank goodness Big John took the hint.

"I guess I'll be leaving," he said. Erica hugged him despite him practically being a stranger. She called him Papaw, which brought a smile to his face and tears to his eyes. I knew that had been a bit of comfort to him. I knew he'd been away throughout Johnny's childhood and spending time with Erica would be his way of trying to make it all up. "I'll be back soon to see Johnny's baby," he said as he left.

"He's pitiful, ain't he?" Mom said as he drove away. "I was scared he might drop dead the way he was carrying on," she added as his car disappeared.

Within hours of Big John's visit, Johnny's only sibling, his sister, stopped by before she went back to her home. They'd never been close, although Johnny desperately loved his three nephews. Patty was a beautiful girl and had been a good student and could sing like a bird. Johnny had hoped she would go on and make something of herself, but instead she had rushed into a bad marriage, and after the boys were born, a divorce.

When Patty came on the porch, I hugged her. She introduced me to her new husband, telling me how much better life was for her and the boys with their father out of the way. She said her new husband worked regular and never touched the bottle, as she squeezed his thigh and threw a wink his way. Her new husband never spoke.

Erica came to the porch and Patty patted her head, introducing herself as Aunt Patty, and explaining, "I'm your daddy's sister." Which, of course, made us all start crying again.

That night I did some laundry and packed a few things to take to Lexington the next morning. Don Hayes, the attorney, who'd represented me in my divorce with Michael, had come to drive me back to Lexington. I was thrilled when Mom said she and Daddy would take care of the girls for a few days while I went back to work and found a new place to live.

In my hurried departure from the apartment, I hadn't thought to bring my waitress uniforms with me. I knew they needed to be washed. I asked Mom if she could loan me a few dollars so I could go to the laundry place before my shift at five o'clock. I told her I'd probably make enough tip money to get a hotel room for the night, but she pulled me aside and stuck a fifty-dollar bill in my hand. "Don't tell anybody you have it," she said softly. "I borrowed it from Granny. I don't want everybody to know how I got it." I thanked her, tucked the tightly rolled bill into my cleavage and kissed her on the cheek.

After a tearful goodbye with the girls, I slipped away.

CHAPTER 9

A Picture's Worth

The two-hour ride back to Lexington with my attorney passed quickly. Don and I talked mostly about the election coming up in the fall. He was running for a judgeship and vowed to change the way things were done around home. He assured me he'd get my divorce finalized before he took office if he was elected. I sensed he was trying not to bring up the murder for fear of upsetting me, but that was all I could think about. So I brought it up.

"Every minute of the day, awake or asleep, the death of Johnny occupies my mind," I said. "So it's better to talk about it."

He looked relieved and began to explain the murder trial and the considerable process of getting Michael convicted. "You know, Jane," he said, "that Michael could be acquitted."

"To me that sounds absurd," I objected.

He cautioned, "It's difficult to speculate how twelve members of a jury will see it. You have to remember that the prosecuting attorney represents the state, not you and the girls. And, when it comes to evidence," he said, "judges can sure foul things up by not allowing certain evidence to be presented. But it's the law and they have to enforce it."

"Great law," I interjected, "that doesn't let the truth be told."

He reminded me, "Since you're still legally married to Michael, even though you've been separated for months, you wouldn't have to testify against him if you don't want to."

"I hate the thought of ever being married to Michael."

"I understand that but some of his family might be upset if you choose to testify against him."

My back straightened. "There's no way in hell I'm gonna let Michael by with murder. I am the only living adult witness and I won't be intimidated by anybody."

When we arrived at the police department, Don took me inside and asked to speak to the person in charge. Although he didn't practice law in this area, Don still knew where I needed to go and who to see. I sat in the lobby, my hair raised stiff on the back of my neck like a scared cat, while he spoke to some of the police in the back room. Sitting there, I grew more and more nervous. It brought me back once again to the day of the murder. I tried to study the faces of the people he introduced me to, but they didn't seem too worried about me or the girls and I knew we'd never have much to talk about.

Our next stop was to the office of the prosecuting attorney, Jeb Lowry. "One of the best in the state," my attorney said, adding, "The prosecutor has recently won a precedent setting case and is the toast of the town." His previous won-lost record meant nothing to me. It didn't matter what his legal credentials were. I was concerned for our safety and wanted a guarantee of Michael's conviction. I believed once I told him how it all happened, along with the evidence the police had, that there'd be little cause for alarm. It was clear Michael was guilty of cold-blooded murder.

Unlike the police department, in the prosecuting attorney's office there were several women who worked closely with crime victims. They seemed very sincere when they spoke to me. One woman whose brown hair was streaked with gray gave me her business card and explained, "My son was killed and I understand how you feel." They invited me to call any time during business hours to talk about the murder. They set an appointment for me to come in later in the week. I told them I'd let them know if I could keep the appointment after I got my work schedule.

The last stop was my apartment. The awful yellow police tape had been removed, but one piece remained stuck to the metal railing out front and it seemed to wave to me like an insulting reminder. Tears filled my eyes as I entered the doorway. Don patted me on the shoulder, hoping to comfort me, but nothing could take away the pain. I'd already convinced myself I wasn't going to break down as I passed over the bloodstained carpet at the top of the stairs.

As I took Don through the ravaged apartment, my nerves rankled, I rambled about what had happened at each step of the fight from the night before until the murder the next morning, stopping occasionally to try to catch my breath and pull myself together.

When we finished the tour, I gathered the things that I needed, including my work uniforms, and Don helped me carry them out and load them into the trunk of my car. While we were packing, Babs, the apartment manager, came out. "How are you, Jane," she said hurriedly, and wanted to know where I'd be staying and how soon I'd be getting my stuff out. I explained that I wasn't sure where I'd stay, but I promised to call her by the end of the week and give her all the information.

After we placed the last items in the car, I walked back through the apartment and noticed Johnny's small nylon suitcase stuck in the corner opened wide. I bent down and nervously touched his shirt that was hanging out of the side. Johnny's scent was still on it. Without hesitation and desperately deprived of any other remnant of him, I buried my nose in his shirt. At least something of his had survived. I dug through the rest of his things and found his shoes, an alarm clock and toiletries, some tapes, another shirt, and a pack of generic cigarettes. The realization that this was all I had left of him caused me to break my promise to restrain myself. I squeezed the bag and its contents against my chest, crying out, and walked aimlessly in semicircles in the dining area, in the exact spot where the fight had started hours before Johnny's murder.

As I turned toward the sliding glass doors, I noticed the burn holes in the carpet where the SWAT team had to blast in the tear gas to flush out Michael. I thought of how horrible the place looked. I thought of how real it had all been. I thought of how my mind had so vividly captured the simplest details over the last few days, like a snapshot of misery. I drew a sharp breath.

I ran upstairs with Johnny's belongings still fixed tightly to my chest. I closed my eyes tight as I jumped over his blood stains, entered my room, and fell to my knees on the floor of my closet. With Johnny's bag placed carefully beside me, I turned over the small box of pictures still hidden in the corner of the closet. With uncertain hands, I spread the pictures in a smooth layer and wiped away my tears, fearing the salty drops from my chin could stain the one picture I might find of Johnny. As pictures of my past covered the floor, an old Polaroid caught my eye. I turned it over and there it was. Finally, a picture of Johnny holding Erica.

Tears of joy and screams of happiness flew from my body for the first time in weeks. At last, I had a picture for Erica, a happy one, one that could help replace the bloody images trapped in both our minds. Clutching it, I ran back downstairs. "It's okay now, Don. I'll be all right. You can leave." I thanked him for his help, got in my own car, and drove off.

Time was getting away from me and I knew I still needed to get my uniform washed and get ready for work. No matter how grief-stricken I was, I didn't dare take off any more time. Knowing I'd need a shower and some rest, I pulled the fifty-dollar bill from my bra and drove to a moderately priced hotel.

After I checked in, I unpacked my few things, washed my uniform out by hand, and dried it with the hair dryer. I tried to nap but, as usual, sleep never came. Over a week had passed since I'd slept for any length of time. I tried not to worry about it, but I could no longer ignore my own needs. I had two children relying on me for safety and now, justice. I knew I'd have to be above my best to get it accomplished. Rather than lay there with muddled thoughts passing through my brain, I decided to get to work early.

I went into the bathroom and washed up. The bathroom mirror was a horrible source of truthfulness. Years of aging had come over my face in just a matter of days. It showed just how tired and stressed I really was. I thought of the tips my modeling coach had once taught me about makeup application and remedies for puffy eyes, but I didn't have the money to order cucumbers and there was no room service, so what good did that bit of education do me, I wondered? Splashing cold water on my face and applying some mascara and a little pink lipstick to my cheeks and mouth, I did the best I could to look nice. I needed the tip money, and I knew I needed to look good to get it. Unfortunately, it was common knowledge good service had little to do with your tips. The right smile and a sure fit of your uniform brought much more money than hot food.

When I arrived at work, my hands shook in my pockets and my eyes searched the faces of my fellow employees who instantly seemed to tense up when I walked in. I knew they'd have plenty of questions to ask and I tried to buoy myself up for them, but I hated to have to tell the wretched story of Johnny's death over again. Several of the day waitresses who knew me were the first to hug me and offer their condolences.

Nevertheless, I could tell I made them uncomfortable. I looked around for something to do so I would look too busy to talk and decided to copy my schedule for the week. I walked to the bulletin board where the schedule pages hung, checked up and down on both sheets, but didn't find my name. I figured fatigue was playing tricks on my eyesight, so I checked the sheets again. My name was gone. I turned to the cook. "Harry, where's my name?" He pointed me toward the boss's office.

My heart felt like it was choking me as I stepped into Andy's office. He was at his desk doing some paperwork when I tapped gently on the side of his door.

"Come in. How are you?" he asked.

"I'm fine, I guess, until I saw the schedule. My name isn't on it, and I, I was just wondering when I worked this week?"

He shifted in his chair, noticeably uncomfortable. "Jane, it wasn't my decision. In fact, I argued on your behalf, but the hotel manager said you were a high risk to us right now. There's still a chance your ex-husband could get out on bond, and since he's been here before and caused trouble, we can't jeopardize the lives of our guests and employees. It has nothing to do with you or your performance. I know you're a good . . ."

Upset, I broke in. "But you don't understand, Andy. I need this job desperately." Tears filled my eyes.

"I know that, Jane, and I'll be glad to write you an excellent recommendation," he said.

"Haven't I been through enough? I don't need ya'll treatin' me like this. I've got to git a new place for me and the girls to live and, hell, I don't even have food for tonight. All the money I had, well, practically all of it, I just spent for a hotel. I don't even know where I'm gonna be staying tomorrow and now you're tellin' me I don't have a job!"

I couldn't hold back my tears. I became dizzy with confusion and tried to think of where to go or who I could turn to. I wanted to believe my manager. Everyone liked him and he always went to bat for us when we tangled with his boss, who only occasionally sashayed through the kitchen wearing trendy clothes he bragged about buying in New York City.

As I sat in the office crying, Andy rose and closed the door to save me from others' eyes. Sitting back down, he opened his desk drawer, pulled out a checkbook, and began to write as he talked to me.

"I know this must be terribly difficult for you. Well,

really, I can imagine it. I guess I've had an easy go of it in life and I'd like to help you out a little. I want you to take this to help you get by for a few days," he said as he ripped out a check from the book. "Don't worry about paying it back. I've got plenty, and I want you to have it."

"But I couldn't," I said as all the pride my mother had ever taught me filled my head. "I can't take your money. It's not right. I'll get another job in a few days. I'll be fine."

"Here, I insist. Finding a new job may take some time, Jane, and you need to eat in the meantime. Do you have anybody around to stay with?"

"No, I don't, but I'll manage."

"Here's my card. Call me in a few days if you need something else. I'll be glad to help. Are you driving? Are you okay to drive right now?"

I shook my head no as I tucked his check in my apron pocket. He extended his hand and helped me from the chair, wiped my tears with his handkerchief, and led me back to the employee dining room.

"Sit here until you get yourself together," he said and brought me a glass of water. "Don't forget to call later this week. And get some rest."

By now, a few of the evening shift employees had come to work and had flocked around me. Harry and Jim were the first to appear across the table and offered to help in any way they could. Jim had to go back on duty but Harry, a plump man in his sixties with gentle brown eyes, sat down.

"Are you gonna be okay?" he asked.

I assured him I would, but the more questions he asked the more he seemed to realize I might not. I talked for a few more minutes and when I felt the urge to cry again, I knew it was time to leave. Harry offered to walk me to the car.

"What are you gonna do? Do ya have anywhere to stay?"

"For tonight."

"Have you applied for emergency housing? Or food

stamps? Ya need to get somethin' comin' in. How are you really doin'?" he asked, after we walked from the sight of the others.

"I don't know, Harry. I haven't slept in days. My apartment is trashed. Right now, I'm just trying not to break up completely. One minute I feel like I'll be okay, like all I need to do is catch my breath or wake from the dream, the next minute I feel like dyin'!"

He nodded sympathetically. "I've been through somethin' like this before. My brother was gunned down in Chicago a few years ago and it almost drove me crazy. It's not easy to lose someone close."

"I know, especially when ya see the whole bloody thing. It never leaves my mind. It never goes away. I keep seein' it all. I just wanna die."

"Jane, don't think like that. Look, I gotta go before they notice I'm late from my break. Where are you stayin'? I'll stop by after I get off work."

He handed me a slip of paper. I pulled a pen from my apron and wrote my hotel room number on it. When I handed it to him, he squeezed my hand. "I'll help all I can," he said.

Inside the car, I checked my rearview mirror and saw streams of black mascara flowing down my partially painted cheeks. The carefully applied makeup had been a waste of time. The road in front of me looked blurry as I struggled with the wheel, trying desperately to keep the car on the road and my mind on my driving. By the time I pulled into the hotel, I'd forgotten my room number and had to dig through my purse to find the key and check the number on it.

I cried nonstop for the next few hours. Sick to my stomach, I heaved up nothing but nerves. I put a cool washcloth to my forehead and another small towel on the back of my neck. My weak and trembling body could hardly carry me to the bed, but once I'd crawled under the covers I finally surrendered to exhaustion.

The knock on the door a few hours later brought panic

back. Could Michael have been released and found me? "Who's there?" I screamed several times until I finally recognized the voice on the other side of the door. It was Harry.

I opened the door after checking to make sure it was him and threw my arms around his neck.

He spoke softly. "It's all right. Don't be afraid."

I needed his hug. Particularly from an outsider, a friend who wouldn't be judgmental.

Harry slowly walked me over to the bed and tucked me back under the cover. "I'll be right back. I'm just going to the car to get something."

I laid still till he came back in with an armful of bags filled with food.

"Ya hungry? I brought ya one of tonight's specials—prepared it myself. Ya got good connections when ya know the cook."

"Sure, I'll eat a bite. I got sick earlier. It'd prob'ly do me good to eat somethin'."

"You never came off to me as the weak stomached woman type," he said.

"I'm not weak. I've been through a lot of shit!"

"Okay, okay. I was just messin' witcha!"

"Sorry. I'm just feelin' miserable."

He handed me the plate he'd readied for me and sat a drink with a straw in it beside me. I reached for it and as I brought it to my lips I got a whiff of alcohol.

"What's this?"

"Rum and coke. You said you couldn't sleep, so I figured this would help."

I swallowed a few sips, shivered as it went down, and picked some more at the food he'd brought.

"So. How's it taste?"

"Good. Very good."

"I thought you needed some nourishment. What do you plan on doin'? Where are the girls?"

"They're back at my mom and dad's house. And I don't have a clue where I'm gonna live. Specially since I lost my job today. That bastard. I really need the work."

"Look, Jane, I know how strong-willed you are. And we've only been friends for a few months, but I know what you're goin' through. I told ya about my brother. Listen, I was raised with seven brothers and sisters, and we were always taught to help each other and people in need. And that's what you are. Don't think of it as charity 'cause I don't have that much to give ya anyway. I'll help you get some assistance. I can't see a sweet person like you left out in the cold. Do you even know where the soup kitchen is?"

"No."

"Do you know anything about welfare?"

"I drew it once, a long time ago when I was pregnant with Erica. But I don't want to go that route. It's so embarrassing. I don't need no more humiliation."

"Well, this ain't about humiliation. It's about surviving, gettin' by, and ya gotta think of your kids instead of your own shame. I'll help ya get it. Tomorrow morning I'll take ya, first thing."

Tears flooded my eyes again. "The kindness of strangers," I remembered a famed playwright saying. In the midst of all this horror, it confounded me.

I knew he was right. I didn't want to be forced onto welfare, but there really didn't seem to be an option. I was broke, homeless, and missed my girls desperately. Erica needed to be with me as soon as possible, but how was I going to get her and Megan back here with me without a place to stay or money coming in regularly? I nodded to him. "Harry, I don't know how to thank—"

He put his hand to his lips. "Shush. Just rest. I'll stay here."

Harry sat by my bed until I fell asleep.

CHAPTER 10

A Voice from Jail

Harry pulled up to the front of the hotel courtyard, ready to go early just as he'd promised.

"I didn't bother fixing my face since all I'm going to do is stand in lines and beg for help," I said, feeling ashamed.

"You look fine despite how you feel," Harry said, and handed me a pair of sunglasses from his glove box when he noticed how much the sun's rays irritated my eyes. I thanked him as he started his car and began to rattle off the day's schedule.

"I'm gonna take ya to the soup kitchen first. They've got full-time social workers that can give ya a check or some cash for rent and deposits. Ya may wanna ask 'em about a phone deposit. I don't think they consider a phone a necessity, but in your case they may make an exception. I doubt ya wanna stay anywhere without a phone."

"Hell no. I gotta be able to call for help if I need to. You don't think they'll let Michael out, do ya?"

"Do his people have money?"

"None close that I know of. Why?"

"'Cause anybody can get outta jail if they got the bucks.

You know any rich people in jail?"

"I don't know anybody in jail. Well, I didn't use to."

"I'm gonna drop ya off up here on the corner. It's that red brick building. I'll park the car somewhere on this street. Just look for me out front when you're finished."

"Why aren't ya goin' in with me? I'm not sure what to say."

"Think of you and your children livin' in your car and you'll find the words. Besides, if they think you got a man around, they won't give ya much. They'll think I'm takin' care of ya and I'm just lookin' out for ya."

Harry really seemed to understand the system, I thought as I walked through the doors and followed the signs to a desk where I was told to take a number. I looked around. The auditorium-size room was full, mostly women with small children. I found a seat in the back, looking over my shoulder every time I heard a noise. Every sound, drop of a book, scoot of a chair, or rattle by a child made my heart pound hard and fast. I hated being there having to crawl and beg in front of strangers.

A tiny baby wrapped in a piece of faded yellow cloth cut from an adult blanket began to fuss. Instantly I missed my girls. I watched the mother as she cradled her baby and slipped a bottle of water into its tiny mouth. I wondered if she needed the money to buy infant formula and had to give the baby water instead. It was nearing the end of the month and I remembered too well how difficult it was making money stretch that long. Lucky for her she was the next number called. But what if they were like me and didn't have a home?

I noticed the woman with stringy brown hair next to her had a sleeping toddler in her arms. Barefoot and sweaty, the child seemed content being held by its mother. The woman looked frayed and tired. On the left side of her face was a bruise, faded slightly, but familiar looking to me. I'd worn those marks many times, tried to cover them up when I could. I wondered if desperation made her leave the house without covering it. Maybe, as it had been for me and my girls, the police ignored her when she called for help, or maybe she's just grown used to the beatings and didn't care what people thought anymore.

By the time my number was called, I felt a nervous wreck. It made me sick to think of how many women with children needed help so badly they were willing to beg for it. I was sure they all had their own depressing stories to tell. Having a family was supposed to be happy, yet looking around me all I could see was misery. And now I was one of the many miserable women struggling to keep my family alive.

The young social worker with waist-length brown hair was very kind and friendly. Shortly after I began telling her my story, she said she recognized the details and excused herself for a moment. I knew the newspaper had run the murder as a front page story, but I hadn't read it. When she came back, she had her supervisor with her and an envelope in hand.

"Here's a gift to help get you back on your feet. We're aware of what happened to you and your children last week. We want to help you. We wish we could help more, but our organization is on a very tight budget. Please accept this and our prayers."

I didn't open the envelope, thinking it would be rude, but I smiled and thanked them as they handed me a list of other groups in the area that could help me with my utilities and food. The intake worker marked a few of the important phone numbers and recommended I call them as soon as I found a place to stay. I cried as I shook their hands and hugged both of them, their embraces warm and sincere. Their generosity and guidance as well as Harry's made me think that maybe there were still good people in the world. I cried even harder as I walked outside and opened the envelope and found a check made out to me for $300, just as Harry's car pulled up.

"They gave me a check for three hundred dollars! I can't believe it!" I told him as tears ran down my face. "They gave me this list and told me to get an apartment and these other agencies would help me out, too!"

"Good girl, Jane, now git in the car before somebody snatches it." I sat in the car and closed the door following Harry's orders as he spun us away quickly.

"Let's grab a paper 'n' a bite to eat and we'll start lookin' for a place for you and the girls."

We drove to the burger stand. Harry insisted, "It isn't a good idea for us to eat inside together. We'll order and eat in the car." It was getting close to noon and I hadn't paid for another night in the hotel. I remembered the check Andy had given me.

"Harry, could we stop at the bank so I can withdraw some money?"

"I'll pay for tonight's room," he said.

"Harry, I can't let you do that." Remembering how quickly and smoothly Michael had moved in on me, I was hesitant to accept anything from anyone, even this grandfatherly man. I appreciated Harry's help, and lord knows I needed it, but I didn't want him to get the wrong idea.

"I understand," he said, and, when we got to the bank, he turned into the drive-through. From the bank we went back to the hotel.

After paying for another night, we went up to the room, cleared the table, and began searching the want ads for a place to stay. I pointed to one, put a circle around it, and handed him the paper.

"Ya don't wanna live there. Too many break-ins," Harry said. "First floors are more dangerous." He gave me back the ads.

I read another out loud. "What about this place? The rent's right, and no references required."

He shook his head. "I think ya wanna stay outta there. That neighborhood's mostly drug-infested, and ya got gunfire at night. It'd drive you and the girls further over the edge."

Harry knew a lot about the neighborhoods. Unfortunately, almost all the apartments that I could afford were in high crime areas, but within an hour Harry and I had narrowed the choices to three, two of which had nice move-in specials. It was early

August and I knew that competition with monied college students would be stiff. I fixed my face a little before we left.

Harry was careful to drop me off out of sight of any of the apartment managers' offices. It bothered me that people would figure he was more than just a friend, but Harry stayed tight-lipped when I asked why he wouldn't go in and look around with me. He recognized danger quicker than I did and, after Michael, for almost every decision I had to make I wanted a second opinion.

The place I settled on was only a few miles away from where I used to work. After I put my money down and signed the lease, I had to get furniture, so I went to a rental place. I picked out a blue and brown couch and a few tables. There was a small stereo and I fingered the price tag, hoping it wouldn't be too much.

Music took me where I needed to be, a safe place where I could think of my good memories of Johnny. I wanted Erica and I to listen to the tapes Johnny had left behind. I could recall all of our other precious memories we'd shared through sound. The spirit and soul of music would give me a place to take my grief and, at the same time, bring me comfort. The salesman must have seen how desperately I needed it. "We'll throw it in," he said. I couldn't have Johnny back, but I could still be with him through our love of music.

After the furniture was delivered, Harry helped me arrange it, until it was time for him to go to work. Not really wanting to be alone, and missing the girls terribly, I left when Harry did and went to a pay phone. More than anything, I wanted to speak to my girls. My own phone wouldn't be connected till the next day.

I called Mom and Dad collect and chatted with Erica first. She put Megan on the phone to hear my voice. Of course, Megan couldn't talk yet, but she did squeal and jabber a little. Erica said her arms and legs were waving as I spoke to her. I choked up with tears. "I'll come back in a day or two, just as soon as I can. I'll bring you to our new home." Erica was afraid our new home would be like the last one and Michael would get us. I needed to be with her, for both of our emotional security.

Mom said she and Dad weren't used to having kids around. I knew it was difficult for them. Just a few more days, I pledged. It was difficult being away from Erica and Megan. I hated our separation just as much as I hated being alone, but I had to get a job before I could go and get them.

I telephoned the old apartment complex next. I'd promised Babs, the manager, that I'd call when I got a place to live and make arrangements to get the rest of my things out. After I gave her my address, she said her attorneys would be in touch with me to pay for the damages.

"What? I have to pay for the mess Michael made when he killed Johnny?"

"Well, you are responsible for all damages," she informed me. "It's in your lease."

The frustration and anger I felt rose. "We've been through enough without you treating us like this. If I were you, I'd call the police department. They're the ones who blasted the smoke bombs in to git him out. That's where the holes in the windows and the burns in the carpet came from!"

I hung up the phone exhausted. How could she hold me responsible for the damages? I couldn't control what Michael did or make the police decision of how to get him or when. If I could, they would have kept him in jail a long time ago. I was the one who'd been beaten and threatened. I had done everything I could to stop the violence. No one had helped me. Now Michael had killed someone and I was expected to pay for the way he'd trashed the apartment doing it.

The conversation nauseated me, but I knew if I was going to get my things out I'd have to do it quick. I dug through my purse and found the number Allan had given me. I didn't have any change on me so I had to call collect. He accepted my call and we made arrangements to meet the next day. Allan arrived early the next morning. We hadn't seen each other since Johnny's funeral so we decided to have breakfast before we began the repulsive chore of cleaning out my apartment. "I spent most of the week looking for old pictures of Johnny," Allan said. "I didn't locate too many but I did find a picture of Johnny and you when you were very pregnant with Erica."

"Could you . . . " I began.

"Don't worry," he said. "I promise to give you a copy."

Allan was anxious to talk about our memories of Johnny, and I was glad to reminisce with someone who had known Johnny so well. "We're still friends, don't forget," he told me. His words eased the tension of all I was enduring.

Allan delighted me with his stories about some of the new music he and Johnny had savored. We exchanged some of our favorites: one-liners Johnny had created, bittersweet, but left for our amusement. "Life won't be the same without Johnny's artistic ability and his sense of humor," Allan said sadly.

We went into the apartment and packed up everything that wasn't burnt or broken. First we loaded the few pieces of furniture into his truck. Then we began loading the other things. We drove the first load to the new place and placed the things in the appropriate rooms. Allan helped me put the girls' beds together. "I miss them so badly," I said, "and now that they'll have a decent place to stay, I can go get them tomorrow." We went back to get another load. Finally we were finished and Allan took me to the market late that night and helped me get food.

I was saddened when he said, "I have to go now, but stay in touch."

I promised I would. "Life won't be the same without Johnny," I added softly.

After Allan left, Harry who'd come by helped me get everything as presentable as possible for the girls' return. We had their beds made with fresh sheets and hung pictures of teddy bears with flowers on their walls. Harry had bought them as a welcome home present for the girls.

I broke the speed limit the next morning driving to get the girls.

Mom had all of their clothes packed and ready to go when I arrived. I didn't stay for a visit. I could tell Mom and Dad needed a rest, and Erica was anxious to see her new room.

Here we were again, I thought as we drove to Lexington. New place, starting all over again, but this time with a mountain of misery heaped on our minds.

Erica didn't want to go to sleep by herself that night after I'd tucked Megan in. Sleep was frightening for us both. Not only did noises wake us easily, but the terror of being awakened again by gunfire was enough to keep us both tense. I went over to her foldout bed and curled up beside her. Her thoughts were still on that awful day.

"Mommy," she said, "do you know what happened that morning when Michael killed my daddy?"

"No, honey, I don't. Mommy was asleep. Do ya want to tell me about it before you go to sleep?"

"Yeah, 'cause Papaw said the papers said that Michael and Daddy had been in a fight that morning, but they didn't. Daddy and I were playing when Michael knocked on the door. Daddy peeped out the hole in the door and saw Michael and we ran upstairs."

"Why did you run upstairs?"

"To hide. I hid in my closet and Daddy looked out my window and said Michael wasn't out there anymore. Me and Daddy thought Michael had left for good, but he hadn't. I got out of the closet to follow Daddy back downstairs and Michael shot him in the back when we walked out." I clutched her closer.

I could hear those shots fire followed by screams over and over in my mind. How close Erica had come to taking a bullet made me shudder. Had she been a step faster, she could have died with Johnny.

"Did Michael say anything to your daddy?"

"He said he was gonna kill you next."

He would have if the gun hadn't jammed, I thought. Erica began to cry hard into my shoulder as rage mixed with sympathy for Erica came over me. Not only had Michael killed her father, but he'd destroyed her childhood innocence. In a flash, that marvel of youth was taken from her. She was still a child, but, in many ways, she was now old beyond her years. We held each other for hours as she cried a cry that no parent ever wanted to hear. Helplessly, I held her. There was nothing I could do. No words came to mind to soothe her broken heart. I knew I had to let her cry it out. I felt a hate come over me I'd never felt in my life. My child was wounded. Her mangled heart and tortured emotions made me hate to be alive. I had failed to protect her. I was afraid she'd never recover. How was I going to help her through this while trying to deal with my own grief? My life seemed useless as long as hers was so miserable.

Finally she fell asleep; even in her sleep she cried. I lifted my aching body from her bed and slowly walked to the kitchen for a drink of water. The gas stove caught my eye. I could end this agony for all of us if I wanted to. I could do it while the children were asleep. They wouldn't feel a thing. I walked to the stove, opened the oven door, and tested the knob to see if it worked. Then I drew back, thinking.

The manager had told me when I rented the place that I'd have to light the oven with a match if I wanted to use it. I didn't want to eat. I didn't want to live. I wanted an easy way out and the gas stove could provide it. We could all die in our sleep, anything to end the pain for all of us.

I reached for the oven doorknob again and opened the door. It wouldn't be difficult. It would be easier than living like this. My confused mind pondered the possibilities. I could open the oven door, make sure the fire didn't catch, and lie down with the girls for one last slumber. Then a jarring thought struck. But what if we don't all die? What if Megan lives and Erica and I die? She'd be an orphan. What if I die and leave them both? Erica would lose what's left of her mind. I'm all she has left. She couldn't handle another loss. My head ached as my mind went back and forth. We'd all be so much better off, especially if Michael gets out with an acquittal. How could they think of letting a cold-blooded murderer out of prison? He'd come straight for me and finish the job his gun had failed to do. At least I could take myself out instead of giving him the pleasure.

The knock at the door startled me. I slammed the oven door, my mind working furiously. What if they'd let Michael out? What if he had come back to get us? I tiptoed to the living room and peeked through the keyhole. Thank God! It was Harry.

"Are you busy?" he said, in his usual friendly tone.

"No. I just, well, did ya git off·work?"

"Ya, I thought ya might need something. I thought I'd stop by and check on ya. How are the girls?"

"They're asleep. Ya wanna come in?"

"Sure. I brought you some leftovers from work. I thought you'd like a hot meal."

"Actually, I couldn't eat." The front I'd tried to keep up finally caved in. Had Harry not appeared, I could've been inhaling gas from the stove.

I began crying and said in a hoarse voice, "I thought of killing us."

"Jane, don't cry. You're not gonna do that. Depression hits us all."

"But, Harry, five minutes ago I wanted it more than anything. I wanted us all dead. I'm tired. I can't take it. I'm afraid Michael's gonna git out and I've already promised Erica he wouldn't. I can't let her down. Do you think he could be set free, even after everything he's done to us?"

"Jane, you don't know he'll git out and none of this is your fault. It's not you, Jane. The rules are different for everybody. Some get by with murder, and some get life for smoking a joint. It's crazy, I know, but you gotta ride it out. Learn to bob and weave. Take your lumps and learn your lesson. Learn to lay low."

"But, Harry, you don't know how hard it is to hold your child whose heart is ripped in half. I feel so helpless. How do I give her hope when I have none of my own? I can't make this go away for either of us."

"No, you can't. But you can't let Michael continue to run your life. You give up, he wins. You surrender and he gits what he wanted all along: control of your life and Megan's."

He was right. I couldn't lay down and die. I'd loved life before, loved my kids, loved my friends, and I was only in my twenties. But I still didn't trust myself. Harry sat me back on the rented couch, put some silverware and a napkin on the smoked glass table.

"You have to try to eat to keep up your strength," he said as he brought my dinner plate in and sat it in front of me. I picked at it, more out of gratitude than hunger. After a few minutes I leaned my head back on the couch.

Harry went to the hall closet and grabbed some sheets. He spread a sheet over me and laid one out on the floor for himself.

When I woke the next morning, both of the girls were in the kitchen eating a breakfast Harry had cooked for them.

"Ya hungry?" he said. "I fixed the works: eggs, French toast—Erica said that was your favorite. Got sausage and gravy and hot buttered grits. May I have your order, ma'am?"

Erica giggled at the performance Harry was giving. I pulled up a chair and tried to eat a little of everything. After the breakfast dishes were done, Harry said, "I need to go, but I promise to check on y'all later." Although I felt sad, I was lucky he left when he did. He wasn't gone five minutes when a thin woman with short gray hair knocked on the door.

"Are you Jane?"

"Yes, ma'am," I said, confused. "Who are you?"

"I'm Clare Buchanan. I'm with the county welfare agency children's services. We've had a report that you're not taking proper care of your daughter and I need to check it out."

I had no idea what she was talking about. Both my

daughters were well cared for. Maybe they think the murder was my fault, too.

"Our confidential report states that you are not feeding your infant daughter. Could I see her?"

A nervous but confident smile came over my face when she mentioned Megan might be underweight.

"Who told you she was underfed? They don't know what they're talking about. She's asleep right now but I'll wake her to show you that she's fine."

I tiptoed back to the girls' bedroom and gently lifted Megan from her crib. I straightened her clothes a little as I carried her back in. Her bright yellow dress accented her dark hair and eyes, and when I sat her twenty-five-pound body on my lap, the social worker began to grin.

"I would hardly call this child underfed, would you?" I said with all the confidence of a good mother. "She hasn't been weighed in a few weeks, but look at the thighs on her."

I rolled Megan's clothes up, exposing her round belly and lamb chop plump legs. Megan giggled a little as I stroked her, and the social worker seemed to melt.

"What a pretty baby! She looks like a china doll, a chubby china doll."

"I told you that report was bogus. Who would say something like that? Was it Michael? It has to be him."

"We're not allowed to reveal our sources, but we are required to make a home visit within twenty-four hours of the report, you understand."

She had no idea how well I understood Michael. Even from jail he was determined to terrorize the girls and me. I took Megan and Erica back to their room so I could speak openly with the social worker. My main concern was that Michael must know where we lived or how else would she have been able to get my address. I wondered where he could've gotten it from?

"I understand you're doing the best you can under such serious circumstances," the social worker said kindly. She gave me a phone number of a day care center where I could enroll the girls in day care so they could play with other children while I looked for work, or rested if I needed to. When Clare Buchanan had finished the interview, she added, "If I receive more phone calls from my source I'll have to return."

I knew it was Michael. It confirmed in my mind that he wasn't finished with me yet. Even from behind bars, after all the beatings, after destroying all my property and ultimately killing Johnny, Michael was clearly committed to make my life and my girls' lives a living hell. I'd tried to convince the police for months of his evil intentions, but they wouldn't listen. Now one murder had occurred, and, if they didn't keep Michael in jail, other deaths were going to follow. I knew it and so should they.

I couldn't dwell on it though. I had to keep my mind on making a living for myself and the girls. Since it was nearly the end of the month, rent would soon be due again. I decided to check out the day care center the social worker had told me about. I didn't have time to worry over Michael's campaign to intimidate us. I had to keep my mind on getting us back on our feet.

I dressed the girls in their Sunday best and drove to the day care center. It was a nice clean place, with bright colors and lots of toys I could never afford for my girls to play with. Erica frowned when she saw the fence around the building. "It's to keep bad daddies out," she said softly, nodding her head and relaxing a little. It made her feel more safe. We arrived during snack time, and Erica's eyes grew enormous when she saw the plate full of goodies. She gobbled down the treats as I spoke with the director and filled out the papers.

"You can bring them in tomorrow. Your social worker has already called and made arrangements to pay for it with emergency assistance money," the director told me. I nodded gratefully.

As we drove back home, Erica chattered excitedly about her new school. I was comforted to see her breaking out a little from her troubled shell. I was even more relieved when she said she wanted to go back and play with the other children. As I put the girls down for a nap, she smiled and asked me, "What can I wear to school tomorrow?"

"We'll pick out something nice after you sleep awhile," I said.

"Just so long as I can wear the new hair bows Aunt Beth gave me."

In spite of all the excitement, they both fell asleep in no time.

The living room was easy to clean and would take me no time to whip into shape. The kitchen and my bedroom were different stories. The bedroom was filled with boxes. Clothes and blankets were piled everywhere. I decided the kitchen was more important and quickly began straightening it when the phone rang for the first time since it had been connected.

"Collect call from Mike," the operator announced.

"Yes, I'll accept." I couldn't believe my brother-in-law Mike would call collect. Something must be terribly wrong with my sister, I thought. My stomach churned.

"I hope to hell you're happy," the voice on the other end screamed. "Look what you made me do. Are ya happy? I'm in jail and it's all because of you."

Michael! I was speechless. I stiffened with fear, petrified that he could get so close to me after committing murder. How could he be calling from jail? As he continued to scream into my ear, I kept wondering how he could call from the jail. Was he lying? Had he been released? My panic finally broke as I heard him promise to get me. That bastard! He's not getting me or going to hurt my girls again.

I slammed the phone down and paced in circles thinking of who to call and where to run. I thought of the card the woman at the prosecuting attorney's office had given me. I grabbed the phone and dialed her number.

She explained that Michael was still in jail but, to double

check, she put me on hold while someone else in the office called the jail. "All prisoners have free time," she said when she came back on the line. "During that time they have a phone where they can make calls. He probably got your new phone number from information."

"I didn't realize he could call me," I explained. "I wouldn't have accepted the charges, but I thought it was my brother-in-law Mike calling. I had been worried something had happened to my sister."

She told me not to accept any more calls from him. By the time we were finishing the conversation, I believed that despite his threats Michael was still locked up.

Overcome by nerves and relieved that Michael wasn't on the loose, I fell to pieces when I hung up the phone. I doubled over at the waist and cried, wondering when it would end. I wanted to get away. But where? I wanted to run. Run, Jane, run. But I'd already been served papers to appear in court as a witness to Johnny's murder. Michael wouldn't be convicted without a witness, and I'd become a fugitive. As it stood now, I wasn't guilty of anything except having bad taste in men. What if Erica had answered the phone? Hearing Michael's voice might have further wounded her emotionally. I had tried to get us away from him. But the very system that had kept me with him was now forcing me to stay around him. I had to find a place for me and the girls where Michael couldn't get us. I had to get away. I had to get out of Lexington. I knew we couldn't go back to Mom and Dad's. They'd looked exhausted after having the children for a few days. Where could we go? How could I find a safe place to stay? And where would I get the money to leave? I pulled out my phone book and began to search for someone, anyone, who would be willing to help us.

CHAPTER 11

No Place to Hide

Finally I reached an old friend; Loren told me to bring the children and meet her at the gas station just off Interstate 64, and I could follow her on out to her house for a few days of much needed rest. It'd been several months since I'd seen her. Loren and I had been friends since we were children. Although few girls in appalachia even finished high school, she'd gotten a college scholarship. She'd earned her degree in English as a liberal arts major. She'd worked at a magazine up north in Cincinnati, but her one sure talent was her ability to sing. She sang Bobbi Gentry songs better than Bobbi Gentry, and she played the guitar better. Some thought she even favored Ms. Gentry with her dark brown hair and sea blue eyes. I'd always hoped Loren would make it big in the music world. She wrote me that she'd been offered a record contract, but she wanted to get married first and felt at twenty-five that time was running out. She left Cincinnati for Tennessee to find her a big ole boy, and that's just what she did. She married Billy McKay, had a baby girl, and came back home.

I had been shocked when she turned up with that mountain of a man with the glassy blue eyes. It was hard for me to believe she'd surrendered a recording contract to marry him. But, like the rest of us girls who'd grown up in the hill country, she was afraid of being an old maid and hauled him back to Kentucky to marry, despite his heroin addiction and two children from a previous marriage.

Loren wasn't there when I pulled into the gas station, but at least I was on familiar turf. I'd stopped at that same station many times before for gas and coffee and just to stretch my legs. It was located exactly halfway between Ashland and Lexington and it made a nice pit stop on my road trips back and forth to Mom and Dad's house. Loren not being there when I pulled in was typical of her, always late, I thought. Rather than sit in the hot car with the sun beating down, I asked Erica if she wanted a Mountain Dew. I figured she did by the way she leaped out of the back seat. The things children will do for a treat, I thought, as a grin spread across my face. I unbuckled Megan, laid her on my shoulder, threw a blanket over her head, and headed in with Erica right behind me.

The air conditioning was the first thing to welcome us when the metal and glass doors swung wide to let us in. The clerk behind the counter didn't pay much attention as we wandered around. I tried not to stare when I noticed how frazzled she looked in her black sleeveless heavy metal T-shirt and bleached blond hair curled probably by a home perm. Her hair was teased up only in front, above her bangs, giving her a bizarre unicorn look from the side. Her worn face surrounded by the fictitious mane that dangled like a worn-out mop across her round shoulders made her look far older than she was. As the girls and I made our way down to the soda cooler, she glanced up and rather than be caught staring, I quickly asked her, "How far to Clearfield?"

I kept a watchful eye on Erica who was skipping around gathering items.

"'Bout twenty miles h'up a bad crooked road. Whut kinda business ya got 'n Clearfield?" she asked as she eyed my clothing and must have recognized I couldn't have been from these parts when she got to my high-heeled shoes. I altered my accent a little to match hers so she'd feel more at ease.

"Just agoin' ta see an ol' friend from school I ain't seen in years." I wanted to tell her about Johnny. I wanted to tell everybody how the system had failed me and the terrible heartache I was suffering. But, by the looks of her tired features, I bet she knew all about hard life.

I paid for my things and put back the items Erica had hoped I would give in and buy her. They always put the toys or candy that tempt kids the most right in front of the cash register, as if mothers didn't have their hands full enough with children in their arms. After the clerk bagged our purchases, I headed for the car, Megan on one hip as Erica ran a few steps ahead of my watchful eyes. Mom used to warn me of the bad stuff that'd been known to happen close to the interstate when children were left unattended. I stepped up my stride to catch up with her bouncing blond head. We'd just opened our treats when suddenly I saw Loren standing beside a pickup truck.

"Howdy! How long ya been here?"

"Not long," I said, and hugged her. "I'm so glad you came. It's really nice of you to invite me and the kids over."

"That's what friends are for," she said, swinging her dark brown, waist-length hair.

"Wher'd ya git that truck?" I asked. I always hated trucks, especially the ones with gun racks in the back window.

"Hell, you can't get by without one here! Get in and we'll head on up to the house, out to God's country!" She laughed.

"Do you have car seats for the kids?"

"Jane, do you know how close we are to Elliot County, the poorest county in the state, maybe the country? People over yonder never heard of a car seat."

"I'll just follow you up," I said. "That way we don't have to unload all this stuff."

"Jane, you've have to have a four-wheel drive to get to

where I live. There's another road that'll get you there a little smoother but it's twenty or thirty minutes longer and there's no damn way that old car a' yours can pull the hill."

I insisted on getting Megan's car seat so at least Megan would be safe. I hiked up my dress and dug my heels into the side of the truck and hoisted myself to the seat. Settling in, I tried to lock the door, but it had been stripped and wouldn't lock.

"Damn, Loren! This is a Hatfield and McCoy truck if I've ever seen one."

She laughed and then grew serious. "Nobody's got jobs in these parts, except when school's in session. This was all rural country until President Kennedy and Uncle Jim had the four-year institute of higher education built here and the locals don't mix with the educators or the students too well. They're suspicious of people with education. They think they're gonna steal stuff from 'em. The main currency here is food stamps. You can buy diapers, food, guns, dope, or even a car with 'em. A man to envy around these parts is one with a wife that works at a grocery store or a fast food restaurant—and they just added a fine new eatery a few weeks ago—just up the street from the Jim Matthews Playground."

I knew well the legacy of Uncle Jim. He'd been the congressman of our district and served his people well for years. My grandpa Charlie had been one of his best buddies. People marveled for weeks when Congressman Jim Matthews came to my grandfather Charlie's funeral in a gray flannel suit to mourn one of his most faithful political supporters. Everybody loved him like family. And his legend was known far and wide in our area. All the older folks around home knew all they'd have to do was call Uncle Jim when some government agency had fouled them up. But to our generation it was different. We always thought of his dentures and how they whistled when he spoke. Sometimes on the weekends, before Loren and I had children, we'd sit around joking and talking like Uncle Jim.

"J-J-Jane," she'd start, "which came firsssst, hisss denturesss or hisss ssson?"

"L-L-Loren," I'd answer, "I'd jussst about bet fer ssssure it wasss hisss ssson, becaussse hisss ssson's name wasss Chrissss, and he wouldn't want to whisssstle at hisss ssson like a dog now, would he?"

Sometimes this type of conversation would go on sickeningly for hours. Sometimes we'd call a dentist from the yellow pages to get some whistling dentures installed. Thank goodness the receptionist that answered always hung up on us right way, or we'd all have our heads full of musical mouthpieces.

"They've got buildings named after him all around these parts," Loren added as I chuckled from the thought of his dentures. "He helped 'em get their draws."

"What's a draw?" I just had to ask.

"First of the month checks. You know, Disability, Social Security, Welfare. Hell, Jane, everybody in these parts have got some type of dysfunction," she said with a snicker.

The truck took a curve that slung us all to one side, and I grabbed Megan's car seat as we regained our balance. Loren kicked the gears down and headed up a winding dusty road. I grabbed the dashboard and covered Megan's face with her blanket, coughing as clouds of dust rolled in the windows. Loren laughed at me, softly at first, but it immediately turned into a belly laugh.

"Your gonna have to toughen up to live here, Jane. No place for the weak-spirited or the frail of body. This is no-woman's land."

"I thought you said it was God's country," I laughed. I was beginning to realize that this was not the quiet hideaway Loren had promised on the phone. But at least there was little chance Michael would find us. "You're really great to let us come," I said and looked out the window. "Some pretty hills through here. What are property and rent prices like around this place?"

"Out where I live is real cheap. That's why we bought there.

Well, that and the fact Billy can hear the helicopters comin' from miles away."

"Why are there helicopters?"

"Dope crops. Dope's the main cash crop here, and the army flies over lookin' for crops. That helicopter sound brings Billy right back into the jungles, back to his days in 'Nam. It's worse in the fall."

Escape from Michael was important to me, but it was beginning to sound like I was heading into a war zone.

As we pulled into Loren's yard, the truck wasn't even shut off when two of Loren's three children ran from the house, partially clothed, and met us as we got out. Right behind them came their daddy, Billy.

"Ya'll git your asses in the house 'n' git some goddamn clothes on. Ya look like a bunch of goddamn Mexicans standing out in the yard waitin' for the rain."

I felt like covering the girls' ears but I didn't want to get things off to a bad start with Billy. I gave him a hug and he patted my bottom as I lifted Megan, car seat and all, from the truck.

"Jane, come in and get ye a bite to eat. Grace, git Jane an ice cold beer out of the refrigerator," he yelled to his oldest daughter. "Got plenty of beer and plenty of food cooked up and I got a barbecue on the smoker." Billy was a genuine Tennessean, and his shitkicker attitude mixed well with most of the locals in eastern Kentucky. Food and beer were the main ingredients of any gathering. I could tell Billy had gone to a lot of trouble to roll out the carpet for us.

Loren and I carried our things into the living room that was swarming with flies as she started making excuses for the house.

"Jane, I figured if Billy's not gonna work, he can at least remodel. For Christmas, we bought ourselves a pump for the well and now I don't have to bail water for baths and laundry. You haven't lived till you've had to bail water to the number three tub for the kids to wash in. Don't drop anything you expect to eat on the carpet. We fantasize and call it the fine Antron, but it's ready for the junk yard. And, we have a bathroom in the house now; you have to go out on the back porch to get to it, but it beats the outhouse."

"Loren, don't worry, we'll be fine," I said to be nice, but I felt embarrassed for her. She'd been one of the most impressive people I'd ever met when I was younger. She was talented and college educated but something had gone wrong. I was grateful to see her, but I had to try hard to ignore the way she was living. She deserved better.

We turned the children out to play on her thirteen acres where there was plenty of room to run. She assured me it was childproof. I spread a big colorful quilt Loren had made in the middle of the floor and laid Megan on it after I washed her up. Then Loren and I finally got a chance to sit down on the couch and talk about my plans for the next few weeks. I'd quickly explained the murder on the phone, but we hadn't had the time to talk about it or my fright over Michael's phone call and the upcoming trial.

Loren patted my shoulder. "Jane, ever since you called me and told me the news, I've been sick and had nightmares, one after another. Of all people why Johnny? He wouldn't hurt a flea. I don't understand how Michael would do something like this. Remember that time we stopped by right after you and Michael got together? I thought he was the perfect man for you. He dressed so nicely and seemed like the perfect gentleman, and waited on you hand and foot. There were dozens of roses all over the house and all those expensive champagnes. Damn, I thought you'd hit the mother lode."

I nodded. "I guess I thought I had, too. He was a charmer back then, but, as soon as we got married, it was like Cinderella had lost her glass slipper. I became his servant and when I got pregnant with Megan, he started runnin' around with other women."

"Boy, there ain't nothin' that haunts a pregnant woman like that does. You feel so fat and unattractive as it is, and they shove it in your face by whorin' around. Damn. I'm lucky Billy's never laid a hand on me. He tried to once. Got drunk and decided he was gonna beat me. I picked up that double-barrel over there in the corner and aimed it right between his eyes and promised to plant one in his frontal lobe if he took another step. I asked him calmly, 'Where do you want it?' That ended that."

My eyes found the gun she'd pointed to, and I felt beads of sweat form under my skin. I stared at it until Loren asked me what was wrong.

"Can we do somethin' with the gun? It makes me nervous with the kids around, especially with it laying out like that."

"Our kids know not to bother it. We have to keep it close in case animals or crazy humans come around. H'it won't bother you!" Loren insisted with a laugh.

I still couldn't take my eyes off of the rifle. Finally, Loren stuck it under the bed. "Boy, you do have it bad," she said.

"What's that?" I asked.

"PTSS, post-traumatic stress syndrome. Most people have it when they've been in wars or gunfire like you've been in. It's perfectly normal, but I'd never seen anybody so soon after they've been traumatized. Billy still has flashbacks from his soldier days. But I didn't meet him for ten years after, and he'd drank whiskey and shot heroin until most of it was out of his system."

"You mean he covered it up. Drugs, even sedatives, are one thing I won't take. I took a few pills before the funeral, but that's all. I'm afraid I'll get hooked on 'em and lose the girls and where would they go?"

"I don't suppose your mom and dad can take the kids."

"I don't want to lose 'em to anybody! I've nearly drove myself into an early grave trying to keep 'em. They're all I've got."

Suddenly Billy started shouting: "Loren, git your ass out here and git these goddamn kids out of the pond!" He was yelling from out back loud enough to hear in the living room. "They're soakin' wet, and Tiny's got a shit-filled diaper. Goddamn, how am I supposed to cook with all these kids under foot?"

I jumped from the couch and ran to the back porch. Erica was hiding behind a tree, not sure what to do with Billy carrying on the way he was. I ran toward her and I motioned her over to me.

"Honey, are you okay?"

She didn't say a word but kept shifting her frightened eyes toward Billy to see what he was going to do next.

"I don't think it's a good idea to play in the pond," I said calmly. "Somebody might get hurt, okay?" She nodded yes and went the long way around Billy to get back to the other kids.

"Does Billy always yell at the kids like that?" I asked Loren when we got back inside.

"They just get on his nerves, and I do the best I can to keep 'em outta his hair. But he loves 'em. That's one thing he's always promised: he'd never walk out on 'em like his ol' man did."

When dinner was ready, it was quite chaotic trying to get five children fed at once. With one high chair we had to take turns with Megan and Loren's baby boy, the only son they called Brother. He was five months older than Megan and Loren was glad to finally have a boy.

"I can reclaim my stomach now that I've borne the male heir," Loren said proudly. "Thought I'd never get a son out, and as soon as he was born, I made the appointment to go out of town for a few days. Billy didn't mind watchin' 'em all that weekend!"

"What do ya mean, out of town?"

"To get my tubes tied. Now, Jane, we are many miles from the land of reproductive freedom. The only hospital in this town is a Catholic one, and you know how *they* are. No birth control pills. No tubals. Gotta drive inta town for that operation. Hell, Estee Lauder's easier to get than it is for a woman to get fixed. Here, cows have more reproductive rights!"

"I knew it was hard to get pills sometimes, but most family doctors prescribe them back home," I said.

"People can't afford private doctors here. Everybody's got to go to the clinics or the hospital with medical cards. Only the professors at the university and a few professionals have regular doctors and some of them drive to Lexington."

It took us hours to get everybody fed, and, before long, it was getting dark and we had to get ready for bath time. Erica didn't like the idea of taking a bath in a tub full of dirty water that all the other kids had washed in, so I cleaned her up real good with a wash cloth. Billy's children immediately put up a fuss, saying it wasn't fair that Erica got to take a sponge bath. "They're company," Loren told them, "so mind your own business." Loren mentioned how low the water got in the summer months and instructed me not to flush the toilet till the last child went to bed.

We tucked the kids in bed. Then when Billy turned in after the sports portion of the news went off Loren and I popped some corn. We sat up for hours and talked about the past, our lives, Johnny's death, and what the future might bring.

CHAPTER **12**

Waiting for Justice

The sound of gunfire echoing through the hills woke me. I sprang from my sleeping bag on the floor as I heard a haunting shrill sound outside the window as another bullet burst from a firearm. The only thing I could think of was somehow Michael had escaped and found us. Crouching low, I ran through Loren's kitchen and up the stairs, praying I'd find Erica. I found her in the kids' room, shrunk down in the corner, her hands gripping her head, her miniature frame trembling. Erica jerked her face toward me as I wrapped my fingers around her tense shoulders. She grabbed my neck and gave a miserable muffled moan as we heard another bullet explode. The sound was coming from the backyard, but I couldn't tell who was shooting or who was screaming after each shot landed. Erica's heart was pounding hard against my own throbbing chest. I tried to stand up to peek out the window, but Erica had wrapped her legs around mine, making it nearly impossible for me to maneuver.

"Honey, let go of Mommy," I whispered. "I need to see what's happening outside." Her eyes were as big as half dollars and her teeth were clenched tight. She couldn't say a word. I picked her up, tucked her head under my chin, and wrapped her cramped legs around my waist. I lifted us just enough to get a look out the upstairs window. Billy stood in the yard below, his gun cocked and aimed at some unknown target. The next bullet left the chamber, striking something and causing it to scream. Petrified by what might be happening, I stomped wildly on the floor, knowing Loren's room was below us. I prayed that she'd wake up.

"Loren," I yelled, "What's goin' on out there?"

I heard her bedsprings bounce as the sound of constant cries came from Billy's victim. Her footsteps smacked against the floor as I crawled below the window and down the stairwell with Erica until I saw her.

"What in the hell's goin' on? Billy's shootin' somebody but I don't know who."

With her mouth hanging open, shocked probably from the pose Erica and I were maintaining, she held up her index finger and motioned for us to stay put. She stepped to the door as the victim's screams grew louder and more intense.

"Billy, what in the hell are you doin'?" she yelled.

"I'm killin' this pig one shot at a time. I landed one 'n each side 'n' one in each of its four legs! Com'ere an' look! I'm savin' the last bullet for its forehead."

"Dammit, Billy, put that gun down. Jane and Erica are fastened to each other, scared out of their wits. And would you mind puttin' that pig and our house guests out of their misery. You were a damn sharpshooter in Vietnam—now get it over with!"

The door slammed behind her as she made her way back to us. I pried Erica's locked fingers from my back and left arm as Loren explained what all the commotion was about.

"He's butchering a pig. Sorry about the scare."

"I thought we were all dead. Is he finished?"

"I think it's over. He'll take a knife and finish it off."

"Loren, save us the gore! Erica's terrified as it is, and I'm not much better," I said.

"Jane, I'm really sorry about Billy wakin' y'all up like

that. I'm used to it. Billy hunts all the time and it don't bother me."

"Loren, I grew up around hunters, too, but it's different now. After ya been in the kind of crossfire we have, I guess ya think about that defenseless creature on the receivin' end of the bullet."

"There was a defenseless creature on the other end, but its name was dinner," Loren said with a wide grin and a chuckle.

I didn't laugh. I looked away from her as I smoothed my hand over Erica's head. Her heart was still thumping and her breath labored.

"I'm sorry were acting like this. It's only been two months since the murder, and we're still edgy."

Erica must have thought it safe now to leave my embrace as she turned my neck loose and climbed back up the stairs. I hadn't noticed she'd wet on us both, but I wasn't surprised. Every night since the murder she'd not only wet the bed, but she'd had at least one nightmare, sometimes two.

"Loren, I'm sorry about the wet sheets. I've got some money comin' this week from the rental property before the bank takes it. I'll take all the clothes and wash 'em at the laundry place."

She nodded. "I hate for you to have to but water always runs low this time of year and Billy gets aggravated as hell when he has to haul water." She looked closer at me. "You sure you're up to taking the stuff over?"

I nodded. "I'm okay. I just haven't been able to sleep much. I'm really nervous about the trial. I don't know what to expect. Both times I've met with the attorney, he told me not to worry, everything'll be fine. 'Just tell them the truth' is what he says, but I think this is somethin' I should be more prepared for."

"Have you made arrangements for the kids?" Loren asked.

"No. I called Mom, but she said she'd be too nervous to keep 'em."

"I'm going to go with you," Loren said insistently. "But you know I gotta take Brother with me. He's still nursing, and I can't leave him with Billy."

"I'm not leavin' my kids with Billy either. I know Erica will be a basket case, and I'd be scared ta death that somebody would snatch her for meanness knowin' I was in court. I'm still worried about Michael's family hurtin' them on account of me testifyin' against him."

"I can understand your fears after everything that's happened."

I nodded. "I gotta be real careful who I leave them with. But I don't know who else to call."

"Jane, we'll just have to take them with us. I'm use to lookin' out for kids. Lookin' out for three'll be like a day at the beach. I don't have anybody out here to help me. My parents are gone, and I don't have any other family within three hours of here, and half of Billy's don't speak to me anyway."

"The prosecutor's office said we could stay in a hotel room downtown. They'll put us all up and feed us."

"Hot damn! A bathtub with water to waste! It's been so long since I could enjoy that luxury. I'm gonna take some bubbly bath and soak for an hour."

It was difficult to listen to Loren talking about taking a bath as a special occasion. I remembered when she'd dress in the finest, her hair and body perfectly kept. We'd had such a good time back in those years. She'd stuck with me through all the emotional havoc in my life but, despite my problems, I couldn't ignore what had become of her. Loren told me one of her only friends was her husband's mistress. It didn't seem to bother her that he had somebody on the side. She said she was glad to get him out of her hair once in awhile. Her trips out of the house were limited to the store, school, to the doctor with one of the kids, or the food stamp office. She woke early, worked all day, and went to bed late and exhausted. She accepted this schedule because she believed she was sacrificing for her's and Billy's children, which offset how he carried on, she reasoned. With all my troubles, I was in no position to tell them how to live their lives, but my heart ached for Loren.

As the days passed and the trial drew near, my awareness of her plight grew. She thought I looked worn and she insisted I rest. She went about bailing water, tending the garden, caring for three kids, mending pipes and repairing the house while Billy drank, ran the roads, chased women, and cussed like a fallen preacher when he got home. I was afraid to say anything to her. I knew Billy's constant bad mouthing was painful for her. His slurs were always about her appearance or how stupid he thought she was. "You with a college degree," he'd say. She had been stripped of her confidence, thanks to him. His verbal attacks brought her down and kept her there.

I tried to take the girls out alone with me when I had the gas money. Erica craved private time to talk about her dad and her fear of Michael. Sometimes she couldn't wait for our getaway and would pull me aside to tell me something she had remembered about Johnny.

"Mommy, ya know what Daddy said when we were at the pool?"

"What did he say?"

"He said after he got a job he was gonna ask you to marry him again. Wouldn't that have been wonderful?"

An awkward silence filled the air as I struggled to give her an answer. My eyes filled with tears as I thought about the years stolen from us. I would never know if Johnny and I could have gotten back together, and the void of doubt crushed me to the core. I propped my face in my hands and released tears of uncertainty and frustration.

"Mommy, I didn't mean to make you cry."

"Honey, it's not your fault." I still hadn't answered her. I didn't know how. As hard as I tried to be strong and have all the parental answers, I was afraid I might say the wrong words and complicate her healing. I wished I could afford a therapist for her, and now I knew it was necessary to find her a counselor as quickly as I could.

The next morning when I explained to the intake operator of the local mental health agency what had happened to us and the problems we were having, she labeled us high risk and scheduled an appointment for the following day. I tried to prepare Erica for the visit. I told her these were nice people, trained to help us talk about her daddy's murder, and not to worry about crying if she felt like it.

At the agency, after we filled out the paperwork, the schoolgirl-looking counselor took us back to an office and spoke to us both for a few minutes until another social worker came in to get Erica. "I'm Cheryl," the counselor said, and grabbed a book from the shelf as I assured Erica I'd be waiting for her when she was finished. My suspicions were raised when my counselor kept her eyes glued to the pages. I watched her browsing through the text and suddenly noticed how young she was, at the oldest twenty-three, I thought, staring at her boyish cut brown hair and makeupless face. Maybe straight out of college, I thought, and here I was placing my child's mental health in her hands. I figured it was best I interview this young woman before she started delving into my unsure thoughts.

"If ya don't mind me askin', Cheryl, are you married?"

"Well, actually, I'm not. I've thought about it but I've never told my boyfriend."

I knew she couldn't be from these parts with that kind of answer. In these hills, I'd never heard of any woman making a man wait for longer than the end of dinner for an answer. It was really a stupid ritual, proposing, because most women in our town jumped at the first chance to get married. If a woman had turned twenty and she wasn't married, people found it mighty peculiar.

"So, I don't suppose you got children either."

"Well, no."

While Cheryl rattled off the problems of premarital sex

and children out of wedlock, I wondered how this inexperienced child was going to help me sort out my complex life. I bet her daddy paid for her schooling. I bet she lived in a fancy apartment off campus, completely paid. I felt like educating her about Appalachia, explaining hard times and the need for a man, particularly if you had a child and no education. If you didn't have a husband, you had no social life. Other women didn't want you around; they thought you were going to steal their source of support and protection. And that wasn't the half of it. An unmarried woman was considered fair game and men from miles around could have their way with you without worrying about court action. An unattached woman had no recourse around here. Who was going to defend them? Even the other women supported the men in the courtrooms, all of whom stuck up fiercely for one another. I'd learned that myself the hard way.

I didn't much listen to what Cheryl had to say after that. She spent the time explaining the field of psychology and the wonders it could work. If it was so wonderful, why didn't they have all the men who rape women and beat their wives in for a mass healing? Make them all well, instead of putting us women up in shelters after they beat us.

The agency asked us to come back every day, and I did until I felt more like an experiment or worse yet a circus freak. I got tired of being blamed for picking bad men. Did they mean that was my only fault? If so, why didn't they carry away the real sick men that beat, raped, and stole from us women. The whole idea of holding me responsible for someone else's violence made me ill. I worried about what they were telling Erica. I thought of how weird it must be for a child, someone who hadn't chosen marriage or birth, to be uprooted and thrown into a shelter and placed on the welfare rolls. It all made me sick and extremely cynical.

Finally, the morning of the trial came. We'd been preparing for several days, trying to get Loren's chores done. We'd washed all the laundry, cooked up enough food to last for a week, and bathed the kids till they shone. The deal Loren had to strike with Billy to baby-sit their children was a costly bargain: Loren had to rent movies, some for him and some for the kids, buy a case of beer, a carton of cigarettes, and plenty of snack foods so he wouldn't have to cook. I felt helpless when I figured how much money it was going to cost her. I didn't have a penny to help her.

Loren made Billy leave the room when she dipped into her "rathole" money. I remembered that trick from when Michael started beating me and I used to keep money tucked up in the drawstring of the ironing board, just in case I had to get away fast, to where I didn't know.

The drive to the hotel in Lexington was frustrating. The hot September sun seemed cruel and vindictive, especially for the three small children. Megan was eight months old and teething. I couldn't afford teething lotion and the hard biscuits I gave her to chew on did little to ease her pain. Brother was always fussing and crying. He'd scream to the top of his lungs forever, but Loren had grown used to it. He sounded so much like his dad screaming and fussing all the time, she'd learned to tune them both out. Erica was quiet and less distracting, but her stillness worried me. She'd created a way of slipping out of reality and drifting off maybe to a safer place, somewhere where no one could reach her. During the ride she curled up in the back seat, her eyes fixed on nothing. What was she thinking, I agonized, on her way to Michael's murder trial for her father's death. What a shocking speech this would make when she was asked to tell her first grade class about her summer vacation.

When we pulled into the hotel parking lot, Brother and Megan were wailing louder than Bob Marley's band. We locked the truck and headed for the lobby with the babies still crying. The clerk passed us our keys quickly across the counter, ahead of several other customers. A bellhop grabbed our bags and took us up on an express elevator.

As soon as we got in the room, I mixed up a formula bottle and rocked Megan in a nice cushy rocking chair. She fell right off to sleep. Poor Megan had been uprooted so many times and we'd had to do without so many things, it broke my heart to think she'd never been able to enjoy the simple pleasure of being rocked to sleep before.

Loren took her luxury bath after we got the kids down for a nap. She'd waited all week for that treat, and I was glad that at least she felt pampered. All I could think of was the trial. Not only was I afraid of Michael's defense attorney trying to confuse me on the stand, but I'd have to see Michael for the first time since the murder. I'd already decided I wouldn't make eye contact with him. After all he'd done, I never wanted to lay eyes on him again.

After I cleaned up a little, I felt I needed some last minute advice from the prosecutor's office.

"I'll stay with the kids," Loren offered.

The office was around the corner from the hotel. "It'll be worth it if I can get a little comfort," I said.

When I stepped out on the street, I felt like a moving target, stalked by anyone who took Michael's side, which seemed like everybody in the universe. My eyes wide and watchful, I scrutinized every sound as I picked up my pace. In my frenzied mind, I tried to make a list of questions to ask the attorney, things I thought were important.

The gray stone building looked intimidating as I approached it. Inside, I asked for Mike Morrison, the deputy district attorney for the case. The gray-haired woman at the central desk riffled some papers in front of her. "I think that case has been switched to Richard Connors," she said disinterestedly. Her words threw me further into a panic. The last-minute switch scared me. I had only spoken to Morrison a couple of times but he'd reassured me of a conviction. He'd said it was a cut-and-dried case. But the kind of justice I'd seen during my whole ordeal assured me that nothing was a sure bet. Poker and the horses were safer bets than just a decision in a courtroom.

CHAPTER 13

Justice?

Finally the trial began. On the day I was called to testify, I stayed in a conference room at the prosecutor's office for hours biting my nails to the quick while I waited. Richard Connors, the new prosecutor, came in to speak to me. His advice about what I could and couldn't say only made me more distraught. The large picture window at the end of the office provided me with a clear view of the courthouse, but I couldn't see anybody I knew going in or out. Thank God Loren was with me. Megan was cutting her new teeth while I was grinding my old ones, and Loren did what she could to calm us both. She took turns holding Megan, then her baby son, and tried to ease Erica's fears while I paced the floor. I'd gotten there at 9 A.M., ready to put Michael away, but it was now close to 2 P.M. Finally, security officers came to lead me to the courthouse.

As we left the office, a few more deputies circled closely around me. One of the officers talked on his walkie-talkie while steering me across the street. They acted like snipers were going to pick us off before I had a chance to testify. Thoroughly unnerved as I walked through the large white doors and into a steel elevator, my heart pounded hard in my chest. They hurried me down the long corridors, whipping me around each of the corners to the chambers at the end of the last hall where a sign read COURTROOM.

The doors opened. Around me the courtroom was filled to capacity. My body trembled as I made my way inside. I'd wanted to come over earlier, to look around and get a feel for the place so I wouldn't be so intimidated but Richard Connors said I couldn't. He explained that witnesses weren't allowed to listen to anyone else's testimony because it might affect their statements. Nothing would have changed what I had to say, and nothing could have shocked me more than I had been already. I was still dazed from being told by Mr. Connors that I couldn't talk about Michael being in jail the night before the murder. He said I also couldn't talk about the warrants for Michael's arrest or the history of him beating me. The judge had ruled it inadmissible, since Michael had never been convicted of the abuse.

But that wasn't because I hadn't reported it and tried. I'd done all I could to stop the violence, to get Michael convicted and behind bars. No one had cared. None of that mattered to the judge. If the police had kept Michael in jail the night before he killed Johnny, I was sure the murder wouldn't have happened. I had prepared myself to tell the truth, but now their orders were like a gag had been stuffed in my mouth, muffling justice, guaranteeing the truth wouldn't be heard. How could I possibly explain what had happened without talking about abuse? How could the jury convict Michael if they didn't know how long the violence had gone on and what it had led to?

The prosecutor had also told me that Michael was using a self-defense plea, which made no damn sense to me. How could the judge possibly allow him to use that type of defense? The coroner's report proved that all three lethal bullets entered Johnny from the rear. He was shot twice in the back and once under his arm. All three bullets pierced his lungs and heart, and all three were fatal. I wondered how in the hell shooting a man in the back could be considered self-defense?

As I began to walk up the aisle of the courtroom, I recognized a few faces in the crowd. Johnny's dad sat right up front. I'd overheard at the prosecutor's office that special provisions had to be made for him. They knew his heart was bad and feared the graphic details of his son's murder might cause him to have an attack. No one seemed to care how it all affected me and the girls.

Reporters and a few of Michael's family members were the only other faces I recognized. The rest of the crowd blurred into a mass of colors as the early autumn sun penetrated the lofty windows behind them, offering a bizarre contrast of beauty and brutality.

After being sworn in, I had to climb on my unstable legs into the boxlike witness stand. The judge sat elevated very close on my left and the jury was lifted high to my right. Michael sat directly in front of me. I tried to avoid his glares, but I couldn't help notice how he looked. Dressed for deception, he was clean cut and professional looking, unlike the stereotypical wife beater and murderer.

Michael was outfitted in his favorite pants which were perfectly pressed, polished pointed-toe shoes, starched white shirt, silk tie, and blue blazer. Probably every stitch of clothing he had on were charged on my credit cards, I thought. Just looking at him dressed so nice reminded me of all those nights he'd leave late, splashed with expensive cologne, to pick up women over drinks and some smooth talk, while I stayed home cleaning and crying, and many times, bruised and bleeding, and pregnant with Megan.

The lumps in my throat choked me as I drew a deep breath. Mr. Connors was the first to question me. He asked me to tell where I lived, how old I was, and what I did for a living. I knew that the meaningless questions were to help me adjust to the microphone in front of me, but there was no way I could relax. Knowing I would have to retell the whole ugly story kept me on edge, as did having to confront Michael again.

I tried to find an object in the courtroom to look at while I answered what Mr. Connors asked me. The first questions about Johnny's death were similar to the ones the detective had asked the day of the murder, just a description of the facts, each time rearranged a little differently, but that soon changed.

"Where did Megan sleep?" Mr. Connors asked.

"With Erica. She had her baby bed set up there."

"You put Megan's baby bed in Erica's room?"

"Yes." The question threw me. I didn't think them sleeping together was unusual. My sister and I had shared a room during our entire childhood. Why did I have to answer that twice? What was he getting at?

"And did you have a bedroom of your own?"

"Yes."

"At the time the children went to bed, were they in the same room?"

"Yes."

"Did you see Mr. Haney again?"

"Yes. He came back after that." Sweat poured from me as my blood ran cold under my burning skin. I was uncertain how I should answer the questions without revealing that the police had arrested Michael the night before the murder.

"Do you know what time it was?"

"No. I don't."

"What happened when Mr. Haney came back?"

"He just came back in and told Johnny to leave, and Johnny said, 'No.' He said he was staying there."

"Did somebody open the door and let him in?"

"Johnny did."

"What did you tell Mr. Haney at that time?"

"I told him to leave."

"Did he leave?"

"Eventually, after . . ." I came close to slipping. I knew I wasn't supposed to say anything about the arrest and it really rattled me.

"Tell us what happened."

"After," I stuttered and had to repeat the word. "After an argument, he started, you know, he wanted to know when Johnny was leaving, and then he kept refusing to leave. He sat down on the floor and said, 'I'm not leaving. I am not leaving.' And he sat on the couch. So then I went outside to one of the nine-one-one phones across the street, and I was going over there to call the police."

I worried about telling them I'd left the girls alone with Michael. What if they used it against me later? I was afraid they'd accuse me of abandoning my children. But how could I get help without calling the police? I couldn't tell them I'd hit Michael either, and I was glad they didn't ask me. They might charge me with assault, take the girls from me, and put them in an orphanage. Not only would that destroy Erica, but I was sure it would've unraveled what was left of my mind. I was only trying to defend us, keep us all safe. Why couldn't they see that? Why did it seem as if I instead of Michael was on trial?

I described to them how the pool gates were locked up when I tried to get to the emergency phone, and, because I couldn't make the call, that's why Johnny had to leave to find somewhere to call the police. Desperately, I wanted to hear that tape, just to hear Johnny's voice one more time. If I could hear it again, like a cherished song I could store every word, every sound, every lyric and verse, and hold onto it forever in my mind. He'd been taken so suddenly, snatched without a last goodbye. If only I could hear his voice one last time!

"Did Mr. Haney go away with the police at some point?"

"He walked outside, and I ran upstairs to get copies . . ."

"No." The prosecutor stopped me. "As far as you know, he went out?"

I didn't know what they'd do to me if I said something I wasn't allowed to, but I didn't want to take that chance. What if they put me in jail? It wasn't worth going to jail and losing the girls. I had to be careful and tell only part of what happened, just like I was told by the prosecutor.

"Yeah," I said, unsure how to answer. "He went out front and was out there. When I walked outside, he was talking to the police."

Before I made another mistake about what I could and could not say, I think the prosecutor intentionally shifted his line of questioning.

"Did you go to bed that night?"

"Yes."

"At the time you went to bed, where were you, each of the two children, and Mr. Eidson (Johnny) located?"

I thought it was more than a little rude when he asked me in front of everybody in the courtroom where Johnny had slept that night, but I answered truthfully anyway. "On the couch," I assured them. Johnny and I had decided to keep it that way, sleep apart, take things slow this time, but out of respect for each other rather than what nosy people would think.

After explaining the screams and gunfire, where Johnny was laying, and where Michael was standing, and how Erica watched it all, Mr. Connors put some very grisly pictures in front of me. I turned away in disgust, sick and queasy, until they insisted that I identify them. The pictures were of Johnny's body, bloody and dead, sprawled out across the steps, his head pulled down toward the front door, his eyes still open, and his feet pointing toward the top of the stairs. The pictures confused me, because I remembered distinctly that Johnny was not positioned that way when I escaped. Suddenly, images of Johnny trying to crawl toward the door filled my mind. Had Johnny not died instantly as I was told? Was he still alive and died trying to get away from Michael?

Looking at the pictures, I began to cry. The judge demanded I gather myself. He didn't seem to understand how horrifying it was for me to see Johnny's bloody, bullet-ridden body spread out again, more vivid than my own memory. Some of the pictures were of the holes Michael had kicked in my bedroom door, when he had tried to get in after me.

"What happened after Michael began kicking the door?" Mr. Connors asked.

"He said he was going to kill me and then he was going to kill himself, and Erica was screaming, 'Don't kill my mommy. Don't kill my mommy.'"

I described how I had to step over Johnny's body, at gunpoint, still hopeful he was alive, while maneuvering the girls and I down the steps and to the door. As I walked, Michael's gun was cocked and pointed at me, at times to the back of my head or rammed into my side, right below the rib cage. I told them about my struggle at the door with Michael, and how I pleaded with him to let the girls out unharmed.

I knew better than to beg him for my own life. I wanted to tell everyone in the courtroom how much Michael had always seemed to enjoy it when I begged him to stop hurting me. During my pregnancy with Megan, he'd slapped and punched me, savagely, almost for sport. If I begged him to quit, my pleas only made him more excited. Then he'd hit me harder, ripping flesh and leaving bruises all over my body. I wanted them to know what he really was like, but Connors had said I couldn't talk about it. I couldn't discuss the hitting or how Michael would rip my clothes off in front of his teenage sons. To me, it made no sense.

After Mr. Connors finished, Mr. Talman, Michael's defense attorney, began. As soon as he stood up, I sensed an attack. He swooped in front of me, his eyebrows arched and knit together, like a vulture after a piece of dead meat. His performance in a way reminded me of Michael, the way he'd try to pretend his inquiry was justified before he'd berate and beat me. I knew Mr. Talman's twisted questions were meant to rattle and confuse me. They did. He kept asking me to remember dates. In my foggy mind this was next to impossible. Even dates that I would normally have at my fingertips like when Johnny and I were married, when we were divorced, and Erica's birthday all flew out of my brain. Then he acted as if my inability to recall if it was the thirteenth or fourteenth showed I was lying. He tried to make an issue out of me being married twice, like I was the only divorced woman in the world.

Mr. Talman kept on baiting me, confusing me, making me seem unstable and incoherent, while Johnny's murderer sat inspecting his fingernails at the defense table. He asked me the day and time of when I'd filed for divorce from Michael. It'd been about four or five months before the murder, shortly after Megan was born, but my divorce attorney was concerned that he hadn't properly served Michael with the divorce papers. Just to make sure, my attorney had Michael served with the papers again the week before the murder trial. That's how it was explained to me. It wasn't my job to file, just my responsibility to pay for it. I didn't understand why they didn't look up the dates themselves. They could've checked the court records and found when it was filed the first time if they'd wanted accurate dates. How could I remember now? After what I had been through such things seemed inconsequential.

After repeated and trivial questions Mr. Talman's interrogation suddenly leaped to personal details about my past. I couldn't understand why my past was important: I hadn't killed anybody. Michael was the one who'd been abusive. Why didn't they allow his past to be examined? He'd been married five times, and I'd often wondered what he'd put his other wives through. His oldest son had once told me Michael had served time on an Indiana work farm for failing to support his children, but that didn't seem to matter. The court didn't seem concerned about Michael's failure to provide for his children, or his deviant or violent past. Meanwhile, the defense did the best they could to make Johnny and my relationship look rotten. All lies contrived for Michael's flimsy defense. Anything to drag me down as a witness.

Over and over, the same questions were fired at me, like an automatic weapon, until I couldn't have answered what my name was if asked. Mr. Talman even made a big deal about Michael giving me ninety dollars a few weeks before the murder. He insisted that I used that money to rent my apartment. Somehow, he figured Michael should've been allowed to come into my apartment whenever he wanted because he'd given me child support. Megan was six months old and that was all the money he'd ever given me, and Michael had even asked for that back. He had changed his mind about paying support when I wouldn't let him stay with me, insisting the money he'd given me was only a loan. He'd followed me to both my jobs, demanding that I pay it back and swearing he'd leave me alone when I did. But that never happened. Michael would catch me after work, knowing I'd have tip money, and demand I give him money. I'd have to beg him to let me keep money to feed the girls or buy diapers, beg him to let me hang onto enough money to get the girls to day care and me back to work the next day. Even after I paid back every nickel of the ninety dollars, he kept hounding me. I knew it wasn't just the money he was after, and I knew Michael didn't give a damn about those children or he wouldn't have tried to break me. He went to great extremes to try to keep me poor, thinking he'd have a better chance of getting me back if I didn't have the funds to take care of the girls. When his plan backfired, he became more violent.

Mr. Connors objected a few times when he felt Mr. Talman's questions seemed out of line or thought my answers had been cut off quickly. There was little he could do to stop the attack. Such techniques were not only allowed, they apparently show off the skills of the lawyer to the spectators, much like in the days of Rome. I was shaken pretty badly and felt dazed by the verbal interrogation.

Suddenly, the judge called a conference at the bench. Whatever they had to talk about must have been serious. Otherwise, the judge wouldn't have given a fifteen minute recess.

When I was helped off the stand, Johnny's dad rushed from his seat, apologizing as he came.

"I had no idea what you'd been through. I didn't know how all this had come about. Can you forgive me?"

I nodded yes, but I couldn't speak. I was too exhausted from the questioning.

The recess was not a relief for me, but only a delay in getting the humiliating ordeal over with. When we were called back into the courtroom, I was put back on the stand. Mr. Talman, poised in front of me, seemed ready to go for my jugular.

"At the break," he began, "we were talking about when Johnny was at your apartment on July 9, and Michael came over there. Michael was upset that he was there. That was not a question, though. And I asked you do you recall Michael telling you the reasons why he did not want Johnny there because of things you had told Michael about Johnny's past behavior." He paused. "You'll have to answer everything loud," he added.

I tried to answer, but I didn't understand why he kept talking about Johnny. He wasn't on trial. He didn't kill anybody. Plus he wasn't even here to defend himself. But the unjust questions pressed on. Talman, to rattle me more, kept saying, "You have to answer out loud. Speak up." As he continued, I began to feel like I was a sacrifice. I was the guilty person ready to be consumed. Johnny and I had had our bad times, I didn't deny that. We were together over five years, most of which were good. When Johnny became unemployed and I was employed and pregnant with Erica, tension built and we argued out of frustration, and would often end the night crying in each other's arms, angry that money was driving us apart.

Marriage to Michael was quite the opposite. It wasn't being poor that drove us apart; a week didn't pass that he wasn't beating me, leaving bruises and cuts all over me. It was true that Johnny hadn't provided for Erica, but I didn't think he deserved to die for it. After all, Michael hadn't helped with Megan. I couldn't believe these questions had anything to do with Michael killing Johnny. I knew Michael was there to kill me but Johnny took my bullets. Nobody seemed to care if I lived or died. Listening to this form of Appalachian inquisition I felt sure if I'd been killed they probably wouldn't have bothered to hold a trial. The urge to cry devoured me as they asked explicit questions about my sexual experiences with Johnny

Why would they ask me these type of questions, questions so personal, so private? Intimate moments between Johnny and I were always consensual. Those tender honeymoon years of our youth, while we were getting to know each other affectionately and passionately, I felt was none of their business. To be forced to describe them, and then have the defense try to pervert them while witnesses and jurors listened and looked on not only embarrassed but infuriated me. Our sex life had nothing to do with the murder. What positions we loved each other in had nothing to do with Johnny being slaughtered. Not to Talman. Our private marital matters seemed to dominate his questioning, as he avoided any mention of the murder.

If he could ask about Johnny and my sexual relationship, why couldn't I tell how abusive Michael was during sex, when I wanted to leave him but couldn't, because I was pregnant and the law wouldn't allow it? While I was trapped by the law and economic conditions, Michael would demand that I say things to him when we were having sex, slapping me repeatedly if I didn't. Michael called them "bedtime stories." He even fantasized about different men having sex with me, strange men. He imagined every man in my life doing sexually violent things to me, and insisted that I enjoyed them. But it was his dirty foul mind and my lack of resources to escape that allowed it to continue. But these answers weren't permitted.

More unnecessary questions kept coming, relentlessly, until I began to wonder how this could be considered a fair trial. I wanted to die. I wished more than ever that Michael would have killed me rather than having to be humiliated on the witness stand. The grinding questioning rendered me speechless, confusing my answers. My whole body shook, knowing they were winning their game even though my life was at stake and Johnny's killer and my abuser might go free. Almost every question, every statement, was picked apart and twisted into something totally inaccurate.

There were so many words that I'd never heard of, big words, words I didn't understand. I felt ashamed and stupid for not understanding them. I'd gone to school, learned how to be a wife and mother, and believed if you told the truth you'd get justice. But I could see this was not how the game was really played. It was more like a stage with actors or a football game with a championship title at stake and a half-blind referee as the judge: suppress evidence, gain twenty yards. This wasn't about getting at the truth. This was a game of egos.

As the questioning persisted, I felt like a piece of equipment, or a hostage tied to the whipping post. Sometimes I got so tired of answering that I said I didn't remember just to get Talman to leave me alone. But the questions went on.

"Did you hear a handgun or a shotgun?" Stupid questions. What difference did it make? Whatever type of firearm Michael used Johnny died from it. Why would they expect me to know that? I'd never been interested in guns. They always scared me.

Talman's and Michael's game was to tire me. To confuse me. The hours ticked by and questions came at me like rapid fire. At the end, I didn't know who the attorney was referring to when he asked me questions. The police? Johnny? The gun? Michael? It all ran together. I worried that my inability to answer the questions would have a negative effect on the jury's decision as to Michael's guilt. Finally, I didn't know what points they were trying to make, or how to answer them, and I felt sure the jury was as confused as I was.

CHAPTER **14**

Despair

Exhausted and dispirited at the end of the day, I climbed into the truck. The ride home to Loren's house seemed to take forever. "I'm worried that my testimony was weak. I'm afraid my blunders will allow Michael to walk," I said to Loren who tried to console me.

In my panic I envisioned Michael in a car right behind us, already on his hunt for revenge. I tried to act calm for the sake of the girls. I knew they were tired, confused, and cranky, but as nervous as I was I couldn't help falling apart in front of them. Poor little Megan looked up at me from her car seat with sad, naive eyes every time I broke down. Sometimes she'd pucker up and cry when I wailed, but I couldn't stop myself. The grief, anger, and frustration of the last few months had worn me down to a helpless child, completely unable to control my fragile emotions. As frenzied as I was, I felt fortunate to be going back to Loren's house. She kept patting my leg for comfort as she drove us home. "At least I have a friend who understands some of my pain," I told her. "You've held my hand through most of the nightmare. I don't know how to thank you."

Mr. Connors had promised to call me at Loren's house as

soon as the jury handed down their decision. I desperately clung to the hope that Michael would be found guilty of Murder One, premeditated murder, and be sent away for life. Mr. Connors had mentioned other possible sentences. Murder Two was a possibility, but surely not manslaughter or reckless homicide, I prayed. As much as I resisted thinking the jury's decision could be anything less than murder, the one word that frightened me most was acquittal. I'd break into a loud howl behind chattering teeth every time I imagined that happening. My screams caused Loren to stomp harder on the gas pedal, forcing her truck engine to groan as she tried to get me to the country where I could be alone and let it all out.

When we got back to Loren's, I called Mom. I tried to explain how overwhelming the trial had been and how scared I was of the outcome. Mom offered to drive out with a friend of hers and pick up the girls and keep them for the night. She could hear the panic in my voice, and I told her, "I don't want Erica to be around me when the decision comes in, especially if Michael is let go. God, I don't want to think about that. I can't imagine him being back out on the street. I know he'll head straight for me and try to finish me off, especially since I've testified against him."

Loren got back in the truck and drove us down to the interstate, almost twenty miles, to meet Mom and her friend at the gas station. Erica didn't want to leave me, but Mom promised to sugar her up real good with treats and junk food, a deal hardly any six year old can pass up. I was glad to see Erica's face break into a smile as she grabbed my hands and kissed my cheek, but when our eyes met I saw the reality of our misery in her sad eyes.

After we strapped Megan in and waved goodbye, Loren drove to the video store to pick out some movies before we drove back to her house. I stayed in the car while she made the selections. It didn't matter to me what we watched. I knew it was just something to take my mind off things. I sat in the truck and cried but dried my tears when I saw Loren coming back.

Getting behind the wheel, she smiled as she handed me a music video she'd picked out: U2's *War*, one of mine and Johnny's favorites. She'd remembered us playing it years ago and must have thought it would be comforting for me to hear it. I clutched it, tears running down my cheeks.

Loren put the video on as soon as we got back to her place. We watched it while we waited for the safety of my future to be decided. Billy grumbled endlessly about the video. "I don't like much music, only Doors and Willie Nelson," he muttered. Loren shushed him when he made fun of the songs or the way the band dressed and danced. I gazed vacantly at the television as it played, crying and sniffling as I watched. Loren turned the sound up a few times, maybe to drown out my sobs. It was still playing when the phone rang. We stared stupidly at each other, Billy in his recliner, and Loren and I on the couch. When the phone rang again Loren jumped up to answer it, but Billy frowned her back into her seat and waved his large commanding hand at me, motioning for me to answer it.

"Is Jane Haney there?" the deep, male voice on the other end asked.

"This is she."

"This is Richard Connors. Glad you made it home safely. I wanted to let you know that the jury has reached their decision."

"What is it?" I blurted out, weak-kneed and sweaty.

"Mr. Haney was found guilty of manslaughter and first degree burglary," he said calmly.

Silence filled the phone lines as U2's *Sunday, Bloody Sunday* played in the background. In a state of shock, unable to speak, I listened to the words of the song, seemingly more amplified than before.

"We'd hoped for a higher degree of guilt, but the jury didn't see it that way," Mr. Connors said, breaking the silence.

"How could this happen? How does premeditated murder get reduced to manslaughter? Maybe I could understand second-degree murder, but I . . . It was my testimony, wasn't it? That other attorney really got me confused. I know it's all my fault, I just know it is."

"You did a fine job, the best anyone could expect, but sometimes juries see things differently. There was only so much you could say because you didn't see what happened before the shooting."

"Yeah, but it might've helped if they could've heard everything, or let Erica testify. She saw it all, every bit of it, and she knew Michael had come in and killed Johnny without a fight or a warning. Damn, I can't believe this is happening. How much time will he do?"

"He was sentenced to thirteen years, and Kentucky law requires anyone with a double felony conviction to serve at least fifty percent of that time. He'll have to stay in for at least six and a half years."

"But Johnny will never live again," I said as I started to weep uncontrollably. "In six years, Erica won't have her father back. It's not enough."

"No, I agree. We thought we had a solid case. We thought for sure we would get a first-degree murder conviction, but the jury decides."

"How long, how long must we sing this song," played on mercilessly from the television. Johnny had died on a Sunday morning, and the irony of the music accosted me.

Michael had gotten away with murder. He'd taken away Johnny's life, beaten me, terrorized the children, stolen my furniture, caused us to lose our home, and now this. Thoughts of Johnny dying, of all the battering and the disgrace it all brought me, with nobody to help and nowhere to turn, raced through my mind as the prosecutor tried to explain what could never be changed. The jury's decision was final. The blow had been struck and would stay with me for the rest of my life.

By the time I hung up the phone, Loren had heard enough of the conversation to know the outcome. She held me in her arms as we cried, until Billy interrupted us.

"What the hell are ya so damn upset about?" he asked. "If that woulda happened in my state, he'da walked for sure. Over there they got pleas like, 'Well, your honor, he deserved to die.' I don't understand why ya ain't jumping for joy. Michael got more than six years, and that's a long goddamn time outta a man's life."

I left the room crying. Flinging open the back door, I ran onto the porch and into the bathroom. I sat there on the floor amongst the flies and dirty clothes and sobbed in disbelief and misery until my throat was raw. I was dying inside. My heart grew cold and my mind numb as a vulgar hardening took over. I lost my faith in people and government, and wondered if there was a God in heaven. How could *He* let this happen?

Later that night, Loren lifted me from the pile of dirty laundry and led me to the couch. Somehow I fell into an exhausted sleep. When morning came, I sat and stared into space, taking a few sips of the coffee Loren had placed in my hands, but nothing would bring me around. When Mom called I couldn't talk to her. Loren begged her to keep the girls for another day, and, kindly, Mom agreed.

After she talked with my mom, Loren kicked into her best cheerleader mode, explaining that I couldn't let Michael get the better of me.

"Jane, it's all up to you. You control your own destiny. The best thing for ya ta do is change your sheets and get on with yourself. Make a clean start. Nobody's gotta know what's happened to ya."

I knew I had a life to live, despite the pain of it all. I knew most importantly I had two beautiful children to love and raise. I knew they needed my support, emotional and financial. I knew I couldn't let the disappointment of the trial verdict get in the way of making a future for my children. Still, I thought about Lady Justice and the myths about her. I thought of those scales balanced from her arms, her eyes tightly blindfolded. It probably would've been more fitting to have a donkey tail in her hand and to spin her around till she was dizzy and hope she'd pin the tail on the end of fairness. The images in my mind were similar to a Salvador Dali painting, with time melting and daggers thrown at me from out of nowhere. I had to get back to real life, the reality of the world I had to live in, but it was getting hard for me to distinguish one from the other.

The kids had started school a few weeks before the trial, and I needed to get the girls settled in and allow Loren's family to do the same, but I had to get work to do it. Loren had warned me not to get my hopes up too high because businesses around town were family run and even company-owned places had managers who hired only their next of kin. As I trudged downtown from place to place in the next few days, it didn't take too many trips to figure out she knew what she was talking about. No matter how hard I looked or how convincing I was at interviews, I couldn't find a job. I was an outsider.

"Jane, best thing for ya to do is sign up for welfare. You're gonna run out all your gas for nothin' lookin' for work that ain't out there. I've been here six years with a college degree, and the food service at the university is the only place I can find work, and that's only now and then for banquets."

"I hate the thought of going on welfare. Most people think you're lazy if you draw it," I protested. However, I knew we couldn't keep going to counseling if I didn't get a medical card, and Erica and I both needed professional therapy to talk about her daddy's murder. We also needed to get out of Loren's house. As good as she'd been to us, Billy was yelling more now than before, and I knew we needed to get out for Loren's sake. Moreover, we couldn't get welfare as long as I was living with them. I had to be on my own before I could quality, but where was I gonna get the money to do that?

Luckily, Loren knew the ins and outs of the welfare system. She offered to give me her house payment to find a place, as long as I'd swear not to tell Billy and promise to pay her back the money with my first welfare check. She'd been my brace and my anchor, and she knew how hard it was. She had nobody but Billy around, and he treated her like a hired hand.

We found a place in town. It took all her money to get it. Then Loren took me to several agencies and churches to help get my utilities turned on and helped me fill out the ten-page welfare application. I felt relieved just to have a place of my own, with a lock on the door offering me a sense of security, but having to accept welfare weakened my self-worth. I needed something to do besides sit in an empty house and dwell on my past. Before long, I didn't even care to see daylight. I didn't want to see people. All I wanted to do was stay holed up, cry, and stare at blank walls.

Loren became my caretaker. She began stopping in to check on me. We both knew my mind and reason were delicate. Loren brought me books, but I couldn't read: every word was gibberish. I'd turn through the pages and not even know what I'd read. I did what I could for the girls, almost mechanically, washing their clothes by hand, hanging them to dry, and pressing them with an old iron Loren had bought at a yard sale. I tried hard to take care of them as I used to, but Loren could see that, despite my counseling, I was sliding into a serious state of depression. She was afraid the county welfare people would come in and take the girls. She knew if Michael hadn't already thrust me into the realm of craziness, losing my kids would surely push me on over the edge. She stopped at our place twice a day if she had the gas, usually having to make an excuse to Billy to leave the house.

"Your mom called me today. She sounds concerned."

"About the girls?"

"Yeah, I told her they were fine, but I also told her y'all were in serious need of some food and diapers and other stuff ya can't get with food stamps. She said she'd come out tomorrow, but she didn't say what time."

"Like I got such a pressed schedule, Loren. You know I'll

be here. I got nothin' but time on my hands and it's makin' me nuts. I feel like I'm fallin' into a deep dry well and the walls are caving in on me."

"Jane, honey, I'm really worried about you. Sometimes it scares me to knock on your door, I'm so afraid."

I sighed heavily. I know she meant well and spoke from concern, but I was as worried as she was. "Loren, I'm reachin' down deep to keep myself together. I got to for the girls."

"No, Jane, you got to for yourself. As far down as I've let myself git, I do things every day like a ritual. I stay tired all the time and sick of havin' to do all the work, tend the garden so we can eat, raise three kids, and look after Billy, especially when he gits on one of them wild ass drunks of his, but I still try to keep my head held high."

Loren stood up abruptly, searching through some papers on the end of the table.

"What are ya lookin' for?" I asked.

"I'm looking for a clean piece of paper, and I need somethin' to write with."

She fumbled through the disarray until she found a pen and a notebook, flipped to a blank page, and began to compose a list. I watched as she wrote.

"Here." She thrust the paper at me. "I want you to keep this at your side at all times. I'll make copies and pin them to your walls. You need to follow this. A simple list to help you keep your dignity."

I glanced over the paper, written with a flare of perfection, love, and meaning. It was titled "Jane's Ten Commandments."

1. I will take a shower every day, even if I have to dry off with a dirty towel.
2. I will wipe the tears and stress from my face every morning. It is a new day, and only I can make it better.
3. I will make my bed.
4. I will brush my hair and promise never to let it mat again.

5.   I will hold the girls, separately and together, for at least an hour each day.

6.   I will wash my dishes at least once a day.

7.   I will try to put on makeup every day.

8.   I will eat at least once a day.

9.   I will brush my teeth at least twice a day.

10.   I will not let Michael continue to destroy my life.

Loren was snooping around the kitchen when I finished reading her list. She whizzed back through the room. "I'll be back in a few minutes," she said, tucking Megan under her arm like a football and heading for the front door. "My food stamps have come in, and I'm going to get a huge healthy salad at the store for us to eat."

The list made me realize how far I'd slipped into my hole. I couldn't remember how long it had been since I'd had a shower, and Loren joked every time she came over about how you could eat off my kitchen floor because there was at least seven different courses on it every day. Megan was at a stage where she enjoyed dropping food from her high chair, not only to hear it splatter, but to get a giggle from Erica. Sometimes I'd clean it up, but as depressed as I felt, it was usually all I could do to get the children cleaned up after dinner and put to bed.

After Loren's truck had pulled out of the drive, I walked into my room, catching a glimpse of my ragged reflection in the dresser mirror as I headed for my bed. I looked ten years older. I sat on the bed and stared out the picture window. I heard Loren come back, but I couldn't move.

Later, I heard Erica come home from school, but Loren told her, "Mommy isn't feeling good, so let her rest." I could hear Loren rustling through the house. She looked in on me several times before she loaded Megan and Erica into her truck. She said she was taking them out to her house for a while, but I didn't answer. I just stared down at my hands.

When morning came and Loren returned with Erica and

Megan, I was still sitting in the same place when Loren opened the bedroom door.

"Jane, have you been up all night?"

I couldn't answer her, but I felt her hand on my forearm.

"Jane, look at me. I've got the girls with me. I've got some runnin' to do, and I'll keep them with me for a while. Don't forget your Ten Commandments, Jane. You've got to pull out of this."

Loren pulled my taut face toward hers and looked deep into my eyes, shaking me gently. Loren said, "I'm gonna help you through it. It just takes time. I wish you'd eat somethin'."

"Water," I said instinctively.

"I'll get you some water." She ran to the kitchen and brought back a large tumbler filled with ice water and held it as I took a few sips.

"Things'll fall into place," I mumbled. "You just . . . I just . . . I have to let them . . . fall into place."

"It'll be okay, Jane. I'll take care of the kids. Just hang on. Don't let them break you."

"It's just gonna take some time," I repeated, but I didn't believe the words I mouthed.

CHAPTER 15

Snakebite

Spiritless and depressed, I reached for my robe when I heard the loud knock at my door. I wrestled the pink poly-cotton wrap over my shoulders and peeked out the side window to see who was there. It was Billy McKay.

I pulled my robe tighter and tied my belt in a loop knot as I opened the front door, squinting as the daylight hit my eyes for the first time in days.

"Hey, Billy. Come on in."

"Loren sent me down ta see 'bout ya. She said you'd had a bad coupla days. I assure ya mine ain't been too goddamn grand with your two kids and my kids runnin' around the house for two days. All those fuckin' kids underfoot'd make a preacher cuss."

"Sorry about the inconvenience. Loren offered to take 'em," I said as I shifted my foot to hold the door open. "I've just been sittin' around losin' track of time. What day is it anyway?"

"It's Thursday and your kids've been at my house since Tuesday," he said disgustedly, but still with a somewhat friendly tone.

"My car still ain't runnin', so I can't go up and get 'em, but tell Loren I can look after 'em now," I said.

"Yeah, I told Loren I'd try ta help ya fix your car, but I think there's more things than your car that needs servicin' around here."

I knew my mind had been unstable, and, at times, I couldn't take care of myself or the girls as well as I once had, but when I shamefacedly lifted my head and saw Billy's expression, I could tell he had other ambitions as he slid his way around my front door.

"Jane, quite frankly I think ya need your brains fucked out, shake all them cobwebs outta your head," Billy said as he locked the door behind him. "That's the best thing I know ta do for ya. I ain't a plumber, but I know a lot about women's pipes and how to clean 'em out, if ya know what I mean."

At first I thought he was kidding me, trying in some sick way to cheer me up, but when I saw the venomous grin on his face, I knew better. I pulled my robe tighter, feeling Billy's eyes undress me as he stroked his chest like he was petting a kitten. I felt dirty, and my stomach lurched as his large scaly hand slid up the back of my neck. I quickly jerked away from him, slapped him, and jumped toward the door. "Git out," I insisted.

"Now, Jane, I know you're my wife's best friend and ya prob'ly think I'm just a sick bastard for comin' here 'n' makin' advances. But, goddamn, if men have killed for it, it must be some damn good stuff. You just got my curiosity up along with a few other things."

"Git the hell out of my house! Git out now and don't you ever come back here and disrespect me like this!"

"Now, Jane, don't git so upset. I'm just a man with a natural appetite, and, besides, I've looked out for you and your kids for the last few months. The least ya could do is let me smell it."

"No! You're wrong! Loren's looked out for us! I don't owe you a thing! Now git out of here!" My eyes searched the room for something to throw at him.

"You look so sexy when you're mad. It makes me want ya more! Come on over here 'n' let me plant a big sloppy kiss on ya!"

I kicked him in the shins as hard as I could and grabbed the antenna off the television set and aimed it for his eyes. "I'll blind ya if ya come any closer."

He laughed at my attempts to fend him off. His body shook with pleasure as I trembled, praying he'd leave me alone.

"Git out, Billy."

But he wouldn't stop. He kept coming toward me. I scratched his face, drawing blood.

"What the hell did ya do that for? I was just messin' with ya."

"I ain't messin' with you, Billy. I ain't playing. I want ya outta here now!"

Without a word and wearing the jagged, bloody scratch and a rejected look on his face, Billy stepped around me and strode out the door. As he spun his truck out of the drive, splattering gravel all over my front yard and door, I worried what he'd tell Loren, or if he'd tell her at all. How would he explain the scratch? I didn't know what I was going to say to her. I had to get my kids back before Billy got home. I was afraid he might take out his frustration on his family, or worse yet, on my girls.

I knew it would take him fifteen minutes to get home; so I threw on some clothes, scraped together twenty-five cents from a basket in my bedroom, and headed for the pay phone at the grocery store.

"Loren, I need ya to bring the kids back," I said as quick as she answered.

"I will after awhile," she said. "They're havin' a big time in the backyard right now. Billy's on his way down there. He said he was gonna fix your car."

"He's already left. He couldn't fix it."

"What was wrong with it?" Loren asked, completely innocent of her husband's real intentions.

"I don't know, but he left a few minutes ago. I need to see the kids. I haven't seen 'em in a few days, and I really miss 'em. Can ya bring 'em right away?"

"Well, I don't know what's got into ya, but ya sound better, like ya got the will to live back anyway."

"I guess when ya git backed against the wall, the fighter in ya comes out."

"By the way, your mom called again. She said she was sorry she couldn't make it out the other day, but she promised she'd come tomorrow for sure."

"I need to git the house cleaned, but, Loren, I need to see my girls. I really need them to be with me."

"I understand. I'll bring 'em down in a few minutes."

"Thanks, Loren."

I walked back to the house. The brisk fall wind blew through my unbrushed hair, tossing it in opposite directions, reminding me that winter was on its way. Images of cold weather, the promise of snow keeping me in, shackling me to the confines of a house I no longer felt safe in after Billy's visit, frightened me. With every step I took down the broken edge of the asphalt road, I thought about Billy's nerve, after everything I'd been through, and him knowing I was his wife's best friend. "That slippery, slimy, two-faced snake," I muttered as I trudged on.

Suddenly I looked up to see Loren's car passing me. I yelled her name and she stopped the car and swung open the door to let me in. Instantly I halted the damning swears I had on my breath for her husband. I was still stunned by the advances Billy had made, but I did the best I could to hide it from her. I didn't know how to tell her what her husband had done. I knew the dangers of keeping such secrets, but I felt I had to wait for the right moment to speak. Even though it had to be said, now was not the time. I hugged my girls tight as I pondered how and when to tell her. Loren waved goodbye without a clue as she let us out at the house.

Inside, I played with Erica and Megan for a while, half playing and half still wondering how I was going to tell Loren about Billy. It was something I felt she needed to know, however painful it would be for us both.

After giving the children a relaxing bath, I put fresh sheets on Erica's bed and Megan's crib and dressed them in their p.j.'s for a good night's sleep. They were tired after a day of hard play at Loren's. The running and jumping caused them to doze off quickly. I curled up next to Erica as she drifted to sleep. I was thankful to have them back, and, as I lay there, I realized that for the first time since I'd gotten word of the trial verdict I'd acted responsibly. The irony of it was it was because of that jerk Billy. He'd made me so mad I'd become sane again. I had to try to hang onto that.

It was late in the afternoon the next day when Mom's car pulled into my driveway. I went out to meet her and opened the car door. She handed me a bucket of chicken. "Carry some of these other things in, too," she said, handing me some of her packages as she got out.

"I can't wait to see those babies. Let's hurry up and bring this stuff in. I brought ya all kinds of goodies." She reached into the back seat and pulled out a green garbage bag, handed it to me, and retrieved the rest of the dinner out of the front seat.

"Lord, Janie, I brought plenty to eat: mashed potatoes 'n' gravy, green beans, cole slaw, biscuits, potato salad, and I even brought dessert. These kids'll eat good today now that their Mamaw's here."

I was glad to see her. I sat the bag down in the living room as Mom carried the food into the kitchen and started filling up plates just like she was at home.

"Run in there 'n' git that bag for me. I brought ya'll somethin' real pretty."

I lifted the plastic sack and carried it to the kitchen table. Mom dug through it and pulled out some place mats with matching napkins and ring holders.

"Aren't they pretty? This'll make ya feel better. Just fixin' my place up always makes me feel better. I know ya haven't been able to buy nice things for yourself lately, so I thought this'd cheer you up."

"It looks real nice, Mom. What else do ya have in the bag?"

"Well, I brought some curtains. I thought these would look good in the girls' room, and I brought ya this rug. I figured we could put it in the bathroom."

"Mom, did ya happen to bring any diapers? Megan has only three left, and it'll be another two weeks before I get a check." I didn't want to sound ungrateful, but I was sure Loren had given her a lengthy list of my real needs.

"No, I didn't bring diapers. Those won't cheer ya up. But look what else I brought ya, a set of matchin' coffee cups! Aren't they gorgeous?"

"Yeah, but I don't have a coffeepot, Mom."

"Well, we can hang 'em over here by the sink. They'll brighten up the kitchen. We'll do that later. Let's get the children fed before the food gits cold."

I put Megan in her high chair and gave her some green beans. She liked most vegetables, and she liked the chicken after sampling it a few times. Mom had already filled Erica's plate and she was asking for second helpings when I sat down to eat. Mom jumped up on demand when Erica asked for more.

There was a knock at the door. It was Loren coming to check on us and probably wanting to see what Mom had brought. Mom showed off all the fancy things she'd given us: the cups, curtains, place mats, and the bathroom rug.

"Where's the food?" Loren asked.

"I brought a bucket of chicken. Are ya hungry? There's plenty left. Go over there and git ya a piece." Mom was so pleased with her gifts. "Next time I come out here," she said, "I'll bring ya some of those little hooks so we can hang up the cups."

"That'll be nice, Mom," I finally said. "But I really need diapers and toilet paper and baby shampoo for the kids."

"Well, Janie, I'm gonna give ya a coupla dollars and maybe Loren'll run ya to the store ta get 'em. Will five dollars be enough?"

"Anything'll help," Loren said quickly.

"Well, I'll try to remember diapers next time I come out. We're not havin' it easy either, Janie, and I spent a lot of money on this chicken dinner."

I caught Loren's disapproving look and smiled. That was my mother, and, in her own way, she was doing all she knew how to help me.

After Mom had brushed the girls' hair and put new blue and pink hair bows on them, she said, "I have to go before it gets too dark. I don't see too well at night." Just as she was leaving, Mom suddenly remembered another package for me: a large manila envelope from my attorney. She handed it to me. "I'll come back next week," she promised.

We all stood outside and waved goodbye as her car pulled away. Afterwards, I hurried the girls in out of the chill and went back to their room to find some warm clothes to take them out in. The early evening air was nippy, and I didn't want them sick. I had to get diapers while Loren was here, otherwise I'd have to walk to the store the next morning with Megan on my hip.

As we settled the girls in the back seat of Loren's car, I could tell she wanted to talk about my mother. "Why did she buy all that junk instead of the things I told her you need so badly?" Loren asked.

I smiled. "You just don't understand Mom's way of fixing things. For Mom, when life's thrown off-course, she buys something pretty, she looks for instant gratification to end her misery."

Loren shook her head. "She doesn't understand what you're going through."

I nodded. "She doesn't understand what she's going through."

I, on the other hand, was desperate to tell Loren about Billy. I'd worked up my courage but was afraid Erica might overhear me. I knew better than to burden her with more complications that adults had created.

I still had the envelope from my attorney tucked under my arm, meaning to read it as we drove to the store. Its contents bulged, and, when I opened the metal fastener, I instantly noticed inside several sealed letters, some postmarked "Kentucky State Prison," and others with uncancelled postage stamps. Passing over the letter from my attorney, I grabbed the letters that had Michael's name, address, and prisoner number in the left-hand corners. My hand shook with fear as I tore open the seal.

"What's that?" Loren asked.

"Letters from guess who," I said, hoping not to alert Erica.

"Are you kidding me! Is he allowed to do that?" Loren asked, shocked.

We talked in riddles to keep the conversation above Erica's understanding. I didn't want Erica to know Michael could have contact with us. I knew it would put her into a panic.

As I unfolded the first letter chills ran through my body. I was afraid Loren would wreck her car trying to gawk over my shoulder as I read it.

"My dearest Baby Doll Megan," the letter began, and my stomach turned into a chamber of churning acid. "Daddy sure does miss his darling little baby girl and can't wait to see you. I love you and miss you so much." Grinding my teeth and trying not to scream, I opened another letter, aware that it would most likely be as foul as the first one. "I wish you could talk your mother into sending me some pictures of you. I'd sure like to know how pretty you are." Megan can't even talk, I thought. You'd think he'd know his daughter's age. "I don't understand why she would want to keep you from the love of your father." At first the letter confused me. Maybe Michael had forgotten he'd killed Johnny in front of us? But, as I read on, I knew it was the only way he had left to make my life a living hell.

"How's your sister Erica?" the letter continued. I felt sick to my stomach. Why would he get concerned about Erica after murdering her father as she watched? "Tell her I love and miss her and give her a hug for me. I can't wait until we can all be together again." That remark did it.

Nauseated and nervous, I asked Loren to pull over so I could throw up the chicken dinner Mom had just spent her money on. As soon as my foot hit the gravel, my insides, tormented and twisted, heaved out my burdens. After emptying my stomach and feeling the burn of the purge and the rage of Michael's attempts to drive me crazy, I pulled my cold, sweat-covered body back into the car. We were close to the store, and, when Loren pulled in, she peeled my fingers from the five-dollar bill Mom had given me and ran in to buy Megan's diapers.

Megan and Erica sat quietly in the back seat as I shuffled the papers that had made me sick. I put the letters from Michael into a neat pile and placed them in the larger envelope, retrieving the letter from the attorney as I did. As I clumsily unfolded the thick stationery, I could see Loren from the corner of my eye returning to the car, diapers in hand.

My attorney told me that he had been elected a judge and wanted to resolve my divorce swiftly. His urgency was nothing to mine, I thought. The urgency I felt to shed the title of Michael's wife was greater than my lawyer's to get his work done. Luckily, I hadn't changed my name on too many legal documents during my short marriage to Michael. And those few could be corrected quickly.

Included in my attorney's letter were some forms for me to fill out in order to make my divorce final. It was going to be a quick divorce called a Putnam v. Fannin, named for the divorcing couple who had set the precedent, my attorney explained. It allowed for a legal divorce immediately and a property settlement later. That wouldn't take long, I thought. Almost everything I'd ever owned was gone, hocked or stolen by Michael.

However, other issues had to be resolved by the court. The custody of Megan had to be decided as did child support and visitation. I figured I'd get Michael's checks for making license plates and finally get to stand before a judge, with Michael now a convicted felon, and tell the courts what I'd known right along: that he was violent, deviant, and deceptive and had not only beaten me, but taken an innocent life. Finally, I thought, I'd get a little piece of justice, but at great expense. Johnny had to die for it, the girls had to watch it, and the memories of the beatings and Johnny's death would haunt us all for the rest of our lives.

CHAPTER **16**

Dark Holidays

Somehow time passed and the leaves turned autumn colors. Poverty forced us to rely on humor to lift our spirits during the holidays. Being thankful, joyous, or optimistic in planning the celestial celebrations in our poor economic and psychic states was hard. Michael being behind bars seemed the only thing to be thankful for or optimistic about. I was still a bundle of raw nerves and bitterness. Not only did Johnny's death still give me nightmares but Billy's outrageous behavior added to them. I still hadn't found the right time to tell Loren what Billy had done. Billy hung up the phone every time I tried to call her. One night in December the slam of his receiver rang painfully in my ear as I walked home in the icy weather with Megan on my hip bundled in blankets and Erica holding my hand with her sock-covered fingers. I couldn't afford gloves for her.

Loren had not only been my trusting friend and source of solace, she was the only adult I knew in town. If by some unforeseeable miracle Billy wasn't lounging in the recliner beside the only phone in their house and Loren did answer, our conversations were over with quickly. Trying to figure out the codes Loren spoke in as she kept Billy unaware, while I shivered in the cold, grew more and more difficult.

Wintertime was not a wonderland in eastern Kentucky. True, the snow-covered mountains dotted with leafless maples and oaks formed a blue-gray mist that was beautiful, but bad roads, freezing weather, and poverty all made winter the more brutal. Some unknown delinquent had sugared my old car's gas tank, and my transportation, already inhibited by icy roads and layers of snow, became impossible. I'd suspected several people besides Billy of doing my car in, but I knew it would do me no good to go around town pointing fingers. A few of the local men who'd tried to move on me at the store or while I was walking on the road, most of them already married or shacked up with someone, were stunned and indignant when I turned down their offers for company. It was a commonly held belief in Appalachia that a woman should never be without a man, even if he was somebody's spouse. None of them liked the fact that I was surviving on my own, and they mouthed obscenities to my face because of it. They believed I was setting a bad example for their wives and daughters.

Christmas morning brought one of the few smiles to my face during that winter. Erica knocked on my door to tell me what Santa had delivered, but all I could think about was how good it felt knowing Michael was confined. That was my real Christmas present. There wasn't much under the tree for the girls, just a few cheap toys, and nothing for me. It angered me that I couldn't do better for my family, but at least Michael was locked up, even if only for a couple of his crimes. I cried when my thoughts turned to Johnny buried in a frozen lonesome grave sixty miles from us. I'd wanted so desperately to go to his grave and maybe put a piece of our tree on his tombstone for remembrance, but I had no way to get there. There was never any time for me to grieve. I had to be strong for the girls and try to put our lives back together.

December ended with a fierce winter storm. Icy January turned to an even colder February. I still had no job, though I searched and searched. Not finding a job further wounded my feelings of self worth, but I tried to remain hopeful for the girls' sakes.

Then what I viewed as a fresh wind blew. Nothing sweeter could have been delivered to my doorstep than on Valentine's Day when the official copy of my divorce papers arrived. It had taken almost two years to get my own name and single status back. It was the first tangible sign, I thought, that the record of my relationship with Michael was being swept away. It didn't represent the end of my court appearances though. I'd still have to hire yet another attorney, since mine had been elected judge. The property settlement and custody of Megan still had to be ruled on. It seemed ridiculous to throw good money after bad for another lawyer while we did without necessities, especially since Michael had probably hocked or sold what was left of my things.

Having my name back and knowing I was legally divorced gave me a feeling of freedom, but only until the next set of Michael's letters was forwarded by my attorney. Just seeing Michael's name and prisoner number in bold print on the envelope was intimidating enough, let alone the assaulting memories reading his words produced. All his letters started out with "My Darling Baby Doll" and made me want to vomit. The nerve of him pretending he cared for his daughter after beating me while she was inside me and nearly killing us after she was out. Killing a human being in front of your child wasn't my idea of expressing love or affection. But I kept every one of his cleverly disguised threats.

As March became April, I continued to try to find work but still to no avail. When I thought of getting on with my life and making a clean start and my parents asked when I would be settling down like I was taught, I thought of the hazards of having a man in my life, or in my house for that matter. No, I couldn't imagine being thrown to the wolves again. I wanted to go to school, make a living for myself and the girls, and never again get trapped in the dangers of matrimony.

As my fruitless search for a way to support my family continued, I began to realize I had to get away from this town to do it. I'd tried every way I knew but no work or way to get ahead existed here, and I had no ties except for Loren.

When Michael's next batch of letters arrived, informing me that he'd been transferred to a prison in a neighboring county, fear coursed through me, and I knew it was time to go. What if Michael escaped? What if Billy decided to have his way with me? How could I fight off either of them? I had to find a place for my children and myself to heal, without worry or the threat of us falling victims again. I'd lost Johnny who I missed terribly. If I stayed around Billy I stood to lose Loren, the dearest friend left in my life.

As spring began to bloom around me all I could think of was getting away. It wouldn't be easy to get enough money together without a job. The rent took all but a few dollars of my welfare check. Then there was my car to worry about. I'd have to figure a way to get it fixed. But the move was something I had to do. I looked forward to going back to work, getting back my self respect and not having to take a monthly handout from Uncle Sam. The idea of making a living for the girls and myself motivated me, gave me something to look forward to, something to live for after months of wallowing in shame and fear. Moving would give me some control over our lives. All I needed was a plan.

It was early May when I decided to "change my sheets and get on with myself" as Loren always put it. I pulled out an old road atlas I'd managed to hang onto, got a pen and paper for notes, and began to plan. I made a list of the things I wanted in a city, a simple list really. Some place that had good schools for the girls, jobs, a college so that I could get the kind of education which would help me earn enough to support my family, a daily paper, and basketball.

Aside from music, there was nothing I enjoyed more than basketball. I used to joke that in Kentucky babies weren't given rattles to play with, just basketballs. Adolph Rupp had made the sport the pride of Kentucky, and the human legends basketball produced lived all around the state. The city I picked was Cincinnati. Though it wasn't in Kentucky, it was just across the river.

I still had a few months left on my lease, and I hated to break it. The landlord had been kind and never bothered me for money when times were difficult. I didn't want to leave him hanging, but I had to move. The least I could do was leave the place in good shape and give him some kind of advance notice. I didn't see any other way to do it. I'd have to leave as the month turned and use my rent money to get my car fixed.

My car would have to serve as our temporary shelter. I made a list of our necessities and planned how to find room for them in the car. I could take the girls' beds, a crib and a rollaway, if I used cord to close the trunk. I checked the fit while Erica was at school one day just to make sure. I lined a single row of milk crates and sturdy boxes filled with our must-have clothes, towels, and toiletries on the floorboard. The girls were small enough not to need leg room on the floor.

I threw some sheets and pillow cases stuffed with clothes and a few of their favorite toys in the back seat and made it look like a playpen. The whole time I packed I prayed my plan would work, not thinking of the dangers of moving to a city of strangers. I didn't want to think about it. Homes had been most hurtful to me, not the streets. Besides, the girls and I had each other for comfort, support, and company.

The first necessity to be tackled was my rickety car. I called a few mechanics from the pay phone and got the lowest bid I could find to overhaul it. Luckily the place was just around the bend, and the guy towed the car there for me free. I knew he could hear the desperation in my voice. He said it was a bonus that he didn't have to rush to fix it. I told him I didn't need it till the first of the month when my check and food stamps arrived.

I needed the food stamps to buy food. I could use them at any market and find a microwave in a convenience store to heat up sausage biscuits for breakfast and burgers or TV dinners for lunch and supper. I had to remember to pack a water jug and some utensils.

What was I going to do with the other furniture? I'd lost so much while married to Michael that I hated to give up even my few acquired yard sale furnishings, but I had to.

I wanted to tell Loren about my plans. It took two days to reach her. Billy kept answering the phone and hanging up. Finally Loren answered and in code I told her it was essential that she come to my place as soon as possible. Sensing my urgency and the need for secrecy with Billy kicked back in his recliner right beside her, Loren performed like an award winning actress. She pretended I was her case worker calling from the food stamp office. She told me later she swore to Billy they'd misplaced a file at the food stamp office and she needed to take some papers into town or they wouldn't eat next month. She knew something serious was up with me and got there within a half hour.

"What's the matter?" she asked as I met her at the door and slipped out into the front yard so the girls couldn't hear our conversation.

"I'm going to move," I told her. "I can't take it here no more. I can't get a job so I can support us. I gotta go."

"Jane, don't ya think ya should think a little more about this? I mean, where are ya gonna go? Where are ya gonna live? And where will ya get the money ta do all this?"

"I've 'bout got that worked out. My car's gettin' fixed this week, and I still should have a few dollars left for gas money. I got a few things to sell, too."

"Where are ya goin'?"

"Cincinnata."

Loren pondered my plan.

"That's a big city, Jane," she said, as if talking to a child. "I know, I lived there. Do ya know anybody?"

"Johnny's cousin Allan lives in the city somewhere. I've lost his address, but I'll look him up when I get there."

"Ya might have to do a lot alookin'. There's over 300,000 people there, and what if the car don't make it?"

"Then I'll live where I land. Got any better ideas? I'm goin' crazy here! No work. Michael the next county over. No family to count on."

A hurt look appeared on Loren's face when I blurted out that remark about the family. I tried to catch my reckless breath and hurried to rectify it. "Loren, you've been a great friend but I've already taken too much advantage and I know it's caused you stress from Billy." I stopped, my mouth dry. I wanted to tell her about Billy, but I couldn't. I knew if I told her and she ran home and squared up with him we both might have hell to pay.

"My immediate problem is what to do with my furniture," I said, hoping to break the space between us that had grown awkward and tense.

Conditioned as a woman to help in times of crisis, Loren's green eyes lit up as the cool spring breeze swept across her face, worn beyond its years.

"We can put it all in my shed, across the street from the house," she quickly decided.

"But what will Billy have ta say about it? Won't he get mad?"

"Hell, he never goes over there. He don't hardly get out of the recliner unless it's hunting season or a pig roast or a deer feast is happenin' up one a' these hollers."

Other unspeakable reasons he'd get his carcass off the chair came to my mind as I thought over her offer.

"We'll wait until he's gone fishin' to take it out there. It might cost us some worms for bait and a few dollars for beer and his gas money, but then he'll never know it's in there." She whispered her strategy to me as if someone was spying on us and might wreck our plan if they knew. She knew Billy despised me although I knew she didn't know why. She just accepted his abrasive ways, either out of fear or despair, maybe both.

We surveyed my house and began to work out the particulars. I started packing right away. Over the next few days, if Billy left their house for any length of time, Loren ran down to my house, grabbed stuff and put it away in hers without him knowing. It took several days of bobbing in and out of my house with boxes and bags, sneaking as we went to get the job done.

By the end of the month we'd packed, moved, and stored the bulk of my belongings, leaving only my most necessary items for the remaining days. The children and I lived in the empty house like refugees.

Loren had a close call one day when Billy came home early one afternoon from a fishing trip. Loren's car was parked on the roadside beside the shed. She was standing knee-deep in weeds when Billy's truck came flying around the bend. As he slammed on his brakes and swerved to miss her, he yelled, "What in the name of Christ Almighty are ya' doin' with the ass end of your car sticking out for hell and all the world to hit?"

She tried to conceal our secret stash. "One of the kids knocked a ball across the road and I'm getting it so they won't get hit."

"Oh, shut up," he said. "You should've parked the car in the driveway first."

But at least he didn't find us out. The recliner was closer than the shed and that's where he wanted to be, with a cold beer in his hand.

When moving day came, Loren had to put her foot down with Billy so he'd keep their kids and she could come down and help me with the final packing. Having all those kids under foot while we moved would've complicated things even more. Pretty much everything was packed but the sweeper, some cleaning supplies, and a few fragile keepsakes I didn't have room for in my car.

"Jane, where are all those place mats your mom brought ya when you and the kids was so hungry? We should open a museum and show 'em off. We can call it the 'It's-pretty-so-we-must-be-happy' collection, or maybe we should donate them to the 'Shall Gather at the River Used Clothing Store,' and put them in the Lord's hands."

"Loren, these two boxes right here, you've got to be careful with 'em," I said, trying to ignore her babble about my mother.

"What's in 'em?"

"It's my collection of Kentucky Derby glasses. I've got more than fifty, and I've drank from 'em festively every Derby Day. It's all I've got left of my special things. My sister Beth's hung onto 'em for me all this time. They're one of the few things Michael didn't break or make off with."

Loren looked proud when I asked her to keep my treasured pieces. She grabbed the box firmly by the bottom, eyeing me sadly before she carried them to her car and stuffed a blanket around the sides for extra protection.

As I finished running the sweeper so the place would be spick-and-span, my eyes welled up with tears at the thought of saying goodbye to Loren. Not only was she my best friend, but I hated to leave her to a wretched life with Billy. I knew I had to tell her what he'd done. It was now or never.

Loren was whistling as she walked through the house checking all the closets behind me while I was working up my nerve to tell her about Billy. I stood in the living room watching the girls play in the front yard when she entered the room, smiling as she came, with a handful of junk I'd overlooked.

I took a deep breath. "Loren, there's some things I need to say before I go."

"Now, Jane, don't get yourself all worked up before you have to drive such a long journey. You'll call me when you get there, won't you?"

"Yeah, I'll call, but what if Billy answers?"

"I'll not let that happen. I'll stand guard of the phone all night if need be."

"Loren, ya gotta know what I've been goin' through here. I mean, I hurt over Johnny and all, but Billy . . . he's been . . . I don't know how to say this 'n' not hurt ya."

Loren froze in her place and looked out the window like she was already starting to ignore what I was about to say.

"Loren, for the past few months it's been all I could do to keep your husband out of my pants. Remember when he told ya he was comin' down here to help me with my car like a good Samaritan? Well, he was trying to have sex with me." The tension of holding it in and knowing I had to tell her made me spout like a percolator of stale coffee. I knew my news would be bitter and hard for her to swallow, but I felt I had to say it. She needed to think about what Billy's betrayals might bring. She needed to put herself first and think of AIDS and other diseases she might catch and what would happen to her kids if that were to happen.

"Ah, Jane, he was probably just playin' around, you know, makin' jokes the way he does. Just bein' playful."

I shook my head. "Remember that scratch across his face?" I said. "The one right under his left eye angled with his cheekbone? I put that there when he didn't take no for an answer. Where did he tell ya it came from, a tree branch in the woods?"

"No. I think he said it was a fence he ran into while he was huntin'," she said, still wanting to believe Billy's story.

"Loren, if you keep swallowin' that garbage he's feeding you you'll be too far gone to know what's the truth. Someday you'll get sick on the lies he's feedin' ya. Damn, Loren, understand I'm tellin' ya this because I love ya, and if ya think it's easy for me, you're wrong. I've tried for months to tell ya, but I was afraid, afraid ya wouldn't believe me, or if ya did and ya ran home mad and confronted Billy, then we might both be buried along one of these ridges, with nobody ever knowin' what happened to either of us. You know how he brags about doin' people in when they've crossed him."

My heart beat hard against my chest. Sweat poured beneath my hair and rumpled clothes. The cold spring air raised goose bumps all over me as I stepped outside to get some relief. Loren stood speechless until the screen door closed behind me, the slamming sound awakening her from a daze. Her lips seemed to mumble as she followed me, as if she was searching for words she couldn't find.

"Jane, I don't know what to say," Loren said, unable to look at me as we talked.

"Ya don't have to say anything, Loren, it's what ya gotta do. Ya can't let this go on. Ya told me before ya don't understand why your old friends don't come around anymore. Maybe ya just got the answer."

"Most of 'em won't come visit because I live too far out in the sticks," she rationalized, still looking at the ground. "They never said Billy had done anything to them."

"Oh, bullshit, Loren. Wake up! You're like a sister to me and I haven't been able to get up the courage to tell you. How comfortable do you think they'd feel tellin' ya?"

"He wouldn't do that, he's not that kind. . . ."

"Loren, ya just want to believe that it's not true and deep down I think ya know it is. God knows how many others there are. Someday it will rear its ugly head again, you wait 'n' see. Maybe I'm the only one that's had guts enough to tell ya how he's actin', or maybe I'm the only one that really gives two hoots about ya, but what's obvious is you have to care more for yourself."

Never had words been more difficult to say than those I told Loren. She didn't speak another word about Billy as she wiped tears from her face and stepped toward me. Her arms hugged me tight. Then we both cried and said goodbye.

"Be sure and call me. You know I'll worry."

"I know, but I'm gonna worry about you, too. Please don't put this out of your mind. Don't shove it back like you have all the other things Billy's done and said to ya. You deserve better."

"We both do," she said softly.

She reminded me again to call her. I promised her that I would, but from where I wasn't sure.

CHAPTER 17

On the Road

"Momma, where are we?" Erica asked as she pulled up on the back of my seat to get a better view.

"We're in downtown Cincinnata," I said, fingering my glasses as I drove on. "See all the lights and big fancy buildings."

Megan had slept most of the way and seemed undisturbed by the neon signs and street lights. But Erica, with her chin and palms resting on the seat, her eyes wide and alert, was eagerly taking it all in. As the red, yellow, and blue lights flashed, she wiggled to the side window to examine the exciting scenery.

"Are we on vacation, Momma?"

"Yes," I stuttered. "Yes, we are," I repeated, trying to be reassuring. I thought the truth would scare her. It terrified me to think of her frail mind and the heavy burdens she had to carry. The painful expression she wore most of the time on her tiny face and in her soft eyes broke my heart. I couldn't tell her the sad facts: Yes, honey, we're homeless, but now don't you worry, the streets are safer than where we've been staying. What troubled me most was that she might agree.

Somehow I'd have to try to get her some more help once

we got settled. She needed to talk to somebody, to try to heal her mind and heart, but who knew if I could afford a therapist or a counselor for her, and would they be competent enough to deal with a child who'd been a witness not only to her mother being battered but to her father being murdered.

As I drove down Columbia Parkway parallel to the Ohio River, I was relieved to be on the north side of the Ohio's banks, glad to be out of Kentucky and overjoyed to be in a place where nobody knew us and wouldn't bring up the painful past Michael left us to deal with.

"Look, honey, over there on the left. See that, that big stadium? That's where the Cincinnata Reds play baseball and the Bengals play football." The sight of the stadium brought up memories of my childhood. My neighbor Nelson Armstrong, long since dead, was a hardcore "Red Legs" fan. He told me he never missed listening to a game. He sat on his front porch religiously with his transistor radio cranked so loud everybody in the neighborhood could hear the game from first to last pitch. All season, sometimes late into the night, I'd fall asleep listening to the games. The roar of the crowd, the Skyline Chili commercials, the sounds of bats cracking and balls slamming into the catcher's mitt rang in my memory as if it was all happening now as we drove past the strange but somewhat familiar coliseum.

We had arrived, but what an enormous task lay ahead of me. I'd put so much energy and faith in getting away from Kentucky, I hadn't given much thought to what I'd do once I got here. Here I was, but now where? I didn't know where to go or even which direction I was heading with the sun down and the moon nowhere in sight.

Nervously, I took a long deep breath and pulled the cool night air into my lungs, hoping to strengthen my fortitude. Gripping the wheel as if it were the only sturdy fixture in my life, I steered off at the next exit. I needed a map, a newspaper, and a plan.

The clerk at the counter hardly acknowledged us when we

walked into the convenience store stiff legged and sore from the tension and the long drive. Holding Erica by the hand and carrying Megan still dozing on my hip and shoulder, I smelled nacho cheese and hot dogs. Instantly, I felt my stomach churn. Erica caught sight of the rack of Little Debbie cakes and broke out of my grip begging to buy one as she ran to the counter. The mention of food made Megan's head and eyelids spring up. Even at barely a year she understood.

"Can I help you, ma'am?" the clerk asked. He didn't seem too happy. The lines on his face looked like a road map of troubles.

"I need today's paper and a map of Cincinnata."

"You mean Cincinnati. What part of Kentucky are you from?" he said as a smirk cut across his face.

"Yes, I mean Cincinnati," I said, correcting myself.

"It's easy to spot your kind. The accent is a sure sign you managed to find your way to civilization. Did ya have an outhouse and well water?"

"Not at the home I owned, but my vacation home had similar features. Why'd ya ask?"

"I make a game trying to guess which holler you hillbillies crawl out of. Seems more and more of you come up here to live these days, even after the auto factories closed down."

I was in search of work, but I didn't tell him why I'd really left. And I sure's hell never aspired to work in an auto factory. Maybe a music store, but definitely not a factory. Of course, Loren's place had hardly been a vacation home! This clerk not only scared me with his patronizing attitude, but he was also getting on my last nerve. The courts had damned me for being a woman, but here I was damned for being Appalachian. I hated people making fun of my heritage. I knew we pronounced things differently but that was no reason for him to poke fun at us.

I paid for the map and the paper and the pop and cakes Erica had talked me into buying. The clerk laughed when I paid for the food with food stamps.

"Food stamps must be the only currency used in Kentucky!" he said.

"What's so damn funny 'bout bein' poor?" I snapped with a thick accent slipping out before I could catch my Celtic temper. Mom had always said the German in me was worse than the Irish, but I thought that was because she despised my grandmother Wells, a Honacker at birth.

His laughter bounced off the walls and into my ears like bad reverb as I huffed out with my purchases.

I sat in the parking lot and read the front page as the girls tore into their treats in the back seat. The clerk's nasty remarks hadn't hindered my determination. If anything, they'd further motivated me. The fresh air cooled my hot aggravated temper, and the new surroundings lifted my spirits.

I spotted a pay phone across the lot and pulled some change from my front pocket. I tried to call Loren but when Billy answered I hung up. I prayed he hadn't hurt Loren for helping me move. I thought of how cruel and childish Billy was and how helpless Loren felt living with him. Maybe I shouldn't have told her how Billy had treated me. I wanted her to get out of her hell hole, but I had to let her go. I had my own hole to claw out of and I knew I didn't have the means or the strength to hoist us both out, especially with our children attached at the hip and breast.

I flipped to the entertainment section of the paper and saw that the movie *Batman* was playing at the drive-in theater. Erica wanted to see it, and I figured that would be a cheap place to sleep for a while and give us something fun to do on the first night of our so-called holiday. I was exhausted from the packing, the moving, the stress of telling Loren, and the drive.

I located the Oakley Drive-in, named for Annie I figured, on the map and followed the trail with my finger until I had the major streets and crossings fixed in my mind. It didn't look too far way, just out Madison Avenue.

We made it there within fifteen minutes. I found a place to park away from the loud music playing down front and the lovers parked in the back row. Even though I knew there'd be constant traffic by the concession stand and restrooms, a well-lit spot was safer. I bought popcorn and got the girls some cool water, changed Megan's diaper, and put the girls up front with the doors locked. I stretched out in the back seat and read the paper, looking for work.

The employment section was incredible. There were tons of jobs and most of them high paying, unlike back home where the only possible fortune came from a crippling work-related injury and a damn good attorney. But as I studied the columns, I became intimidated by the qualifications. Some required a resume, which I didn't have. Some wanted me to call for an interview. What number would I leave for them to call back? I couldn't handle a career position. Now wasn't the time to look for permanent work considering my present circumstances. I just needed a check coming in by way of a mindless job until I could get settled.

I circled a few jobs that I might qualify for, intentionally skipping over the maid positions. I'd been cleaning up other people's messes long enough, and I vowed to take such work only if all else came up empty.

I located my stops on the map, darkened the most promising ones, and fished through a milk crate for something decent for the girls and me to wear the next day.

With tomorrow's schedule planned, I curled up and watched part of the movie, but I couldn't pay attention to it. I couldn't stop worrying about my predicament. The girls were sound asleep, and, with the windows slightly cracked, enough air was getting in to keep us alive. Survival. That's all I had in mind as I finally drifted off to sleep. I reminded myself I'd gotten through a lot worse.

Sometime in the wee hours of the morning the roar of other cars leaving awoke me. The burst of their ignitions, rumbling exhausts, and tires screeching sounded like an enemy attack. It probably didn't help that I'd been dreaming of

Michael's gun firing round after round while I tried to get my children away from him. I pressed my hair down with my trembling hands and moved the girls to the back seat as I traded bad memories for thoughts of my day's horrendous schedule. I had mammoth moves to make before the day ended if we were to survive.

As the sun peeked through the east hills, I got a better look at the area of town where we'd spent our first night. The four lane street was lined with old buildings, probably from the 1920s, some freshly painted, others looking like they should be condemned. Traffic was heavy, considering the early hour, a sure sign it was a working class neighborhood.

I pulled the car into the parking lot of a convenience store and bought some coffee for me and breakfast for the girls. They gobbled down Jimmy Dean sausage biscuits topped with Smucker's jelly. I sipped my coffee, pulled out my makeup bag, and prayed for a miracle.

My face was a mess. I looked stress-ridden and lined from not having the time or the mind to look after myself or eat right. "I look like a rundown work car," I murmured. I filled in the creases under my eyes with a bonding-type concealer followed by a layer of primer coat and powder to knock off the shine. I finished with a light enamel coat on my lips, perfect in color. I realized I thought like the men back home who treated their women like their cars. They'd take them out to show off if their paint jobs still looked good, but if the body was rusted or dented they were bound for the junk yard. Really, they'd park their wives in the living room and kitchen till death do them part while the men drove around sometimes with younger models.

Looking at the paper again, I drove to the first job ad I'd circled. Megan had snuck in some sticky leftover breakfast and presented it to the less than amused receptionist who quickly informed me this was no place for children. I didn't bother to explain my situation as I retrieved Megan's half-eaten biscuit and tucked it in my purse. The well groomed, thirtyish personnel director was tolerant but quickly picked up that I didn't have child care, otherwise I wouldn't have brought the girls with me.

"What happens when they get sick?" she asked, probably already knowing what my answer would be.

"Well, they are very healthy children," I assured her.

"Yes, well, all children get sick and someone will have to take care of them."

"But I really need the job, to help me take care of 'em so they stay healthy."

"I can appreciate that, but maybe you should have stayed with their father a while longer, until they were a little older. It's difficult for mothers with young children to work."

She wasn't telling me anything I didn't know, and I didn't dare tell her about their fathers. It might've curled her straight bleached red hair if I'd told her the truth about my past. Thoughts of living in our car and eating from the freezer of a 7-Eleven the rest of our lives were unnaturally changing my own hair color to gray.

The next two interviews were almost identical, although Megan didn't give away her food. The fourth interview angered me so bad I felt like giving up. The manager wouldn't even see me with the kids. He told me to come back when I could talk privately. My nerves were growing paper thin as each rejection jolted my senses. They didn't care what happened to us. Nobody did. The whole ugly mess had been dumped on my wobbly shoulders.

But looking at my girls I knew I couldn't give up.

After a quick lunch, I scoured the morning paper looking for child care. I picked a couple of numbers and went to the pay phone. Megan needed a nap, but the starting and stopping of the car and the slamming of doors wasn't much of a lullaby. She cried so badly I had to hang up on one woman because I couldn't hear. We all needed one of those bubble baths Loren loved, the kind that took all the tension away. Everything was so complicated, especially with Megan so young.

I folded the paper under my arm and decided to get a hotel room and call it a day. It would be easier to look for potential baby sitters and get directions to their houses, plus I could get acquainted by phone before I drove over to their homes for an inspection. Putting my children in the hands of strangers was nerve wracking.

As I searched for a hotel, I couldn't get Allan and Candy Harris off my mind. I knew they lived around there. Maybe they could help or give me some direction. Just seeing a familiar face would be soothing. I had forty-six dollars and a couple of books of food stamps left after I paid for the room. Clearly I couldn't afford the luxury of staying more than one night in a hotel, so I had to hurry.

Allan and Candy's name and address were listed in the phone book, but nobody answered and they didn't have a recorder. I knew Candy worked but I couldn't remember the name of the place. I tried to reach them in between day care calls and settling the girls down. All the day care centers had long waiting lists and required money up front, and by then the clock caught me. Business hours were almost over.

I'd bought dinner at another convenience store and fixed it in our room. Erica took control of the television, whizzing through the channels like she was playing a video game. After I bathed Megan she toddled around the room until she stumbled over the rest of the day's paper. She wrestled with it like a birthday toy. How pitiful it made me feel to look at her like this. The child was barely a year old and this was the second hotel she had lived in. The image of Michael rocketed into my mind's eye as I gritted my teeth and crammed my tightened fists into the bed until I thought they'd pierce through to the springs.

The next few days brought no relief. We slept at the drive-in and washed up in gas station bathrooms. Every day I filled up my milk jug with warm water and sponge bathed the girls. I tried several times a day to reach Allan and Candy, but no luck.

Then my car's brakes went. I took the car to Midas for a free estimate and they told me someone had poured who knew what into the brake line. Where was I going to get money for a brake job? Every time I pushed on the brakes I'd have to use both feet to pull the pedal off the floor. I dug deep sores into the tops of my feet but I worried most about having a wreck and hurting the girls. We needed some serious help. I looked up the address for social services. Here I was, in Dad's beat-up old Cadillac, going to the food stamp office. Some of the old jokes about Cadillac-driving welfare recipients came to my mind. I laughed lamentable laughter as I hurried downtown.

I sat in the waiting room trying to keep Megan off the filthy floor and Erica cheered up during our two-hour wait. It took an hour to fill out all the forms, page after page of the same questions, but, finally, in cattle auction fashion, they called my number.

"I'd like to sign up for financial assistance and food stamps," I told the social worker. I cringed looking over my shoulder to make sure I didn't know anyone. The social worker glanced over my paperwork.

"I'm sorry, ma'am. But we can't give you assistance at this time."

"Why? I don't have anything comin' in."

"Yes, that's true, but you also don't have an address."

"That's why I need it. I need some help." I couldn't believe what she was telling me as I squeezed the girls closer. What if she called someone to come and take my girls since we had nowhere to go?

I thanked her quickly, leaving behind the list of food pantries and shelters she'd tried to give me. I ran from the building and drove to the highway with my foot heavy on the gas pedal, but careful not to get a speeding ticket.

I drove out the interstate with Megan bawling louder than I could sing. Erica did the best she could to calm her, but to no avail.

My last hope was Allan and Cindy. I drove to the part of town where they lived. I pulled up to the first street pay phone I saw and dialed their number. I let it ring for several minutes, my eyes overflowing with tears and my head swimming in confusion. No answer. I hung up and smeared the salty liquid, wiping it from my face, got back in the car, and took the girls to eat.

My appetite was as withered as my wallet, but I made sure the girls ate. Megan made funny faces when she tasted the dill pickle she'd pulled off her burger. It was a relief to see them smile. I'd splurged an extra dollar and bought them the kids' meal with a toy inside. I was down to my last twenty and felt desperate and doomed as I watched the other families eating around me. I sat amongst them, the ones with homes, cars, and jobs to keep them going. I wanted to talk to them, get to know them, ask for help. But I was afraid. I was petrified they might not understand and call the police.

After we ate, I put three dollars worth of gas in my car. I had just enough money for two more nights at the drive-in. We knew almost every scene and line from *Batman*. Megan babbled "Batman, Batman" throughout the day as we drove from pillar to post looking for help and security.

It was nearly dusk when I dialed Allan and Candy again. This time, Allan answered.

"Hello."

"Allan, it's Jane. How are ya?"

"Hey, Janie, how are you? Where are you calling from?"

"A pay phone on Madison Road. I came up a few days ago, but I haven't been able to get hold of you."

"Well, we're in and out a lot. We've been on a trip for a few days. Where are you staying?"

"Well, actually, we're stayin' in the car. I did manage a hotel one night, but since then we've been sleepin' at the drive-in."

"Do you have the girls with you?"

"Yeah, they're settin' in the back seat lookin' at me now."

"Come over here and stay. We've got plenty of room and an extra full-size bed. You won't be a bit of trouble."

I thought he'd never ask. I didn't want to beg, but he must have known we were in dire need of shelter. His gently familiar voice brought tears to my eyes. I fought hard not to break down in the middle of our conversation.

"Are ya sure it's okay?" I asked with a noticeable quiver in my voice. "What about Candy? Shouldn't ya check with her first?"

"Janie, she'll be thrilled you came up, and I know she'd love to see the girls."

He gave me directions, but I'd already looked up the street on my map so many times I knew where they lived. I hadn't wanted to appear unannounced on their doorstep. Fortunately, Allan's invitation kept me from such a desperate move.

CHAPTER 18

A Respite

Staying with Allan and Candy for a few weeks made life
seem livable again. Candy, a nurse, worked an early morning shift and then went to dancing class. So she came home
well after dark, but Allan came home every evening. He spent
time with us and checked on the day's progress. With their help
and encouragement, I went back to look for work and child care.
I was determined to become self-sufficient and, with their support, I finally had a safety net in place. Allan and Candy said I
could stay as long as I needed. They didn't expect me to pay rent,
but I knew the difficulties that could develop when two families
lived in one house. I wanted to keep peace amongst us, and I
searched every second of the day for a job, sometimes going back
to the same place three or four times.

Finally, Quickstop, the convenience store where I'd
bought breakfast several times while living in the car, hired me
as a cashier. Never had anyone been more grateful for a job. The
manager, Ted Morris, asked if I could start right away, 6:00
A.M. to 4:00 P.M., Monday through Friday. That was impossible,
since I didn't have a sitter. Mr. Morris gave me a day to find someone to keep the girls, but if I didn't he'd have to hire someone

else. The hours were long, but I didn't care. The paychecks would soon enable me to get a place of my own.

Luckily, I found Jill Baker. She lived in a well-kept, older two-story frame house located midway between Allan and Candy's house and the Quickstop. Allan took time off from work to check things out and to pay her in advance when I decided to let her keep the girls. Jill and I had talked on the phone and I had a good feeling about her before we even saw her.

The other children Jill was minding clung to her while we visited. She explained the daily routine and showed us the sun room with heavy shaded windows where the children napped. As we walked through her dining room, I saw that she had converted it into a safe play area filled with puzzles, play sets, and a miniature table and chairs with a basket of crayons in the middle. The kitchen had a row of high chairs adjacent to the windows, and the floor was spotless.

I was really impressed when she showed us the backyard. The larger than average city lot was filled with riding toys and a playhouse. The yard was surrounded by a tall fence and safeguarded from the sun by sprawling shade trees. Erica ran straight for the playhouse. Megan was getting hugs from Jill. I could tell Jill really loved children, which made it a lot easier to leave mine with her and start to work.

I had to get up at 5:00 A.M. Not only did I have to drag myself out of bed and get presentable, but I had to get Erica ready for school and Megan changed. I usually left Megan in pajamas and just wrapped her in warm blankets to take to Jill. But soon I had the routine down. I could leave at 5:40, drop the girls off quickly, and make it to the time clock by 6:00 A.M. on the dot.

My first day working at Quickstop revealed why Mr. Morris needed help so urgently. It was hard for him to keep employees. Three doors away from the store was a crack house. I'd never been around crack before. I knew it was a dangerous drug, but I didn't know what to expect. Plenty of people back home used marijuana, which was Kentucky's main cash crop.

However, the slow and sluggish potheads didn't scare me like this bunch of gun-toting drug dealers. They were radically different, and their operations were hi-tech. Guys with beepers attached to their belts waited outside the store by the pay phone, inches away from the cash register I operated. When their beepers squeaked out the high-pitched sounds, they returned the calls and scurried away in cars or on bikes to make their deliveries. It made me nervous watching them, and Mr. Morris must have noticed my reaction.

"Don't worry about those guys," he said. "They're kinda like snakes. They won't bother you if you don't bother them. The morning shift's not as dangerous as the evening shift. That's when most of the robberies and shoplifting happens and the drug trafficking picks up."

His words weren't comforting, but I was glad to have a job and I tried to ignore the unmistakable dangers. I reminded myself constantly that this job was only temporary. I had to keep it if I wanted to get the girls and I a place of our own.

Opening the store presented other problems, too. Each morning I was greeted by six, eight, sometimes ten men, most of them older, waiting outside. During the first thirty minutes of the day I rang up cigarettes, lottery tickets, and half-pints of Mad Dog or Wild Irish Rose with hot coffee chasers. I'd shiver as I watched them swill down their red liquid breakfast, thinking this was hardly a breakfast of champions! Soon, I got to know who drank what and what size bottle they required. I'd have it in a brown bag before they had to ask.

Business stayed steady throughout the day, but the busiest time came just before I was scheduled to leave. Mothers with babies at the hip and hand, with hopes of winning a fortune in their eyes, formed a long line behind the lottery register just as the big yellow bus delivered our underage customers. The school children usually ignored the sign on the door: "Only Two Students at a Time!" It aggravated Mr. Morris so much that he'd come out of his office and play traffic cop as they shuffled in, making a ruckus as they entered.

I didn't mind the late afternoon rush. It made the last hour of work pass quickly, but it was frustrating that most of the children, some in high school, couldn't count money and purchased one item at a time until their pennies, nickels, and dimes had disappeared into my cash drawer. By day's end, I was exhausted and couldn't wait to get home to my own children. I vowed to teach them how to count change.

Staying in the basement at Allan and Candy's gave me some privacy, but there were problems. I had the girls' beds and a full size bed set up in a semicircle from the cinder block wall. I placed the girls' toys in the middle of this roughly constructed playpen. Megan was developing her crawling, walking, and climbing skills, and the old rickety stairs in the basement leading to the kitchen became one of her favorite play places. I made blockades at the bottom, but she could usually work through and make her way up the steps. When I'd turn my back to throw in a load of laundry or to make a bed, she'd make a mad dash for the stairs. I had visions of her falling back and cracking her head on the thick concrete floor. She'd giggle when I caught her, but for me it was a frightening game.

Sometimes, after the girls were asleep, Allan and I would hunt through his house for pictures of Johnny, or sit on the front porch and talk for hours like the three of us had when Johnny was alive. As in his visit a few months before in Lexington, we spent most of our time talking about music and art. Reading his books and flipping through his albums reminded me of the years when he'd hung out with me and Johnny. We'd take turns playing our favorite tunes or reading aloud our favorite book or lyrics. I was comforted by our evening chats, and Allan seemed to enjoy them as much as I did.

I was glad Candy didn't seem to mind either. "I like having you around," she insisted kindly.

I was home in the evenings to fix dinner, a chore Candy despised, and she'd play for hours with the girls. She bought them paper dolls and miniature toy horses at the store where she worked. They loved being with her. Erica ran to the door every evening when Candy's car pulled in. Sometimes after dinner Candy would get her scissors and help Erica cut out the dolls. They'd give them pretty names, dress them up in assorted costumes, and pretend they were riding off to some faraway place. We had to keep a close eye on Megan during these play times. Not just because of the scissors, but she liked to taste and tear the cardboard and parchment figures.

I appreciated the help they were giving me. Being away from Morehead finally gave me a place to grieve and try to make sense of a senseless death. Nevertheless, images of that fatal morning still ruled my nightly sleep and kept me drained of energy and wit. Images of Johnny drawing his last breath, blood running from his mouth while Michael looked down in anger, waiting for his turn at me, dominated my dreams. At night in my sleep, I'd try to imagine a way I could've prevented the murder from happening. Regardless of my mind's efforts, the dreams always had the same disastrous ending.

It helped being around Allan. If I was down and crying, or just unusually quiet, he'd cheer me up by telling a joke or recounting a crazy stunt Johnny had pulled. Allan was not as outgoing as Johnny had been. He was kind of quiet, but not shy, and had admired the energy that Johnny had possessed. I knew Allan missed Johnny terribly. Listening to him made me realize how important it was to remember Johnny's uncanny ways. So, I thought of some silly stories to tell Allan.

"Did ya know about the time Johnny and cousin Sammy were drivin' out Interstate 64 comin' to Lexington?" I began one night. "We'd been livin' there awhile before Erica was born and Johnny had gone to get Sammy for a visit. We'd been havin' car trouble, an oil leak, I think. Anyway, on the way back with Sammy, Johnny pulled off an exit and checked it, and it was okay, but he'd not shut the hood tight. Well, Johnny was gunnin' the car up a mountain on the interstate somewhere around Olive

Hill, and wouldn't ya know the hood blew off, snapped at the hinges 'n' flew off like a frisbee. It sailed across the guardrail, tumbled down the side of the hill, and landed in a valley on what we're not sure. Sammy said Johnny didn't flinch and was as blank-faced as a scarecrow. He just kept drivin' for home. Sammy didn't know what to do other than laugh. But right before they got into town, Johnny realized he'd have some explainin' ta do. It was my car, and he knew I'd be upset. But he also knew my mood was quickly changed by a laugh or a good song, so he combined the two. When he walked in, Sammy right behind him, Johnny broke into song to the melody of *San Francisco*: 'I left my hooood in O-live Hi-ll.' I started to get mad but I couldn't. I was laughin' too hard."

"I know what you mean, Janie," Allan said sadly. "He was ornery at times, but always good for a laugh, and I loved him like a brother. I wish he was with us, but we gotta learn to go on without him."

I loved trading stories with Allan. It was, in some small way, a place where we could still visit Johnny. But I knew Allan was right that I couldn't dwell on it. I had to find a way to get on with my life.

It took me three paychecks to have enough money for the security on an apartment. I found a place on Chestnut Pike, only two miles from Candy and Allan's house. The complex was on a wooded hillside in a good school district. They were making some needed renovations when I went to see it. And because of the noise and the unfinished condition, they had a good move-in special. The apartments were located in three-story brick colonials. They had two small bedrooms and two baths with a tiny eat-in kitchen. The only one I could afford was in the base-ment, but, when I signed my lease, I received a much needed microwave for free. The complex had a playground, adult and baby pools, and the lawns were well-groomed.

Allan and Candy took time off work to help move us in. They had some spare furniture and gave me a couch and two chairs for the living room and a bedroom set for my room. I set the girls' beds up and used milk crates for shelves and storage until I could get back to Loren's shed and bring back the chest of drawers and toys we'd left behind, though I dreaded seeing Billy again.

I called Loren as soon as I got settled.

She was glad to hear from me at last and said, "You better get up here before the snow hits. It'll be a foot deep before you know it, and I'm not sure how leak-proof that shed is, Jane. You better get here soon."

"I will. I've still got a lot of things to do, mainly work and the kids and getting unpacked. The bad news is we're in the basement, three-quarters underground, but the good news is the porch is enclosed with three sides of concrete wall. I can let the girls play out there without worryin' about one of 'em gettin' away, or bein' snatched by strangers. And there's lots of new appliances."

"Jane, while I'm sitting down, will you answer me this: do you have a dishwasher?"

"Yes! And a microwave! Loren, I'm gettin' my life back."

"I'm proud of you, Jane. You're no longer living in the Third World like I am. I can't wait to come up and see you. Send me a map and I'll start makin' plans to get away for a visit."

"How ya gonna do that with Billy? Won't he get mad?"

"Ah, he can just get mad. The hell with him. How are the neighbors?"

"The neighbors are great. They've helped me get Erica settled in school, and they're real friendly."

That was an understatement. Some of the nicest people I'd ever met lived in this small community. Gayle, Pat, Nancy, and Evita helped me with everything from getting around town to keeping the kids if I needed to run a quick errand. After getting to know them a little better, I'd explained to some of them what my family had gone through over the last two years. The beatings, the loss of my entire savings and possessions, and

Johnny's murder shocked them. They couldn't believe I was still sane. They understood my dire need and helped whenever possible.

Gayle came to see me shortly after she learned of our hell on earth. Gayle worked in social services and she wanted to help me develop a survival strategy.

"Have you signed up for welfare?" Gayle asked.

"I tried, but at the time I didn't have a place to live, and they turned me down. Now I can't take time off work to go during business hours."

"You need to get a medical card and be checked by a doctor. You've been under a lot of stress. Think of Erica and Megan. You need to be able to take care of these beautiful girls."

I knew she was right. I had begun passing out at work. One day it got so bad they had to call an ambulance. I realized Gayle's superior view even more when the bill for $150 from the ambulance service came. I begged Mr. Morris not to call them if I passed out again. All they had done in the emergency room was set me up on a stool, check my blood pressure, and make me drink orange juice on an empty stomach until I threw up.

My fainting spells got to be a regular ordeal at work. I'd fall down at the register. Then my boss would move me aside and ring up the purchases of whoever was standing there until I could be revived. Afterwards, he'd go back to his office and finish his paperwork. And if my health problems weren't bad enough, my car was constantly breaking down.

When the brakes finally went, Allan paid to have them fixed and said I could pay him back in installments, whenever I could afford it. Having them repaired was a relief and made it easier to drive. I no longer had to push with both feet and pull back to reengage them. I felt ashamed at having to rely again on Candy and Allan to pay my bill, but I didn't have even a dollar extra after paying for rent, food, and necessities for the children.

Then the alternator went. This time I went to the library and checked out an auto repair book. I had to keep working, and

I didn't want to ask Candy and Allan for more money. I hadn't paid them the first dollar back for my brakes. Repairing the alternator wasn't really that hard. I talked to the clerk at the auto parts store after I read the library book. I borrowed tools from our maintenance man at the complex, put Megan down for a nap, and got it done by nightfall. I had to stop when Erica got off the bus and when curiosity overcame some neighbors who didn't think women should fix cars. It irked me when a couple of men kidded me from their balconies that I'd end up having to get a mechanic to do the job. Some of them made bets I couldn't do it. I loved proving them wrong. I revved my engine and knocked on their doors when I got the car working.

Eventually I called my lawyer, now Judge Don Hayes, to tell him I was getting reestablished. I knew the final property and child custody hearing would be soon, and I worried my car wouldn't make it there and back. The judge said the divorce hearing would be soon, and he would represent me for that, but I'd have to find another attorney to take care of anything that blossomed later. I didn't understand what else there could be in the way of legalities, but I contacted another attorney, Craig Hollingsworth, who had worked for my parents. I hoped being established with Mr. Hollingsworth would help when dealing with serious legal problems at a distance. His secretary assured me he could handle any problems I'd have after the divorce was final. Meanwhile, I did what I could to keep us afloat.

"Jane, why don't you go down to the river and get a waitress job?" Loren suggested during one of our biweekly phone conversations. "Those girls down on those fancy river boats rake in the bucks. You still got your looks and personality going for you," she added.

"Well, the problem is I'd have to work nights and be away from the kids, and it would be hard to find a sitter during the evening hours. Still, we need money bad. What kinda bucks are ya talkin' about?"

"At least a Franklin a night. More on weekends."

"God, that sounds good. But a sitter. How'm I gonna work that out?"

"Jane, you got me on that one. That's what keeps me from working. They don't have day care in the country. Our legislators beg for food benefits, and the heck with the other subsidies. I think what you need is a wife!"

We both giggled at the suggestion she'd made.

"Yeah," she said, "you need someone to cook, clean, and keep the girls while you work."

"I sure don't need a husband!" I insisted. "I can't afford the legal expenses or puttin' up with the hassles. Did I tell ya I think I got arthritis in my shoulder and knee? When it rains or gets cold and damp the pain 'bout sends me through the roof."

"It isn't any wonder the way Michael threw you around, and all that fainting at work doesn't help much either. Yeah, once you get Arthur in your joints it's a lifelong pain. Arthur's one of those men you can't get rid of. You'll always suffer with him. Jane, why don't you look into welfare? They might just sign you up now that you have a place to stay."

"Loren, I feel like a clod of dirt just goin' in the place."

"Yeah, you and that damn hillbilly pride. Go up there and get yourself a draw. You didn't put yourself in this mess. You need to take a break and let somebody look out for you, even if it is your Uncle Sam. Jane, honey, I know you have to be wickedly worn."

I knew she was right. My fainting spells were getting worse. I thought hard about what she had said. I even called in sick one day just to rest and be home when Erica got off the bus. I vacuumed the house, did some mending, and watched my game shows like I was a kept woman. Just for a day, I could relax and watch with a smile when Megan woke up and not have to hurl her into the cold morning fog. It was fun pretending I was a mother with a high-paid working husband. But reality snapped back quickly. My next check was a day short, and I had to find a way to cut back on an already tragically stretched budget.

While Megan napped one Saturday afternoon, I worked on a costume Erica was going to wear for Halloween that night. She'd been invited to an overnight party the apartment complex was sponsoring. The maintenance crew had worked all day raking up the colorful autumn leaves, setting up tents, and piling up wood for campfires. The complex provided hot dogs and marshmallows for roasting, and each child was to bring a can of pop. Erica was thrilled to be going. She pulled out several heavy blankets to keep her warm during that night. She was only a first grader, and I was a little concerned about her staying out at night, but most of her friends were going and I talked to several other mothers who said they'd keep an eye on her.

I could see the campsite from the girls' window. That night, every time I checked on Megan I'd pull back the blinds and look and listen. Sometimes the children were singing. Other times I heard screams and giggles. I figured they were telling ghost stories.

After the circle got quiet shortly after midnight, I turned in. I slept soundly until the phone woke me at nine.

"Miss Wells. This is Ann Cohen, the apartment manager. I wanted to call you and explain a very bizarre occurrence that happened last night."

"Is Erica okay?" My heart raced as I wiped sleep from my eyes and tried to grasp every word she said.

"Yes, Erica is fine. All of the children are in the clubhouse having hot chocolate and donuts for breakfast."

I could tell by her somber tone that something was wrong. She seemed upset, but unable to spit out what was really on her mind.

"What happened last night?" I asked.

"Well, the children were telling ghost stories. The parents who chaperoned assured them the stories were just silly Halloween stories and not to worry. But when it came Erica's turn, she told the group about her father's murder. At first some of us thought it was just her vivid imagination, but she insisted the story was true. We felt you should be aware of this."

I took a deep breath and tried to sound calm. "I do appreciate your call. I'll have a talk with her as soon as she gets home."

I hung up in a panic. I didn't tell Mrs. Cohen that Erica was indeed telling the truth. What if they kicked us out fearing Michael would find us, kill us, and make a mess of their apartment? I walked slowly to the kitchen and put some coffee on to perk. I tried to think of how to approach Erica. I certainly didn't want to scold her, but I needed to talk to her. We had spoken about not telling anyone about the murder, and why. Although I had told some of the women I made friends with at the complex, I didn't want it to become general knowledge.

When Erica walked through the door, she seemed surprised that I was waiting for her.

"Momma, what's the matter?"

"Honey, I need to ask ya somethin'. Did ya tell the other kids about your daddy's murder?"

Erica's head lowered as her left foot drew designs in the nap of the carpet. I knew she was ashamed, but I didn't want her to be. My stomach flinched with pain. I gently placed my hand under her chin and lifted her small face toward mine. Her eyes looked sad and disabled.

"Yes, Momma, I told them. They were tellin' stories. Some were real scary. When my turn came, I told 'em the scariest one I knew. I scared them, too, Momma. Their mouths flew open when I told 'em. It was the scariest one they'd heard."

I took her in my arms and held her close. I couldn't agree with her more. Our life had been stranger than fiction.

CHAPTER 19

Bad Tidings

My day had been better than usual until the envelope with an official return address came in the mail. I opened it and cried as I read it:

Jane Wells Haney, Petitioner, VS: Jerry Michael Haney, Respondent: Findings of Fact, Conclusions of Law and Judgment.

The document concerned the issues of division of marital property, custody, support, and visitation in my divorce from Michael:

The Respondent is presently incarcerated in a Kentucky State penal institution and has very little income, if any at all, and to set child support at this time would only build up a large arrearage. Money can be paid to the Petitioner through Aid for Dependent Children since the Respondent is incarcerated. Child support is hereby reserved by the court until the Respondent has been released from the State penal system.

The real estate in this action being two pieces of real property was owned prior to the marriage and is nonmarital property belonging to the Petitioner.

The personalty acquired during this marriage has been

moved about, some lost, some returned to satisfy debts and obligations and some sold. The Respondent testified that he had no real interest in the personalty. The only thing he desired was to have some type of visitation and contact with his infant daughter. The Court finds that the Respondent is giving up any and all interest in the personalty except for that personalty which has been picked up by his family or being held for him by his friends.

There seem to be considerable marital debts. It is pretty obvious that the creditors would have a hard time collecting any monies from the Respondent unless he is released from the State penal system. Some of the debts have been jointly incurred and both parties are jointly responsible for those debts incurred during the marriage. The Court finds that each party has an obligation to pay the marital debts. Any debts incurred prior to the marriage or after the divorce shall be paid by the individual incurring said debts.

The Court finds that although the Respondent is incarcerated he is still entitled to have contact with his infant daughter. It is true that at such a young tender age taking the child to the institution is not advisable at this time but the Respondent is to have contact with his daughter by telephone and correspondence and should be given some photographs so that he will know what his daughter looks like.

JUDGMENT
IT IS HEREBY ORDERED AND ADJUDGED as follows:

1. The Petitioner shall have the care, custody and control of the parties' infant daughter. Child support is reserved by the Court until the Respondent has been released from the Kentucky penal system.

2. The Respondent shall have contact with his infant daughter by correspondence and telephone. The Petitioner does not have to furnish the Respondent with her address but this contact can be made through the Petitioner's parents. The Petitioner shall furnish the Respondent current photographs of his infant daughter and periodic photographs during the period of his incarceration. The Court feels there will be complaints that this is not being done and will take a dim view of any reasons that are not supported by facts. Failure to abide by this

Court Order will cause the Court to invoke its contempt powers. Personal visitation is reserved by the Court.

 3. The two pieces of real estate are nonmarital and belong to the Petitioner.

 4. The Petitioner shall have title and possession to any and all personalty in her possession at this time.

 5. The Respondent shall have title and possession to any and all personalty being held by his friends or family at this time.

 6. The marital debts shall be paid jointly by the Respondent and Petitioner. Any debts incurred prior to the marriage and after the divorce shall be paid by the individual incurring said debts.

What had I done to deserve this? I'd never killed anyone. I didn't have a criminal record. I didn't know the judge, never harmed him or angered him to my knowledge, but I knew Michael wasn't friends with him either, so there was little chance the judge was playing favorites as far as I could figure.

When I contacted Don Hayes, who was on the bench now, and begged for an explanation, he said that was how the judge saw it. When I pressed him further, he said maybe I should see a women's group, but I wasn't sure what he meant by that. I thought maybe he suspected I needed counseling, so I didn't press the issue. Before we hung up, he asked if I had someone new to represent me. I told him I had contacted Mr. Hollingsworth. "Call me if Mr. Hollingsworth doesn't work out," Judge Hayes said.

Erica was upstairs playing with Gayle's daughter Kristin when the papers arrived. I was glad she didn't have to witness my reaction to the judge's decision. I paced through the house mumbling "Why me?" and "How could the courts treat a child this way?" Megan was sleeping soundly in her crib when I looked in on her. I could think of nothing to do but call Loren and rant about this dimwitted decision.

"Ya got a minute? You're not gonna believe this. I got my final divorce papers and it isn't fair," I said.

"Oh, no, Jane, what have they done now?" Loren said. She

assured me she had time to listen if I could just hold while she pulled the phone and herself into the kitchen away from her kids and the television so she could hear better.

"What's it say, Jane? I'm ready for the worst."

As I read her the dreadful document word for word, I heard Loren's grunts and mumbles grow louder the closer I got to the judgment part. She seemed as upset and puzzled as I'd been when I tried to absorb the contents. It sounded harsh when I'd read it to myself, but out loud it rang in my ears like a death sentence.

"Jane, this can't be real. It's like a bad dream. Is this what the definition of a good father is? What in God's name does it take to become a bad father?" Loren cried.

"I don't know, Loren. I thought a parent's job was to teach their children to obey the law and stay away from felons. But here the court says that when Michael gets out of prison, they're gonna set visitation. Like he's a fine example of a father. Like nothin' ever happened. Like he didn't pull the trigger on Erica's father."

"Is Megan not supposed to eat for seven years or have a place to live?" Loren added. "He can claim her, she has to bear his name, but he doesn't have to pay for her."

"I don't know what to do, Loren. Is there something I don't understand, something I did wrong?"

"Yeah, Jane, they're punishing you for havin' bad taste in men. Hell, go back to court and terminate his parental rights. Then you'll be done with him once and for all."

"But, Loren, how can I find the money to do that? It might be several hundred dollars, maybe a thousand."

"Yeah, but what an investment. You've got at least six years before he gets out to save up and get it done. Then ya won't have to deal with Michael again, you can change Megan's name to Doe or whatever ya want, and he'll have to leave ya alone. You could move away and wash your hands of it all. That'd be a wise way to spend your dollars."

"I like this idea of Jane Doe, but it ain't that easy," I said. "You make it sound like a first grade primer: *Run, Jane, Run.* But where am I gonna go? How do I get there? Who's gonna foot that bill to our safety?"

I lost sleep for several nights worrying over the court's decision and how to protect the girls and I from Michael and the legal system. But they had me. I couldn't just walk away. It would take money I didn't have to fight back. It seemed unfair that I should have to continue to be terrorized by Michael, let alone dread the day he walked out of prison and back into our lives. At least I had a few safe years, while he was behind bars, to find a way, whatever it might be, to get help for us and put an end to his continuing abuse.

In the meantime the dangers at my job multiplied, and one day we were held up.

Frightened that next time I'd get shot and leave the girls with no one to care for them, I quit the convenience store. With no other job prospect in sight, I went to the welfare office to apply for aid until I could get back on my feet. I filled out the AFDC application, unsure if there were special provisions made for children whose fathers were in jail. I thought it was based on need. And I was right. The fact that Erica and I drew Johnny's Social Security made Megan ineligible based on our household's below-poverty income level. The smartly dressed Black social worker became annoyed when I pressed her for a better explanation.

"You can't qualify as long as you get Social Security," she pointed out to me. "And you'll draw that until your older daughter is eighteen or until you remarry."

"No chance a'that happenin'," I said in a low voice, not intending for her to hear.

But she did. "Listen here, darlin'," the social worker said. "I don't know why you want to mess with public assistance. Look at you. You're young, pretty, and White. If I was you, I'd get me a rich White man. Then you can give those children what they need."

I stared at her. She thought that would end all my problems? I hadn't told her how I came to draw Social Security or why my ex-husband was in jail. She thought being White somehow put me above the dangers and risks of everyday life. That I could marry security and be rid of the nightmares of poverty struck me as ludicrous.

I knew I'd have to get a job, maybe two jobs, and save up the money to get things done. I needed a job and I needed an education, but, right now, I needed help with the girls. The idea of inviting a stranger into our home to care for them was not something I could easily do. Jill Baker had helped when I worked days, but she couldn't take care of children at night, and none of the day care centers stayed open past 6:00 P.M.

On the way home from the social services office, I thought about where I could get work. I bought a paper and began scouring the ads again, looking for a new job.

The more I read, the more frustrated I became. I didn't have a profession other than mothering and my skills were entry level. I'd waited tables before and knew the money waitressing could bring, especially at night and serving liquor. Finally, I decided I'd have to find a roommate who could baby-sit, not an easy chore.

After I placed an ad in the paper, my phone rang endlessly. I got calls from runaways, women fleeing abusive hubands, retired women, a few men, and some people whose words I couldn't understand over the phone. I finally settled on Carita.

Carita had just moved from Puerto Rico and was staying with her cousins in town. Carita's mother was an attorney and her father was a doctor back in Puerto Rico, and they wanted their daughter educated in the continental United States, to learn the American way of life. Loren and I joked when we first learned this. We thought about how Carita would someday go back to visit her family, them expecting a sophisticated and enlightened daughter, and there she'd be making chicken and dumplings and grease gravy and announce to them when the food was all gone, "Now, hush up, they ain't na more fer ya ta have." We used our Sunday manners when she moved in with us. She fit in just fine and soon fell in love with my children.

I found a job at Diamante's Restaurant, across the street from The Glass Slipper, a concert hall that pulled crowds from all over, even from our old neck of the woods. I could earn money and be close to a music atmosphere, one of my few pleasures left in life.

Diamante's was near the University. The six block area consisted of several pubs and restaurants, clothing and record stores, a Kroger, a Walgreens, a liquor store, and a small business section that catered to campus life and college students. Diamante's was one of the older establishments on this strip. Most of the day customers were business and university personnel. At night, concert goers from The Glass Slipper, students, and seasoned music lovers packed our club to hear their favorite local bands.

In this area you could see every kind of person, from fraternity boys and their cute sorority sweethearts, to leather-draped skinheads and punks on skateboards with their hair dyed in colors unknown to nature. But the pulse of the streets came from the musicians, some of whom I came to know soon after I was hired at Diamante's.

Ned Burke was the club manager and, lucky for me, a Kentucky native. He was from across the river, not from the eastern region like I was, but he had a deep sympathy for the mountain people who traveled to Cincinnati in search of jobs. He knew most of us were hardworking, dependable, and trustworthy, traits that any good restaurant manager prized in an employee. Of course, we all had country accents that sometimes were hard for city folk to understand. Ned picked up my accent right away, and told me not to be ashamed of my heritage. He said, "Hold your head high, and tell 'em to kiss your ass if they cross ya and always be ready to fight 'em." Ned was a sharp dresser, a real man's man who had a touch of John Wayne about him, but he was unusually understanding to both men and women if you played fair and worked hard.

Over my months in Cincinnati I concentrated on my speech, trying to rid myself of an accent that made me stick out like a marijuana plant in a cornfield.

I respected Ned right away, especially after meeting my fellow employees. He'd assembled a fine work crew. Brock, a journalism senior, and Brian, from Bermuda, were the main bartenders, and they worked together like a finely oiled machine. The waitresses were mostly college students or recent grads. One of them, Irene, was always giving me things like suckers and toys for the girls, extra clothes I could wear, and household items she didn't need.

Todd was a cook and a history major whose father had died when he was a very young boy. He was quite a talker. Aside from philosophizing about every ponderable question under the sun, he told me stories of his mother's plight of raising children on her own, and he became one of my more sympathetic ears. He introduced me to Aaron, the barback, an engineering major who was kind and generous, but considerably more quiet than Todd. His quiet nature allowed him to slip in and out of places unnoticed. If the bar wasn't stocked with a beer one of my customers had ordered, he'd sneak down to get it from the beer cooler in the basement without Ned ever knowing he was making a special trip. They understood I wasn't just working for beer money like most of the others, and they made my life easier through simple deeds of kindness.

Everyone I worked with was friendly, and we worked well together as a team. We had mutual respect. Everyone looked out for each other.

Most of us worked long days. I tried to make as much overtime as I could. My feet felt like fire some nights, but giving the girls some extra niceties and the burning image of getting enough money together to petition the courts to end Michael's parental rights kept me going. I couldn't endure the picture of

Erica answering the door one day and Michael shoving past her into our home. Even if he had supervised visitation at another location, Erica or I wouldn't have a minute's peace knowing Megan was with a killer.

When the next letter came from Mr. Hollingsworth, I had a premonition before opening it that there would be expensive and terrible news enclosed. His letter said it was urgent to contact him by telephone after he returned from vacation. That's just what I needed, something else to keep me on edge while my rich lawyer was vacationing at who knows what exotic paradise. I circled the date of his return on my kitchen calendar and was at the phone early that morning, anxious to know what was so urgent, yet could wait until after his vacation.

It took most of the day to reach him, at almost three o'clock in the afternoon, after a half dozen costly chats with his receptionist who tirelessly explained Mr. Hollingsworth's busy schedule.

"Mr. Hollingsworth," I said, "what's wrong?"

"I have some unpleasant news for you. Did you know there's a warrant for your arrest?"

His news paralyzed me. A troubled pause passed through the hundreds of miles of telephone lines. I'd never been in trouble with the law.

"What do you mean, a warrant? How? Who took it out on me?"

"Well, it's a bench warrant. Michael wrote the judge and said you hadn't sent him pictures of his child, and he didn't think you were reading his letters to Megan."

"I sent them months ago."

"Do you have proof that you sent them?"

"No, I don't. My dad mailed them. I think he sent them certified, though."

"You get hold of him and get copies of the receiving signature. Meanwhile, be careful. If you get pulled over and the police run a check on your license, they could lock you up. If you come here, they'll arrest you for sure."

"How could the judge do this if I've already sent Michael the pictures?"

"Michael can tell the judge anything he wants. The burden of proof is on you. You must show the judge that you are complying with his orders."

"But Michael's a convicted killer. Do judges usually take their word for things?" I thought of the warning the judge had written in the divorce decree. He'd take a "dim view" if his orders weren't carried out. Too bad Michael killing Johnny didn't dim his view.

"Prisoners have rights, too," Mr. Hollingsworth said. "Listen, Jane, some of the guys in jail with Michael are lifers. They know the law inside and out, and they keep their fellow prisoners well informed of their rights. They trade smokes or whatever else of value they have in exchange for free legal advice. I hate to break this to you, but you may as well get used to it. Every time Michael gets a court date with you, he gets a trip out of prison and a stop at McDonald's with a Big Mac and fries, while you pay court costs and the fees of both attorneys. This will likely go on until he's out and has to pay for his own legal counsel."

"How long is this gonna take to get this warrant cleared up?"

"Well, you'll have to get copies of the certified letter that verifies you sent the pictures, and then we'll have to get a court date and ask the judge to hear your side of the story."

My head spun as if I had a fever. I felt like I was in a country where laws were made and broken by despots.

"But what if they throw me in jail first?"

"You'll have to keep a low profile. Meet me at my office and we'll go to court together. I won't let them arrest you."

I took a deep breath. "How much will this all cost me?"

"Three hundred dollars."

I thought about the fee, knowing this could go on until Michael's release.

"Do you think, after we get this warrant business straightened out, we could terminate his parental rights?"

"I'll look into it. That's a more complicated case."

"How much will that cost me?"

"If we can do it, I'd charge you five hundred dollars. But I'll have to look into some things before I make any promises."

After hanging up I tried to pull myself together and not dwell on the unfairness of it all. I called Mom right away and asked her to get a copy of the receipt from the post office. She called back the next day to say that it would take a few weeks to get a copy. Meanwhile, I waited.

Every time I saw the police or heard a siren my heart pounded and sweat poured from me. I shivered when the phone rang, not knowing what new legal nightmare might be at hand. Little daily tasks became a dread. A simple trip to the mailbox made me shake with fear. I was careful of every move I made in the car, fearing the slightest illegal maneuver could result in my being pulled over, thrown in jail, the girls taken to foster care, and all on account of Michael lying to the judge, and me without the resources to prove the truth.

But, though I was afraid, I was more motivated than ever to work. I posted a notice on the board at the restaurant asking for extra shifts. I felt awful since I didn't get to see the girls much, but I kept my mind on my goal to rid our lives of Michael's abuse.

As time went on, overwork and pressure wore on me, making me thin and nervous. One night I got off work in the early evening when business was slow. The others were going to Vito's, an Italian restaurant that had a dungeon type basement and a jukebox. They convinced me to go with them. Irene said, "The early evening crowd is extremely different from the late night gathering, but still, most of the regulars refer to it as the 'Star Wars Bar.' At anytime, day or night, any kind of strange looking creature might walk in for a shot or a beer or a game of pool or darts. When musicians and their herd of groupies and cohorts huddle within the concrete walls, the place is wild. But the evening crowd is mostly college professors, lawyers, nurses, and doctors."

Feeling out of place in the atmosphere, I leaned against the wall near the bar sipping the coke I'd ordered. A fortyish, balding man in a blue serge suit carrying a legal brief sidled up to me. "I haven't seen you here before," he said.

"I just moved here a few months ago. I have a job at Diamante's, and Irene and the others convinced me to come with them and have one for the road."

"Ah, famous last words. Frank Piccolo. And your name?"

"Jane," I said cautiously.

"Where did you move from?"

"Kentucky. You don't sound like you're from these parts either."

"Actually, I grew up in Chicago and here and there, really," Frank said. "I've been here nearly six years. It's home to me. I'm an attorney and I teach part-time."

"What do you teach?"

"Criminal justice. What else would an upholder of the law teach?" He patted the brief he carried.

"I could use a few lessons in justice," I said.

"Well, you've come to the right place," Frank said. "Could I interest you in securities management? How about espionage?"

"No." I shook my head. "I need to know about divorce law and custody rights, visitation, stuff like that."

"Oh, just your average run-of-the-mill law," Frank said, a little disappointed that I hadn't selected one of his favorites.

"Not exactly," I said. "Have you always been an attorney?" His animated movements and fast talk reminded me of a talk show host or maybe even a preacher at a tent revival. Except for his city accent.

"Actually, I worked as an auctioneer to put myself through law school. It's really the same kind of work, only as an attorney one wears a suit to work."

I laughed at Frank's jokes and drank too many cokes, which he kidded me about. He was tall and fidgety, and he shuffled his feet when he spoke of law or sports. Everyone who passed by us he spoke to by name. I pulled a dollar from my pocket and went to the jukebox as he broke into a long conversation with the bartender.

"You like music?" Frank asked as he came up behind me and watched my selections, arguing that number four was a better selection than the number seven I'd played.

"Yeah, my husband was a musician," I said.

"Divorced, huh," Frank said, making an assumption.

"He's dead," I said. "It's a long story. After these songs play I've gotta get home to my children." I was hoping to scare him off, but he didn't move.

"I'm listening," he said.

"Look. I'll tell ya some other time. I don't like to talk about it here. Tell me more about your teachin'. I wanna go to school, but I'm torn between studyin' music and law."

"Bingo!" Frank said as he threw his hands up in the air, excited by my interests. "Did you meet the right person! Besides my law practice, I have a small studio at my place. How about ya come over sometime. I've got some great equipment."

I laughed. "Do you know how many men have told me they've got great equipment back at their place?" I thought of just walking away, but, despite his aggressiveness, there was something likable about him. "Thanks, but no thanks. I gotta go. Some other time."

I thought about Frank as I carefully drove home. I had questions about the law, and I really did want to go to school. He seemed to know everyone, so I felt sure I could talk with him again.

I set my alarm clock for early the next morning. I wanted to see Erica before she left for school and I had to reach my attorney before he left for court to ask again about terminating Michael's rights. I couldn't wait until late in the day when he was usually free to talk to him because I was scheduled to work a double shift.

"I had lunch with Judge Morgan yesterday," Mr. Hollingsworth told me. "I asked him what the odds were of you terminating Michael's parental rights. The judge said he wouldn't be inclined to rule in your favor on such an action. He says he wouldn't take a man's child from him just because he was serving a manslaughter sentence."

"But this isn't just a manslaughter sentence. He tried to kill me, and he did kill Johnny."

"He's aware of that, but that alone isn't enough. The crime has to be more severe, more people killed."

"There would've been more people killed if the gun woulda kept workin'. Does that judge know Michael killed Johnny in front of the girls? Doesn't that matter?"

"Apparently not. The judge doesn't read the murder trial transcript. He just knows the decision and Michael's sentence, and, since it was only manslaughter, he says he won't consider termination."

It was only manslaughter. It was only manslaughter. Flustered and irate by how the judge and Mr. Hollingsworth had callously reduced Johnny's death to "only manslaughter," I slammed my body down on the couch and cried bitter tears, wondering how and when this was going to end. If the whole story could have been told in the courtroom, Michael would've been convicted of Murder One and held in jail for life. But, to them, it was only manslaughter.

I'd forgotten about my glasses. I lifted my shuddering body and saw the twisted frames and cracked lenses. I'd crushed them beyond repair. I didn't dare drive without them. My license restricted me to driving with corrective lenses, and if I were caught breaking the law, I'd probably get the electric chair.

I was sitting at the dining room table weeping about my broken glasses when Erica came in.

"Mom, what's wrong?"

"Oh, nothing, baby. Mom's just having a bad day." I would die rather than tell her how the legal system was treating us.

"What happened to your glasses?" She'd picked several pieces of glass up and was inspecting the mess. I couldn't help the moan which escaped from my lips. Erica placed her small hands on my shoulder for a moment. She stood silent, probably thinking of how she could be a big girl and help Mom.

"Don't worry, Mom. We can get another pair of glasses."

"Honey," I said, sniffling. "I know we can, but right now Mommy doesn't have the money for a new pair." Erica stood quietly again, and then drew air in excitedly when she thought of a solution.

"You don't have to buy a new pair! All ya have to do is kill somebody. The government will buy ya some then. Remember when we went to court and Michael was there? They said he was a good student in school and he was wearing new glasses and had on new clothes. We could get that, too. The government will pay for school and everything if you kill someone!"

"What? Honey, it's never right to kill someone. . . ." I couldn't believe I'd heard Erica say those horrible words. My head was spinning with the chorus of the judge's decree filling my mind. *It was only manslaughter. It was only manslaughter.*

CHAPTER **20**

Lessons in the Law

F rank Piccolo was not difficult to find when I tried to see him again. He was quite the creature of habit. According to my fellow employees at Diamante's, he arrived at Vito's every evening around five thirty. With the warrant for my arrest heavy on my mind, I wanted Frank's opinion. I couldn't risk relying on my unschooled mind.

It took several visits for me to explain to Frank all that had happened to me since I'd married Michael. Frank preferred drinking shots of tequila and beer when we talked. He didn't refuse when I offered to pay for his drinks. I figured it was cheaper than consulting Mr. Hollingsworth back home. I'd never been much of a beer drinker, never drank tequila, and concentrated on imbibing Coke while we conversed.

As I watched him digesting the facts of my sorry life, it was obvious that Frank had a knack for teaching. He beamed at the sight of me, his pupil, grasping a concept or working out a complex question he'd crafted. His delivery was more like a stage show. He paced the floor of the bar and made wild expressive hand gestures as his loud voice boomed out. Between discussions of my legal problems, he explained the First Amendment, due process, and the Full Faith and Credit Clause. Frank guided me through hundreds of years of monarchs and presidents and their overthrows, through vetoes and voting, through legislative bills and legal blackmail, gerrymandering and jawboning, and through the depths of the Civil Rights Movement in a way that was easy for me to understand. His lessons were articulate and eye-opening, his voice thunderous. However, when I circled back to that nagging question, "So why did they do this to me, Frank?" for the first time Frank had no real answer.

"Jane, it's an imperfect world and an imperfect system," he said sympathetically. "It's the machine. It runs a lot of people through, and now and then good people get screwed."

"But this is my life!"

"I know that but, Jane, it's better than it used to be. Believe me. Not that long ago we had trial by ordeal. Imagine a jury of your peers forcing a newt down your throat. If you swallowed the newt you were innocent, but if you spit the newt out you were guilty and sentenced to death. Do you want that kind of justice? And they didn't have a humane lethal injector or a quick jolt in the electric chair. It was execution by torture. Jane, it could be a lot worse. Maybe you need to find an attorney who will push for you to get what you need. Do you have money?"

"I've saved a few hundred dollars."

Frank chuckled and rolled his eyes at my answer. "I mean do you have anybody in your family that can cough up some serious bucks for a heavy-hitter, an attorney with a reputation for kicking butt in the courtroom?"

"I haven't asked, and nobody's raised their hand to help me. How much are ya talkin' about?"

"Thousands to start."

I shook my head. "No chance," I said. "What are you sayin'? You mean if I was rich, I could get justice?"

"Look, Jane, my practice is small, and at times I thought I'd have to take down my shingle when tough times came along. I thought about working for corporations, but it went against my convictions. I know too well what you're saying, Jane. When I'd go to interviews with major corporations on my way I'd repeat over and over: the rich need justice, too; the rich need justice, too. Being rich gets you justice. It's not fair, I know. But how do you think women do in Iraq or China? You couldn't even drive a car in those countries."

"That doesn't make it right."

I spent months learning about and debating law and politics with Frank. When the reality of my life overwhelmed us both, we'd switch to lighter subjects of common interest: basketball and music. Every time I'd have a little extra time or a day off when the kids were taken care of, I'd head straight to Vito's for a short while before going home and absorb all that Frank had to teach me so that I could be more knowledgeable about my legal puzzle. He taught me the history of our legal system. He spoke of great philosophers from Aristotle to John Locke, but Nietzsche was his favorite.

Frank emphasized how knowledge enlightens and elevates man above all creatures. And the beauty of knowledge, he emphasized, was that it could never be taken away once you possessed it. I was starved for that knowledge. It seemed to offer a way to find a solution to my maddening legal problems. The more I understood the legal system, the more I was haunted by my testimony at Johnny's murder trial. Frank said I must not have made myself clear to the jury, otherwise Michael would've gotten a life sentence. I explained to him, "I was so confused by the questions the attorneys asked, plus I was still in shock from the trauma of the murder, but since then I blame myself not only for Johnny's death but also for Michael's lenient sentence."

Frank looked at me sadly. "The attorney was simply doing his job by confusing you." He added, "Of course, some trial attorneys are venomous and slithery. But if one of those same attorneys is on your side and you win the case, they're heaven sent."

He paused. "Can we get a copy of the transcript?"

Later, I called around and found out that I could, but they were expensive. One set of transcripts would cost me over a thousand dollars until after Michael's appeal was heard. Then the price would drop sharply, but that was months away.

The more Frank unraveled the legal process for me, the more the legal system seemed to me like a sporting event with human sacrifices. Increasingly, we used sports metaphors to illustrate the functions of the legal machine.

"So, if an attorney can convince a judge to suppress condemning evidence from a trial, it's the equivalent of a ten-yard gain in a football game?" I asked.

"Exactly," Frank answered. "And if you're already close to the end zone, it might be just the right play to score a touch-down and win the case."

These simple analogies clarified the process but frightened me. Not only were the courts playing law like it was a game, but my family's safety and future were at stake and I didn't have the money to assemble the game-winning staff of attorneys that Frank had suggested would help me win.

Now I knew that the only way out of our poverty and legal turmoil was for me to get an education. The following spring quarter I enrolled at Raymond Walters College, a small branch of the University of Cincinnati. The challenge and excitement of learning, combined with Frank's tutoring, helped me overcome inferior feelings about my education. In my Appalachian high school, most of my teachers had said it was a waste of money to send women to school because they'd only end up married with babies. Strange, I later realized, since most of them had spouses that worked. Even if I had wanted to be a stay-at-home mom, wouldn't I better serve my children with a well-rounded education instead of hiding behind an apron of ignorance?

I filled out the financial aid papers at the college, sent for my high school transcript, and registered as a matriculated student. An appointment was made for me to see an academic advisor.

"So," gray-haired Dr. Winters began, "you've decided on Raymond Walters. I think you'll like it here, Miss Wells. It's a good place for a second start."

Dr. Winters was a very nice old gentleman. I had heard him talking to other students while I waited for my appointment. He was patient and worked hard to help people make sound decisions about their education. He looked over my files and asked if I knew what field of study I wanted to enter.

"I'm kind of torn because of my family's legal problems. I think I might want to go to law school, but I think I might like teaching, too."

"Well, both are good career choices, and they're both in the liberal arts curriculum, so you're safe taking the same classes until you decide. Have you had much math?"

"No, not really. I had one year of algebra in high school, but that was years ago."

"Where did you go to high school, Miss Wells?"

"Russell High in Russell, Kentucky."

"I've never heard of that school. It's not on the other side of the river, is it?"

"No, sir. It's in the eastern part of Kentucky, but it is on the Ohio River."

"I see. What about science?"

"I love science. I took biology in high school."

"I'll sign you up for Dr. Schultz's class. She's quite a professor. What about your foreign languages? You must have one year of intensive study or two years of classes that are a little slower paced."

"Wow! I have a choice of any language? I'll take English. It's a foreign language to me." I laughed with Dr. Winters, but I doubt he realized how desperate I was not only to gain a decent future for Megan and Erica but to learn. Inside I was dying. I was ashamed of the way I spoke. Some people thought I was stupid because I talked differently and because I knew so little about literature, history, and other subjects. Frank said my speech problem was mostly syntax and phonetic differences, but it was still embarrassing the way strangers reacted to me and made me feel. I worked hard to lose my hill accent, and eventually made progress.

I tried to balance my daily schedule between family, job, and school work. Free time for me was pretty scanty.

I was lucky that the children's bedtime came early and I could study at night. When finals approached, Loren promised to come up that week and help me with the kids, but I didn't plan on it. I figured Billy would throw a fit and make her stay home if he knew she was coming to see me.

Carita was back in school as planned and had decided to move into the dorm. We missed her, but I was proud of her choice to work with disabled children. She had to go, but it did make life harder for us without her help.

My financial aid barely covered my tuition and books, and even though I worked every shift I could, it was difficult to keep the lights on, but I believed the end result would be worth it.

I relished my class work, and listened intently to every word my professors spoke. I worked hard to make good grades. Math was difficult and psychology bored me at first, but I enjoyed biology and especially European history class. We studied the period when the French Impressionists were on the cutting edge of change. Just as today, those times were turbulent, and I was inspired by the people who rebelled to get better conditions.

My legal experiences were pushing me toward rebellion, but not too many around me seemed the least bit bothered by the conditions of the world. When I told some other students about my legal difficulties and explained how I continuously fell through the cracks of almost every social service agency, they didn't seem concerned. I asked them how they would feel if these things happened to them. Many replied, "My boyfriend would never hit me," or "Women should leave in that situation. It's their own fault for staying." None of them blamed men for hitting women.

Their indifference was even more baffling when I spoke of the hardships of my people in the mountains.

"I don't feel sorry for them," some would comment. "They've got cable. They can see how the rest of the world lives." They didn't realize that television hadn't reached many rural areas. Even if people had cable, it was difficult for women to wrestle the channel changers from their two-hundred-pound husbands who faithfully watched the *Dukes of Hazard* or *Championship Wrestling*, or whatever other macho show they wanted. Many of the students had grown up in the safety of middle class suburbia and in the lap of luxury, and had no understanding of poverty.

Frank's recommendation that I find a new attorney led me to look this time for a woman. I had known of Pat Jamison from my first attorney. She was one of the few women practicing law in my home county, and I hoped that she would understand why I wanted to protect my children.

My hardest challenges during these months were keeping my frustrations under control and focusing on my studies. Between working, spending time with the kids, the endless loads of laundry, homework, and fixing meals, free time was practically nonexistent.

But one night I took a break to catch the news and weather and found an interesting show about condors. In Dr. Schultz's biology class, we were learning about the dangers of extinction and how the rain forests were being destroyed and how overpopulation was threatening us all.

As I watched, the show described how the condors had been taken from their natural habitat and held in captivity to protect them from extinction caused by overcrowding and the habitat's destruction. The poor creatures lived in cages, were fed daily, and were kept safe in an unnatural but protected environment. The scientists who were interviewed were extremely proud of their successes. The population had grown to safe numbers and they were ready to take the first set of condors back into the wild.

I watched intently as the scientist took the birds back to a region where they had once thrived, with tall trees, good nesting, and an adequate food supply. The frightened birds shook their feathers and squawked when the gloved scientist pulled them from their cages. Once out, the birds sat helplessly on rocks. Bewildered, the scientist tried to shoo them back into the wild, but the birds couldn't fly. They'd been caged so long they no longer knew how to survive. It reminded me of the welfare system. They only give you enough to survive, not the training or money to break free and become self-sufficient. Here I sat, unable to fly because of the repeated injustices by Michael and then the courts, and it took all the money I could scrape together to keep us going, and even my education was putting us further into debt as we went along. And as desperately as Erica needed counseling, she didn't qualify for a medical card because of her small monthly Social Security check. It was times like these I thought we would never fly again, and remain forever strapped in the cage of poverty.

To my surprise, Loren and her children arrived the weekend before my finals. I was a nervous wreck from not having taken tests in almost eight years, and her arrival gave me a much needed hand. Billy's children were already out of school for the summer and they acted like my children were long lost family.

Loren cooked all our meals and loaded all our kids into her car every day that week taking them to city parks and playgrounds while I studied, caught a few hours of sleep, or took exams. She said the children were no trouble, unlike Billy, who continued to be a problem. He'd call once a day, never saying hello when I answered the phone, but yelling into my ear, "Is my goddamn wife there? Put her on the phone!" Loren said he'd started a fight when she left, but she figured he'd cool off by the time she got home.

As happy as I was to see her, I was afraid of what would happen when she left. Billy made it impossible for Loren to call me from home. He stood guard over the phone and she had to wait until he left the house the next day before she could call and let me know they'd made it safely. I hated the way she and the kids had to live. My deepest wish was that some day she'd leave Billy, as I'd left Michael, but I knew it wouldn't be easy for her. Not only was she poor, but she believed once you married you stuck it out for the kids, and since his abuse was verbal and he'd never laid a hand on her, she stayed.

I had a week off from school between spring and summer quarters. I also took the week off from work at the restaurant. I cleaned house, did laundry, mended clothes, and played with the girls late into the night. I enjoyed my break and tried to put the ugly part of my life out of my mind and enjoy my family. But it was hard to look at the girls and think of the dangers we had ahead of us. No matter how hard I worked, I knew we'd have to continue to struggle to provide for our safety.

I was looking forward to my upcoming class schedule, especially philosophy. This was the first core class that examined the origins of our legal system, and I was anxious to begin. I knew the history of our laws was important, and I knew it was an extraordinary leap from Athens, Greece to a Catlettsburg, Kentucky courtroom but, hey, I had to start somewhere.

My expectations were thwarted a bit when Dr. Barton didn't start class as Frank had with the Greek city-state, and swiftly shifted into contemporary law. But I found Dr. Barton's lectures fascinating, as well as the books he'd chosen for us to read. One was writings by Kant, who Frank had already briefed me on. The other text was by Diana H. Coole, titled *Women in Political Theory*. The title surprised me, but its contents set off a three alarmer in my mind once I started reading.

I was stunned by Dr. Coole's description of the development of the city-state, early Greek mythology, and the origins of misogyny, the study of the hatred of women.

I had to keep a dictionary at hand as I read, looking up every multi-syllable word and rereading its usage carefully. And such words! I'd have gotten run out of town without hopes of catching a man if I'd have used words like those back home. They'd have thought I was an alien creature. But that didn't matter to me anymore. I immersed myself in the readings and realized firsthand how the hatred of women played out in a courtroom. It was no wonder most attorneys and judges viewed women in a negative way if Greek mythology had been the foundation of their educations.

Dr. Coole's review of the dualistic nature of Western philosophy revealed volumes to me. By dividing every possible element of the world into conflicting categories of good/bad and male/female, Western civilization placed women on the wrong side from the start. Women were viewed as the Other, as evil. Then oppression of women became valid, and patriarchy flourished. I was bitterly awakened to why I'd been mistreated at every court appearance. This mind-boggling material was overwhelming, but I knew I'd found the source of what I needed to learn.

Dr. Barton required us to write reaction papers after each reading. The papers I handed in were a jumble of muddled scribbles, unhinged thoughts, and rambling questions. Yet I knew from personal experience the principles I'd read. I wasn't used to writing down what I felt, and the confusion with me sparked by the readings made writing more difficult for me.

After class one day, Dr. Barton stopped to talk as I was pacing the pavement, disturbingly aware of what I was learning in his class. He listened patiently as I spit out my bitterness, telling him all that Michael had done to us and the bad law that had been dished up for us since. The hot July sun was cool compared to my enraged feelings as we sat for hours talking about my past. "Until now," I told him, "I couldn't account for why Michael could kill, beat and steal, and get away with it. And to think that his kid glove treatment was only because of one chromosome. It didn't seem to matter to the courts that children were involved. Michael's deeds were justified because men thought his actions were appropriate, regardless of the loss of Johnny's life or the example he set for the children."

"Go on," Dr. Barton said as I thought out loud, sorting through what I'd learned from men, subconsciously recognizing their power and shunning the lifestyle hill women were expected to conform to.

"I grew up knowing sports," I said. "And I could work on cars and swear with the best of them, but, when puberty hit, I was separated by nature from their world of power, privilege, and justice."

I explained to him how, with my newly acquired knowledge, I was beginning to analyze every aspect of my life. Biology had enlightened me to the difference one chromosome could make.

"My psychology class was equally revealing. Now I understand why men around my area keep women away from education."

"You must have studied Maslow's hierarchy of needs this semester," he said, and I nodded.

I went on, "The basic biological drives for all humans are the needs to be safe and to satisfy the hunger, thirst, and sex drives. Only when these needs are met can we begin to find security in our psychological needs: our esteem needs, to achieve and be competent and acquire a sense of belonging, to have friends and feel loved. At the top of this hierarchy is the need to self-actualize.

"I want to find my own potential," I said. "I want to gain knowledge and do something with it. But the judge in my case didn't consider my needs, not even the most basic ones. When I was living in my car with two small children, the judge thought only of Michael's needs. When the judge was threatening me with arrest for not supplying Michael with pictures of Megan and for failing to read his menacing letters to her, Michael's needs were clearly—and painfully—more important than ours.

"I realize now," I went on, "that this knowledge has been kept out of my reach. None of the court's decisions would have stung or confused me so profoundly if someone had told me from the start that there was justice for all, unless you're a woman or minority."

Dr. Barton nodded. "Or get an education and empower yourself." His brown eyes held mine.

CHAPTER **21**

Learning to Stand

I couldn't wait to get to see Frank and tell him all that I'd learned in my philosophy class. Dr. Barton was the first male feminist I'd met, and I was anxious to get Frank's reaction. He was standing at the end of the bar when I arrived, and I wasted no time spilling out my new found knowledge, strikingly different from the philosophy lessons Frank had given me.

"So what are you going to do, Jane?" Frank asked. "Stake off a piece of land, proclaim yourself sovereign, and declare war against the entire U.S. government? What good is that going to do you? If women had been strong in the first place, they would not have lost power."

"Strong? You mean brute strength?" I shot back. "When was the last time a war was won or a court decision was made by a damn fist fight or rasslin' match? This isn't about justice, Frank. It's about the manipulation of power."

"Yeah, but who in this world wants to give up their power? Do you think men are going to surrender power just to make you happy?"

"No, I don't," I admitted, "but what about the Civil Rights Movement you unfolded to me in this very bar. It was you

who said how unfair it was the way African-Americans were mistreated because of their skin color. Shouldn't that same theory
apply to gender? Are you tellin' me now my situation is okay, that
men can kill and basically get by with murder and still be
considered good fathers?"

"What if a man's kids are hungry," Frank rebutted, "and
he robs a convenience store to buy food and the gun accidentally
goes off? He'd be a good father trying to get food for his kids."

"Yeah, but this is a totally different set of conditions,
Frank, and you know it. You think it's the fault of women that
the system fails them the majority of the time? I think it's
insane!"

"Wait a minute. Why do you think the ERA failed?"
Frank contended. "Women represent more than fifty percent of
the vote. If they'd have stuck together you wouldn't be going
through this. Don't come blowing your steam my way. Women
need to unite and then we'll see what they're made of. And may
the best man win!"

"See what I mean, Frank. It's another damn war over
somethin' that, accordin' to your precious constitution, should
serve all people whether they're made of sugar and spice or shots
and beers! I'd hate to see what your cell tissue looks like!"

"Yeah, well, it worked for Ernest Hemingway," Frank said
confidently as he downed his beer and looked at me. "Look, Jane,
I'm not your enemy."

"I know that, but do ya think I married Michael thinkin',
Ah, he may be a killer, but at least I'll have a husband? No, I
don't think so, Frank. Once I got pregnant the damn system
wouldn't let me out of a violent marriage!"

"Jane, will you calm down. You've got everybody at the
bar looking at you. Listen to me. I understand what's going down
here. Believe me, I want to help you. I just want you to understand the enormous battle that's ahead of you. I'm not sure
you're up to it."

"I'm still breathing. They haven't stopped me yet. Oh,

sure, they've cost me lots of money. It's like they're tryin' to bankrupt me so they'll win by default. They aren't thinking of our best interest. The money I've spent shoulda been for stuff the girls needed. Plus we lost Johnny because they didn't keep Michael in jail."

"I told you, you should file suit against the city for wrongful death," Frank said.

"With what, Frank? They talk those damn big words and act like I'm stupid while they have their way with me in the courtroom. But I'm learning. I may be down, but I ain't out." I paused to catch my breath and put my head in my hands.

"Jane, call your lady attorney tomorrow. We'll go down for a visit and see what she has to say about terminating his parental rights. Meanwhile, get a grip on those language skills. When you get mad and you sound like you just moved in from the hills."

"Oh, I do? And why is that, Frank? They've kept us women ignorant so they can use us and we won't even realize we're gittin' screwed!" I knew Frank was playing devil's advocate most of the time, although his slant on women played havoc with his sense of fairness and my temper. But he wanted to help me and I didn't want to kick my gift horse in the mouth.

Meanwhile, the girls' and my own situation spurred me on. I worked hard at school, taking every class I could to help me get a better understanding of how the legal system functioned, or, as in my case, malfunctioned. My appetite for knowledge grew stronger.

Yet, the more I learned, the more troubled I became. My main reason for being in school was gaining ammunition to battle Michael and to understand the legal system in order to protect my children. If my own legal knowledge didn't work, I thought I could get a better paying job and hire a good attorney who could help me get justice. I pressed on. I had never studied women's history. The only woman I'd learned about in school was Betsy Ross, who dutifully made the American flag for her male patriots. Now I took a course on women who were leaders.

Aside from class work, Andrea, as my professor preferred to be called, was an excellent source of information. She gave her students more than just pages of notes. She taught us how to find our history through the library and took us to the local feminist bookstore, Crazy Ladies, which was filled with titles I'd never heard of or seen. I couldn't get enough information after hearing Andrea's lectures on women's history in the areas of work, marriage, sexuality, and political movements. This, combined with my other classes and research, soon brought me to a frightening discovery: wife-beating had a history all its own.

European common law had greatly influenced our American courts. When women attempted to flee their abusive husbands, or even prosecute if their state allowed it, they were met with the "Rule of Thumb," by which men were authorized by law to beat their wives to keep them in line as long as the flogging instrument used to clobber them with was no thicker than a man's thumb. If women were thought to need beatings to control them, it was not surprising to me that women were viewed as wild beasts, untamed and unsuitable for equal treatment under the law.

Andrea's office door was covered with clippings of announcements for new movies and books and upcoming lectures that involved issues relating to women and children. It became a habit of mine to pass her door between classes. One day I noticed that a Women's International League for Peace and Freedom (WILPF) meeting was being held on the main campus. The topic was worldwide violence against women. I had to skip Andrea's class in order to attend, but there was no way I could miss a lecture on this subject.

The classroom was nearly filled with people who, unlike the other students I'd met earlier, cared about the plight of women. I managed to find a seat down front. The guest speaker told of the violence women were suffering in every corner of the world. She spoke of the millions of women who were missing, tortured, or had been slaughtered. I felt like Erica must have felt that night around the campfire when her friends were telling scary stories, because when the floor was opened for discussion, my arm flashed straight up, almost lifting my body out of my seat. I told those in the room about my legal troubles and beatings as I fought back tears and clenched my fists and revealed my tiny, unjust corner of the world. Fortunately, my vocabulary had grown some, so I didn't jumble my words like I had with Dr. Barton and Frank. I felt better as I released my burdens. It felt good and I was surprised by the people who approached me after I spoke out.

"It's great to hear survivors speak out," one woman said. "I was very impressed by your courage. I'm Kathy Huff, and this is Hana Hejma." Kathy spoke while Hana handed me their business card.

"We're with the local battered women's shelter and we'd like you to come and speak to the women in our shelter," Hana said. "It's empowering and they need to know that there is hope. They can learn from you."

Later that week I met Hana downtown and signed a confidentiality waver, promising that I wouldn't reveal the location of the shelter. Hana gave me the address and the name of a contact person and a number to call.

I met the shelter director and spoke openly about my experiences to the women who were currently in the house. Some of them broke down and cried as I spoke, while others looked away in a daze of denial. It was difficult listening to their stories, but I felt good helping them find ways to work through many of the same problems I'd been burdened with.

Over the next few weeks, I went back to the shelter several times to speak, and when I learned that a position was open, I decided to apply. A week later, I worked my first shift, without a day's training.

It was a nerve wracking experience. With all the barred windows and bolted doors, I couldn't help but reexperience my own shelter stay with Megan and Erica. Usually, the office was very busy, with the phones ringing, people coming and going, and me trying to answer questions that many times had no answers. By the time women came to the shelter, they usually had so many problems that it was difficult to work them out quickly.

When time permitted, I read everything available in the office about domestic violence. My personal experiences and knowledge helped the women through their own crises. I knew how they felt. It was confusing that we had to stay in this prison of a house while the abusers, the real criminals, ran free.

It was frustrating hearing the stories the women told, many so similar to mine. The women had tried to flee their batterers, who'd threaten to leave or to commit suicide or even kill the women or their children if they tried to get away. If women did manage to leave, the violence toward them escalated, and stalking often followed. If the abuser didn't catch up with her physically, he still had the courts to drag her through. He could go to court and swear she was the culprit, making her look like the problem for not conforming to his demands and threaten to take the children, anything it took to wear her down and get her to return to him. It was always a miserable day when a woman would lose her children to an abusive man by way of a biased judge.

Intakes were difficult, but the women and children were finally safe and out of their houses, if only temporarily. When incoming women arrived, I had to get vital information from wives who were sometimes bandaged, bloodied and bruised gruesomely. Sometimes, part way through the interview, they'd think of how enraged their husbands would be because they weren't home, or dinner wasn't cooked. Fearing a more severe beating would be in store, they'd beg me to call them a taxi so they could return home before their husbands noticed them gone. The luckier ones, if you could consider them lucky, wouldn't have a scratch, escaping before their abusers could leave their marks. And the children were heartbreaking. They'd hit their siblings so casually, or even their mothers, calling them names that turned my face red. Most troubling of all were the women who couldn't talk. These were women who were too afraid to speak of how they had been violated, who sat numbly unable to explain their years of abuse, and who were too scared to think of their own needs.

All the intake workers tried to educate the women and help them find options and safety. We described the explanation of the cycle of violence developed by Lenore Walker. There were three basic phases, beginning with the tension building phase. I could explain this graphically from my own experiences. You know it's coming again. You can feel the strain, you know he's about to come unglued. Then comes the second stage, the battering or verbal abuse, usually followed by the final "honeymoon," or loving and contrite stage. This is when they try to kiss and make up and swear it will never happen again. It always happened again. Some of the abusers, if they have the money, buy roses or other nice gifts. Some women said these were the only times their men were intimate with them.

Teaching women the cycle of violence was a way to get some of them talking. They'd understand right away what had happened to them. For some women, the cycle had been spread over months. For others, it occurred three or four times a week. Over time and endless beatings, some men stopped the honeymoon phase altogether. Each story was different, but similar elements were usually present. Rarely did a woman come into our shelter after a first beating. Some thought they were safer staying rather than leaving. I saw it over and over again. It was based on ownership, and if she left, there'd be hell to pay.

We'd do the best we could to help them find safe shelter, but it was usually complicated. Politics and budget cuts to social programs during the Reagan and Bush administrations left most public housing complexes with long waiting lists. When wealthy women came into our shelter, they didn't like the option of living in a housing project. I couldn't blame them. It was like going from the frying pan to the fire. If these women left their abusers, they'd have to live with children in a drug-infested high crime complex. Some of them went back, taking their beatings with the children watching. They could cover up the scars with makeup and still drive the Beamer to the country club for cards with the other women and attend parties with the very men who beat them, convincing themselves they were doing the right thing for their children.

On good days you'd reach someone. Women who'd taken years of abuse and had lost their self-esteem often lacked the confidence to leave. Others were so used to waiting on men they didn't know any other way to live. Some of the older women were married before President Johnson's War on Poverty and the advent of social programs, which at least gave them options if they needed to flee with children. They hadn't had the option of leaving abusive homes with children and getting some help surviving until they could get on their feet. These women had few alternatives and were eventually beaten down until their strength and their wills were pounded out of them.

Once, while working the early morning shift, I walked into the dining room of the shelter to see a woman who had just learned her husband was being held in jail with a $10,000 cash bond for biting five chunks of flesh out of her body. She was crying. "You're safe here," I assured her.

"No, that's not it. I'm just so worried about my husband," she said tearfully. "He smokes cigarettes. I know he's stuck behind bars with no money. I need to send him a money order so he can buy some cigarettes."

"Look, he just bit you like an animal!" I said. "If I bite you, will you buy me a pack?" I froze after saying it. She stared up at me, and I'm still not sure which one of us was more shocked by what I'd said.

Later that day I was called to the office and nearly lost my job. I deserved the rebuke. But, a few days later, the woman knocked on the office door and thanked me for waking her up. I knew that wouldn't have worked on most women, and I wouldn't support that kind of treatment as a general rule, but that day my intuition was right. She got out of the relationship, joined a therapy group, got a job, and moved into her own place.

The bad days were many. I often spent sleepless nights after a shift of terrified hotline callers. Sometimes women called speaking in whispers because their abusers were in the next room. I'd try to help them, give them emergency numbers, help them make a getaway plan, and then I'd hear a scream and a struggle, the whacks and thuds, a beg for him to stop the hitting, and then the phone would be hung up or yanked from the wall.

One night I almost landed in jail after a former resident called our hotline. She had gone back to her husband believing he was going to change, but he hadn't. She told me her husband had threatened her and wouldn't let her leave in her car. She had small children and was afraid to walk out in the cold night and afraid to stay in her home. While she talked, I pulled her file. I read the history of her husband's violent past and paid close attention to what was happening on the other end of the line.

She wanted to know what to do. I asked her a few questions. Did he have weapons? She wasn't sure where the guns were. Did she think he was going to hurt her or the children? Yes. Were there neighbors at home? Yes. Were they afraid of him? Yes. Did she want me to call the police? Yes.

Throughout the conversation she kept referring to me as her therapist. He had insisted that she was crazy and needed help, and he said he didn't mind if she called her therapist, as long as she didn't call the police.

I could hear him screaming and swearing at her, her children crying while objects smashed and broke. She asked me to hurry and make the call. I grabbed the other phone, putting it to my other ear, and dialed 911, then kept both receivers to my mouth so she could hear what I said and know help was on the way.

I explained to the 911 operator that a woman and her children were being held hostage and gave her the address. She asked for the woman's phone number so they could make contact and try to negotiate before the police arrived, which meant I had to hang up and wait by the hotline while everything unfolded.

I paced the floor and waited. The hotline rang. It was a new emergency. I had begun another phone conversation when the other phone rang. I put the caller on hold and answered it. It was an officer from the local police department.

"Is this Jane Wells?"

"Yes, sir, it is."

"I ought to come down there and arrest you for wasting our time and inciting a riot," the officer screamed at me through the receiver. "I got a report of a hostage situation. I called out a SWAT team and several valuable cruisers only to find it was only a domestic dispute. What the hell do you think you're doing? You violated the First Amendment by nearly inciting a riot and I should hold you responsible!"

"But, Officer, he was holding her hostage against her will!"

"But it was her husband!"

"How stupid of me," I said. "It was only his wife and children that he could have killed. What was I thinking?" Too bad they didn't respond to all of the domestic violence calls that way, I thought, trying to shake off the officer's threat to arrest me. If anyone should've been held responsible, it should have been the abuser, the jerk who repeatedly beat his wife and made it necessary for the police to respond.

None of the daily events of the shelter had anything to do with right or wrong or who inflicted pain or harm. It all came down to power and perspective, and since many thought wife-beating was acceptable, often times we were helpless.

More sickening were the many times that we had to turn women and children away because we didn't have any room for them. Sometimes our waiting list had as many as twenty-five women and children, sometimes more, who were doing all they could to stay safe. This ugliness bore deep into my spirit. I wanted to find a way to help.

As my court date was nearing, I began to hunt through law libraries to investigate the legal treatment of children, thinking that surely there was a clause that could save children from the nightmares of an abusive home.

I crossed the Ohio River and visited the Northern Kentucky Law Library. I had to dig deep since some of the laws applying to children hadn't been changed since the 1920s. And the laws I found horrified me. In Kentucky, in case law, the child's best interest was not even considered, only the father's. Even if the father was abusing the child, physically or sexually, the courts would not terminate his parental rights. Clearly, the child was his property to handle however he wanted.

Termination of parental rights was still possible, but the terms were vague, and much was left to a judge's discretion. If the father abandoned or neglected the child, defined as failure to feed, clothe or shelter, or failed to pay support for one year, action could be taken if the judge deemed it necessary. To me, judicial discretion was a phrase that represented a gamble similar to the roll of the dice or the horse races.

I contacted the shelter in northern Kentucky and became friends with Bonnie Flaherty, a psychologist and women's rights activist, who helped me collect various pieces of Kentucky law. We had lunch and discussed our war stories. She was very knowledgeable about the conditions women faced in Kentucky and the laws that were on the books. After I explained my own legal nightmare, she gave me the number of a state advocate. Bonnie even offered to attend court hearings with me. I appreciated her kind offer. It would be nice to have someone who understood beside me. But I turned her down. I didn't want a counselor going with me to my upcoming court appearance. This time I was going to stand alone.

CHAPTER 22

One Step Forward, One Step Back

Michael's word had been all that it took to get the judge to issue the warrant for my arrest. Luckily, Dad had sent the pictures to Michael certified mail. Otherwise, I wouldn't have been able to prove my innocence. On February 15 my new attorney, Pat Jamison, had the warrant for my arrest set aside. It was really a small victory. However, it took more than my word to be vindicated in all areas. With the warrant cleared from my record, we were ready to attempt the termination of Michael's parental rights.

Frank and I made the three-hour trip to meet with Pat before she filed the motion. Pat was glad to have Frank helping us plan a strategy, but he wasn't licensed to practice law in Kentucky, so he couldn't appear with us in court.

We knew going into the case that there would be a clash of powers. Fortunately, Judge Chin was assigned to hear our case. I didn't know what to expect from him. I was just glad we didn't have to appear before Judge Morgan who had told Mr. Hollingsworth over lunch that his inclinations weren't in our favor. At least we stood a chance with Judge Chin.

Termination of parental rights was a puzzling process.

The hearings were closed to the public and the findings were not considered public record. If termination was approved, the name of the parent whose rights had been taken away was permanently removed from the child's birth certificate. The child was given a new name, and all the previous records were destroyed. To me, the replacement birth certificate was a legally falsified document, but one that I was glad existed. If we were successful, Megan would not have to know the truth about her father until she was older and better able to understand, and Erica and I wouldn't have to be confronted by Johnny's killer and my batterer.

In May, Pat motioned the court of our plans to try to terminate Michael's parental rights. In the petition, Pat listed our grounds for seeking termination:

> The Respondent, Jerry Michael Haney, is presently serving time for the slaying of the Petitioner's former husband, John Eidson, and will not be eligible for release for at least four more years.
>
> That the Respondent showed complete disregard for the safety and welfare of the minor child who was present in the house when the slaying occurred.
>
> That the infant, Megan Renae Haney, has not seen her father since the slaying.
>
> That, in addition to the foregoing, the Respondent, due to his present situation, has paid nothing for the support of his daughter since entering prison.
>
> That said minor child does not know the Respondent, Jerry Michael Haney, and it would be in the best interest of the child for the said Respondent's rights to be terminated.
>
> That at the present time the infant resides with her mother and her half-sister, Erica, and to allow the Respondent to maintain contact with the minor child would totally disrupt the relationship she presently shares with the only family she has ever known.

A guardian-ad-litem attorney for Megan and an attorney for Michael were appointed next. Michael immediately filed an Affidavit of Indigency stating that he was imprisoned and penniless, meaning I had to pay everything. The court costs, Megan's attorney fees, Michael's attorney fees, my attorney fees, my trips to court, countless long-distance phone calls to prepare for the hearing, all would have to be paid by me. The sick irony of it all was that we were getting by on my waitressing income, student loan money, and Erica's Social Security. Nevertheless, the judge ordered me to use Johnny's death benefits to pay for Michael's court expenses. It was to me another example of punishing the victim instead of the perpetrator.

After Pat filed the petition, the legal slugfest began. Most of the early filings and hearings didn't require me or Michael to be present, so my mailbox was the source of my knowledge about the court happenings.

Our petition had given me hope. I liked that it was brief and to the point and specified why Michael's rights should be terminated. Aside from the disturbing facts that were always difficult to read, I'd never called the girls "half-sisters." I'd correct strangers on the street who'd question Megan and Erica's blood relationship because of their different looks and coloring. Megan had hair that was straight and dark like mine, with matching brown eyes, while Erica still had her baby blond hair. Her gold locks and blue eyes often raised the curiosity of rude strangers.

The next step for us was to interview with Mr. Bauman, the attorney appointed to represent Megan. He seemed like a sincere person. He had children of his own, and he shuddered when I explained our legal torment. We spent an hour in his office talking while Megan and Erica played with books and crayons on the coffee table behind me.

Mr. Bauman watched them play as I explained how Michael would bring more misery if he was allowed to reenter our home and Megan's life. After he talked to Megan privately, Mr. Bauman agreed that termination was in her best interest, and filed his findings with the court.

Meanwhile, Michael hadn't gotten his court-appointed attorney yet, but he had received our petition for termination.

Possibly using the help of what Frank referred to as the "jail-house attorneys," lifers who read the law to pass time, Michael quickly fired off a motion for Modification of Visitation to the judge through the mail. The contents, which would have made a humorous travesty of the law in a sitcom, were in reality a tragedy for those like my children and I who were forced to live with the comic portrayal of a "perfect loving father," who, in his own words, was a model citizen completing many educational programs from the jail where he was incarcerated for killing his stepdaughter's father in cold blood while she watched. He characterized me as a harassing parent who refused to effect their relationship.

Reading it, I didn't know whether to laugh or cry:

> Comes now the Petitioner, Jerry Michael Haney, *pro se*, and requests this Honorable Court to modify its judgment. As grounds for this request Petitioner states the following:
> At the time of Petitioner's divorce proceedings his daughter was just a matter of months old, and she is now three years of age.
> The Court stated in its findings that it felt, due to the young tender age of Petitioner's daughter, taking her to an institution was not advisable at this time.
> Petitioner has not seen his daughter since she was six months of age, nor has he spoken with his daughter since the incarceration.
> The Court stated in its judgment, Paragraph (2), "The Respondent shall have contact with his infant daughter by correspondence and telephone. The Petitioner shall furnish the Respondent current photographs during the period of his incarceration. The Court feels there will be complaints that this is not being done and will take a dim view of any reasons that are not supported by facts. Failure to abide by this order will cause the Court to invoke its contempt powers. Personal visitation is reserved by the Court."

Michael's ridiculous assertions went on and on as he tried to prove he was a good citizen and had a caring family who would back him up:

Petitioner would like to point out to the Court that both his mother and brother are very trustworthy, and very respected in their community. His mother is a member of her church, and she owns her own home in which she resides. Petitioner's brother has been employed for fifteen (15) years and owns his home in which he resides.

Since Petitioner's incarceration, he has maintained an outstanding institution record he has completed many educational programs, he is presently enrolled in an eighteen (18) month college course in which he is majoring in Business Communication and Drug Counseling, further, he is assigned as a teacher's aide here at the institution (see attached progress/job report).

Petitioner wants very much to begin a relationship with his daughter, he cares very deeply for her and he feels that any further delay might cause mixed emotions and a state of confusion upon his daughter. Petitioner has no way of knowing or understanding the Respondent's motives for not wanting his daughter to have and know the joyment (sic) of having a father, he does realize that this behavior on Respondent's behalf is in the future going to hurt his daughter. Again, Petitioner does not understand how Respondent could in a reasonable state of mind wish to impose such pain and suffering upon her own daughter just to hurt and prevent Petitioner from seeing her. It would appear that the Respondent, as a warm loving mother, would want her daughter to seek and know the care and love of her father.

This Court in its judgment reserved the right to grant visitation Petitioner feels that the requested action herein this motion should be granted at this time. Further, Petitioner hereby gives the Court permission, and urges it to review his institutional record, as well as the background of his mother and brother as to sustain their reliability as to their roles herein this motion.

As I read Michael's attempt to make me look like an unfit, villainous mother, I knew his retaliation had nothing to do with his love for Megan. It was filled with his hate for me. I was disgusted by the way he tried to make me look bad after he had killed Johnny in cold blood and left us to live a pathetic life.

While Michael was safe, well fed, comfortable and warm in his jail cell, with free medical and dental care and a free education, we had been living in the car and didn't have money to have portraits of Megan made, let alone buy stamps to mail them. He grumbled that the pictures I'd sent him were fuzzy while we struggled to survive.

Michael reminded the judge of his previous dim view warning. Michael asked that another warrant be issued, even after he had the court-ordered pictures of Megan in his possession. Where would I get an expensive camera? I hardly had pictures of Megan's early years, a sad reminder of our impoverished lifestyle. If Michael had succeeded in his efforts to have me thrown in jail based on his hatred for me rather than fact, where would Megan have ended up? But Megan wasn't his concern. Getting back at me mattered most to him, not how his daughter might be passed around in foster care or orphanages.

I knew how Michael's mind worked when it came to destroying our lives. He was quite successful. I knew that his actions were just another form of abuse. Even from jail he controlled and drained our lives of hope and money. How could I expect this to change once he was released from jail? Did the courts really think that his serving time for killing Johnny was going to change the way he mistreated me and the girls?

Michael's threats seemed even more demented when he said he didn't understand my motives for not wanting him to have a relationship with his daughter, insinuating that I couldn't be in a "reasonable state of mind" and that I was "imposing pain and suffering" on Megan, and "a warm, loving mother should want her daughter to know the love and care of her father." A decent father but not a cold-blooded killer, I thought. Children don't need the abusive rearing Michael had given them in the name of love.

Pat called me at home that night, angry at the waste of time and expense Michael was imposing on us both. She read me the highlights of the response she would be filing the following day in order to rebut Michael's contention:

> The Respondent is *not* imposing pain and suffering on her three-and-a-half-year-old daughter, but rather is thinking of what is best for her daughter. The infant is being raised with her half-sister Erica and shares a loving relationship with that sister. Confusion, pain and suffering would be imposed on her if she is aken to the Petitioner at a Correctional Facility at her tender age and is confronted on a continual basis by the man incarcerated for killing her half-sister's father.

The fear and frustration during the pretrial nonsense pierced every sense of safety and security I had been painstakingly building. I had tried in vain to protect us when Michael had battered me, and now it seemed that my every attempt to stop him through legal means was fruitless.

Court-appointed attorneys were selected from a pool that came up in regular rotation. As my luck would have it, Michael's new attorney, Mr. Ira Gotler, was recently divorced and his wife had moved away with their child. His emotional loss must have fueled his efforts to fight for Michael's rights. He helped Michael win the right to appear at the hearing, another trip out of prison at the state's expense.

Frank explained that this was really a plus for us, in spite of how much I dreaded looking at Michael. He said if the court didn't let Michael face his accusers, he could bring us back to court after his release and say that his rights had been violated and the entire case would have to be heard again.

After his first success, Mr. Gotler decided to try again. He filed another motion to dismiss, denying several of our allegations, and claimed we had no legitimate grounds to terminate Michael's parental rights. Strangely, they added that Michael wasn't guilty of murder, that he had shot Johnny, but was only sentenced to manslaughter.

Immediately, he filed another motion to redocket their request for modification of visitation. Pat was furious that we hadn't had time to respond to their first motion. Her response to dismiss was stronger than her initial response.

The judge overruled Michael's attempt to stop our case and a date was set for the termination hearing. Pat reminded me that this would only be a preliminary hearing, to prove that we had grounds for termination. If Judge Chin agreed, a court date for a full trial would then be set and, hopefully, an end to Michael's abuse would come.

CHAPTER 23

Face to Face

T he day of the termination hearing I was scared just knowing Michael was out of jail and in the same building. Win or lose, I dreaded having to face him. Most of all, I was worried he'd find a way to get loose and hurt me.

Pat Jamison had agreed to meet me at her office, ten miles from the courthouse. She thought it would be a good opportunity to discuss last minute legal plans. Despite my earlier plan of standing alone, I felt safer having my lawyer walk into the courthouse with me. As we drove, we talked strategy and rebuttals, and reviewed Michael's criminal past. Our conversation lifted my hopes that we could win the case, but when I saw the courthouse my high hopes collapsed as I recalled the decisions made there in Michael's favor in the past. I had never had a positive verdict in this building, and I wondered if today could possibly be different.

We stepped from Pat's car and walked slowly toward the courthouse. I was distracted by the tree-covered hills behind the building. The Catlettsburg Cemetery was less than a mile away, just behind the trees. I couldn't help the tears which rose to my eyes, knowing that Johnny's grave was up there. I thought of Johnny's shortened life, of his funeral, and of his tombstone with "Johnny" engraved on it as Pat opened the heavy wooden doors of the courthouse.

Following Pat down the long hall, I thought back to the first time Erica and I visited Johnny's grave. I'd waited until the grass had grown over the dirt pile before I took her. I didn't want her to see the clods of earth heaped in front of her father's marker. I wished I could be near him now, by his grave, but I had the court hearing to attend. I could only think of our misery. Wasn't it enough that we had lost Johnny, and in such a terrifying way? Why did we have to continue to relive not only his death but be confronted by the man who killed him?

As Pat and I walked on the tiled floor our heels clicked out an edgy, unsteady rhythm. The gray walls were lined with dark wooden benches with knee-high ashtrays stationed at each end. We passed the clerk's office and the men and women waiting for their turn at justice. For a moment or two I stared at them. Some paced the floor. Others waited on the benches. But all of them had looks of doubt stamped on their faces.

When we came to the entrance to the courtroom where our case was scheduled to be heard, I peeked through the window of the double doors. I didn't see Michael.

"Jane, have a seat and try to relax," Pat said. "They'll call us when they're ready. Michael's probably being held in the back. They won't bring him in until the judge is ready to come in."

We sat on a bench outside the courtroom doors and waited to be called. I was more jittery than ever knowing Michael was somewhere in the building and unsure where he was and even more uncertain of what Judge Chin would decide.

I jumped to attention when the bailiff threw back the doors and motioned Pat and me to enter. Beads of perspiration dotted my forehead as we walked toward the table. Michael and his attorney were already seated in front of us. I'd decided before I got there not to look at Michael. I didn't want to give him the opportunity to look me in the eye and try to intimidate me as he had in the past. Nevertheless, I couldn't help but glance his way to see what he looked like now. Had prison changed him? No. Nothing about him seemed different. His face was smug and confident, his appearance was calm. I'd hated his cocksure manner after all the pain he put us through, even more after he'd killed Johnny.

I moved my head in the other direction when his eyes fixed on mine, but not before he could give me one of his squinting, hate-filled looks. The same hate that used to scare me into silence and submission when we were married. It was a look that had always meant his next move would be cruel and violent. As if any minute he could stuff his hand down my throat and pull my heart out without a second thought. Even though I knew police and the law surrounded him, I felt afraid.

I followed Pat to the long table adjacent to the one where Michael sat with his attorney, Mr. Gotler. After I was seated, I leaned over and asked, "Pat, why isn't Michael in handcuffs and ankle chains?"

"It isn't allowed," she whispered back, "because it might appear to prejudice the judge."

To my left, the court reporter was organizing papers as the bailiff walked across the room, stood at attention, and called, "All rise!"

I watched Judge Chin stride by the United States and Kentucky flags and ascend to his bench, where a carved eagle sat on a shelf behind him. Michael was visible out of the corner of my eye.

The judge read our names and introduced our respective attorneys. His voice was calm, almost soft, barely audible. He cleared his throat, shuffled his files into a neat pile, and laid them precisely in front of him.

"We're here on a motion to dismiss?" Judge Chin asked, looking at Mr. Gotler.

"Yes, Your Honor," Mr. Gotler said.

"All right, Mr. Gotler. Do you want to state what your position is with regard to the motion to dismiss?"

"Yes, Your Honor," Mr. Gotler said as he rested one hand in his pocket and fiddled with a pencil with the other. "The motion to dismiss would be, basically, if the court will look at the pleading filed by the petitioner, it would note that the first six allegations are nothing but the normal information set forth with no allegations of wrongdoing by my client. In paragraph seven, it says that my client is serving time. Well, we will agree that my client is serving time and our only exception to that would be as to the slaying, no, excuse me, he would not be eligible for release for four more years. Our evidence we would produce would show that that would be much sooner."

Listening, my heart pounded harder against my chest. I felt hot blood rise to my face at the mention of Michael's eligibility for early release.

"In the divorce decree between the parties," Mr. Gotler continued, "it was ordered that my client was to have no visitation or pay no support. Now, I want to bring up Kentucky law, in *Wright v. Howard*, and that would be cited as seven-one-one-SW-second. I have copies for everyone."

"All right, let's see what you have," Judge Chin said as Mr. Gotler handed copies to him and to Pat.

"In that particular case, Your Honor," Mr. Gotler said as he flipped to the page, "the only differentiation in this case is agreed we did not have an individual who is charged with a crime."

Minor difference, I thought, as Mr. Gotler continued.

"But nonetheless, he did not see his child and had paid no support. The court in its ultimate finding held that where a Court Order or where the decree specified no visitation and likewise where there was no support, that this completely negated any finding of abandonment, desertion or neglect and those would be the grounds upon which they would be asking for my client's parental rights to be terminated. Now, going further on the complaint, the allegation in paragraph nine, that he has not seen the child, again, that is per Court Order. Has the Court seen a copy of the decree of the parties?"

"Ah, no, I don't believe I have," Judge Chin answered. Pat nudged me slightly when I rolled my eyes at the judge's admission. I thought it strange that this judge was making such a critical, possibly life-threatening, decision about my family, and he hadn't read the history of the case!

"The Court will note that in the very beginning of the second paragraph, the Honorable Judge Morgan sets forth that my client was incarcerated in a Kentucky state penal institution, has very little income, and therefore would not set child support at this time. He mentions money to be paid through Aid to Families with Dependent Children during the period of incarceration."

"I see," Judge Chin answered. I had to fight my urge to jump up and tell them we weren't eligible for welfare, that you had to qualify, and a judge's order meant nothing to that branch of the system.

"Now, in this judgment, he specifies there would be no visitation during this time period due to the age of the child. Our position is that because of this order, we cannot find abandonment, neglect, or abuse at this time. And to no support, that is likewise our position. Judge Morgan did not say that my client will never be able to pay child support, but he said at this time there is no support obligation."

Gotler went on and on. He told the judge that I had once terminated Johnny's rights and suggested I did it because Johnny'd sexually abused Erica, which was nonsense. I had done it because he hadn't been able to support us, and I needed welfare. It was something that I had grieved over since. I'd hoped that Johnny could be more responsible, put his artistic needs aside, and become a breadwinner. As I grew older, I began to realize how unrealistic that was for him. In college I'd read many stories of artists and thinkers, from Aristotle to van Gogh. Some lived tragic lives, while the lucky ones were appreciated and nurtured by their community. But that had never happened to Johnny. While he was a compassionate and fiery creative person, Johnny never managed to find the means to be a financial success. And these factors, in a courtroom where social position is valued above all else, made Johnny look like a worthless bum.

Johnny had never sexually abused us, and what angered me more was that Johnny was not even here to defend himself! Pat squeezed my forearm to try to settle me. Frank had warned me that Michael's side might try something like this: throw out blatantly false statements to try to anger me so I would lose my composure and yell out. They would use that against me, Frank had said, to suggest I was the parent out of control. I tapped my foot quietly on the floor, attempting to release some of my hostile energy as Mr. Gotler went on and on.

"Now, in her response," Mr. Gotler went on some more, "there have been other allegations that were set forth such as the letter that Michael has written to his daughter. I myself am divorced and wrote a poem to my one-year-old girl on her first birthday. Now, obviously she could not have read that, but later on maybe that will mean something to her. The fact that my client continuously tells his daughter that he loves her is the only way of showing his little girl that. Although his daughter didn't hear from him because Ms. Wells wouldn't let him.

"We feel that the petitioner, Your Honor, has simply failed to set forth any grounds to terminate Mr. Haney's parental rights."

"All right, Mrs. Jamison," Judge Chin said as he turned to look at us. "What do you say?"

I didn't have a chance to whisper to Pat the lies we needed to correct. But I didn't need to. She knew the case. Pat stood straight up, laid her notes in front of her, and began.

"First of all, Your Honor, there are numerous statements made by Mr. Gotler that we would take exception to. Going through the petition, we understand that it is Kentucky law that incarceration is not sufficient to terminate parental rights and that is why that is not our only allegation for termination.

"The reason Mr. Eidson's rights were terminated was because of non-support and that is the only reason. There was never any mention of sexual abuse, because that did not occur. In fact, the abuse that occurred was at Mr. Haney's hands. He has continuously abused the petitioner in front of her children, in front of his own daughter! At the time the shooting occurred, Mr. Haney came into Ms. Wells's house and killed Mr. Eidson in front of Erica and Megan!"

It was my turn to calm Pat down. She was so angry she was stamping her feet. I was afraid any minute she was going to scream and Judge Chin would find her in contempt of court. I understood her frustration with this case, but then I saw she was creating a mood of righteous indignation at that moment and would not go over the line. Pat glanced down at her notes, patted my shoulder and paused to let her words sink in. Then she continued.

"As far as Megan being fed poison, there is no proof whatsoever that Ms. Wells has not read the notes to her daughter. She has in fact read them to her daughter. But Ms. Wells has known Mr. Haney for a very long time and from reading these letters and cards she sees threats. There was no poison fed to her daughter.

"As for the phone calls that my client would have to pay for, she receives no support from Mr. Haney and she does not qualify for Aid to Families and Dependent Children. She provides for her children on her own, without welfare, and it would be extremely difficult for her to pay for long distance so that Mr. Haney can talk to his daughter.

"It is our position," Pat continued, "based on the report of the guardian-ad-litem and based on the petition, where there will be proof provided that there has been continuous abuse in the past, that at the time the crime was committed for which Mr. Haney is currently incarcerated Mr. Haney was under a restraining order from the District Court not to come around Ms. Wells or the children, and he did in fact violate that! He has violated numerous orders of the court and continued to come around her when he has threatened to kill her and was told to stay away. Unless his rights are terminated, this abuse will likely continue.

We would ask that the Court overrule the motion to dismiss and set it for a full hearing on the merits so that both parties would have the opportunity to present the evidence. We believe that we can show by clear and convincing evidence that Mr. Haney's parental rights should be terminated. That is all, Your Honor." Pat folded her notes while Judge Chin turned and asked Mr. Bauman, Megan's guardian-ad-litem, who I hadn't noticed sitting in the back of us, if he had anything to add.

"At this time, Your Honor, I have nothing to add further to either one of them," Mr. Bauman responded.

"Can I respond, Your Honor?" Mr. Gotler asked Judge Chin. "Yes."

"Your Honor, the allegations involved only Mr. Haney and the petitioner. There has been nothing said that Mr. Haney ever abused the child, even they don't allege that."

Pat quickly rose from her chair.

"Your Honor, we are not saying that Mr. Haney beat his child, but I would submit that there has been abuse occurring if he is beating the child's mother in front of the child."

"Your Honor," Mr. Gotler pleaded, "I would point out that the daughter was six months old the last time my client saw his daughter when the incident which placed my client in the penal institution occurred. Six months old. Now, unless Megan Haney is being told over and over and over again that this happened, I hardly believe that she's going to have a vivid recollection of any type of alleged abuse."

Judge Chin nodded in agreement with Mr. Gotler and turned to Pat.

"Anything to say to that?" he asked.

"Your Honor, Megan may or may not have any recollection," Pat answered. "The six-year-old child whose father was killed in front of her and who has also witnessed the beatings must also be considered. You can't very well gag a child. This is something this little girl lives with every day. Erica will carry this trauma with her all her life."

Judge Chin seemed to be thinking for just a second. He rolled his chair from side to side as if he was deciding who to side with. Finally he scratched his chin and said, "Six months of age: she's not going to be seeing a whole lot."

"NO!" Pat said as she stamped her foot. "The six-year-old, Erica."

"You're not trying to terminate the parental rights of the six-year-old," Judge Chin remarked.

"No," Pat persisted, "but we're talking about the fact that they have a relationship. They are sisters. Megan's only family has been her mother and her sister."

"There's got to be neglect, abuse, or abandonment," Judge Chin said.

"Now, the problem with her argument, Your Honor," Mr. Gotler said without waiting to be recognized, "is you've got to draw the line somewhere. All a person has to do is allege that one of my relatives was abused and then the relatives get together and they talk to each other and this would create a problem.

"Our position all along has been that my client has done nothing but try to establish a relationship with his daughter. If the Court wants to place a restraining order that he can never go around Ms. Wells, that's fine. All we ask is that he be allowed to continue the court-ordered contact, and that is to include phone calls, and he can write letters and she in good faith reads them, like Mrs. Jamison says she does, and not poison the girl so that when he has a chance to see her, they can be father and daughter."

"What other proof've you got?" Judge Chin asked Pat.

"Pardon me?" Pat's face reddened

"What other proof do you have?" Judge Chin said, correcting his grammar.

"We will have the testimony of the six-year-old," Pat said confidently. "We would submit that the actions of Mr. Haney, to the petitioner and Mr. Eidson in front of the six-year-old, are going to have an effect and have effected and are abusive to her sister. Although he is not physically abusing his daughter, everything he has done in the past has caused her mental abuse."

"Well, I can't buy that argument," Judge Chin said. "That's like saying you can have a nine-year-old tell her sister, and the mother can tell the daughter that the father's bad and because they tell the child that her father's bad we should terminate his parental rights? I have a tough time buying that argument. What other proof do you have?"

"We have hospital records where he has abused the petitioner while she had the baby in her arms," Pat answered, knowing she was about to get her last try. "We have the other two District Court petitions where he threatened to kill her with the children there. He told her that if she took the children and left, he would find her and kill her. We would ask the Court for an independent medical examination of Mr. Haney."

"Your Honor, we object to that," Mr. Gotler said, not objecting to the abuse but to the medical exam.

"He has continued to show violent behavior in the past," Pat persisted, growing increasingly impatient with the lack of understanding on the bench. "Up until his incarceration it was nonstop. The entire time his daughter has been alive he has shown abusive and violent behavior! We do not believe that this will stop when he gets out. We want a medical exam done and that evidence to be submitted to the Court!"

I could tell by the questioning look on Judge Chin's face that Pat might have been bringing him around. His jaw moved from side to side.

"Well," Judge Chin stated, "what you're attempting to show is that he will in the future be violent and abusive. You don't actually have proof that he was violent or abusive to the child herself. I think it's got to be something that's already happened, that's got to add up to abandonment in the past tense, neglect in the past tense, or abuse in the past tense. I don't think it can be what's going to happen in the future."

"There is nothing to say that this has not continued since

Ms. Wells was pregnant with his child until he was incarcerated," Pat argued. "He continued to abuse her in front of the child and that is abuse to the child."

"Then keep my client away from Ms. Wells," Mr. Gotler suggested, forgetting that we had tried that suggestion before the murder. Did he think Megan was going to drive herself to the destination of visitation? I'd be a sitting duck for Michael.

"A child under six months can't possibly have been affected by that," Judge Chin remarked, somehow leaping from his expertise as a judge to being a psychologist.

"They have stated that incarceration alone does not constitute abandonment," Pat said, realizing she was failing on Erica's behalf. "The record will also show that prior to being incarcerated, during the first six months of his daughter's life, he did not support the child in any way when he was in a position to do so."

A mental picture of a calendar appeared in my head as I tried to calculate again the days when I'd left the shelter to the day of the murder. It was fast thinking for Pat, a last ditch effort, but I knew that we would fall days short of that proof. It was true that once we entered the shelter, when Megan was only a few weeks old, Michael had never paid a penny while he was working, but that fact wouldn't help.

"Your Honor, he didn't have to support," Mr. Gotler claimed. "There is a court order stating that there is no child support."

"Yes, but prior to being incarcerated, he had an obligation to support his child," Judge Chin countered.

"I would beg to differ where the Court has said there is no child support that legally there is no child support," Mr. Gotler contended.

"There's no place where the Court has said there was no child support from the time the child was born until his incarceration," Judge Chin snapped. "He did have an obligation to support the child and he was in a position to do so, and he did not."

The arguments went back and forth as to whether Michael had a duty to support his child before being jailed. I wondered how in the world there could be a question as to his obligation as a father. Was this the justice I had been brought up to believe in?

Finally, Judge Chin decided. "I'm not going to go on failure to properly plead and set the case on the merits, if there are any merits. I don't know whether six months of failure to pay child support and nine months of failure to support a mother during pregnancy is sufficient to constitute neglect or not. If you put that with the other factors of incarceration, a pattern of abuse, physical abuse may be sufficient to overrule the motion to dismiss. When do you want to have a hearing?"

Simultaneously, Pat and I released our held breath. A date was agreed upon, and Pat shoved her paperwork into her brief-case, flashed me an off-the-record grin and said, "Let's get out of here!"

We hurried out of the courtroom, not even looking at Michael being escorted out, and raced for Pat's car.

"How can I stand the crazy remarks they made about me, about Johnny?" I asked her once we were safely inside.

"It's not a perfect system," she said sadly.

"It's not a fair system," I said definitively.

As we drove to her office, we spoke of the difficulties ahead.

"Jane, I don't think we can prove he didn't support you during your pregnancy. And we know we're a few weeks short after Megan's birth."

"I know, Pat. I know you were trying to make the point that he abused me during the pregnancy, but that doesn't count. If they think Megan wasn't injured by what happened when she was six months old, they sure ain't gonna believe she was injured in the womb."

After Pat dropped me at my car, I felt light headed. The tension from watching that impaired brand of justice unfold got to me. My adrenaline rush from the judge's fast turnabout was wearing off, and my head was spinning. I wasn't sure if I could make it to Cincinnati without a rest. It was still early and the girls were safe at day care. I decided to stop in and see Mom and Dad before I drove back.

I needed to rest, but I also needed to vent everything that had just happened.

Dad was on the porch swing when I pulled up at the curb, but not before scraping the whitewalls on my tires. I could see Dad wince.

Mom must have heard me pull in because by the time I sat down in the high-back rocking chair on the porch, she was handing me a cup of coffee.

I blurted out my day in court. Mom said she couldn't believe they'd let that son of a bitch visit her grandbaby after all he'd done to us. But Dad knew better.

"Janie, honey, when are ya gonna learn that ya can't fight city folk?" Dad asked. "These attorneys and judges are like kinfolk. They got their own laws and that's just how it is."

"No, Dad, I think they make some of 'em up as they go along. This is insane! You can't do what Michael's done and still be considered a fit father. It doesn't make sense!"

"But that's the law. And when that gavel comes down, it's written in stone and there's nothin' you can do about it."

I sat and listened to his sermon as I rocked the chair harder and faster on the porch. I'm sure their neighbors several houses down could hear the creaking boards and the rolling of the rocker blades.

"But Dad, Erica and Megan! How do I teach them right from wrong when you have this kind of justice being hurled at us? What part of this is right? Why is there a Congress? They could change these laws. Do they just go up there and stand around and stroke each other's egos and wait for a national crisis so they'll have something to do?"

"That, and ride in parades, decorate war heroes, and work on gettin' reelected," Dad said as he smiled bitterly.

Anger seemed to burst from my body. By now I was rocking so fast I jumped up, fearing I might hurt myself or break something. I thought I was losing my mind. Was I crazy? Why couldn't I understand all this?

Looking at my watch, I finished my coffee and hugged them both goodbye. It was early still and I could make it to Vito's right about the time Frank usually arrived if I hurried. I was beginning to feel like K in Kafka's *The Trial*, which Frank had me read. Maybe he could help me comprehend this nightmare.

CHAPTER 24

Fight or Flight

"It's time to leave the ship, Jane," Frank advised me as I explained what had happened at the hearing. Only a few other people were at Vito's at this early hour. I was glad of that. I didn't want everyone to hear me telling the ridiculous contents of my court hearing.

After listening to me, Frank ordered his usual shot of tequila and beer and watched me as I sat speechless now, exhausted yet ready to cry out in pain and somehow vent my frustrations. Frank's suggestion to quit the legal fight was not something that I hadn't thought about. I dreaded the court battle but I couldn't give up. I wanted to push through the legal quagmire, even though I knew that was no longer realistic.

"Look, Jane," Frank continued. "What good is it going to do to keep fighting? This has drained you financially, without mention of your emotional expense. There's nothing you can do to keep Michael from seeing Megan when he gets out and, besides, what good is a piece of paper saying Michael's not Megan's father? Those pieces of paper aren't a guarantee of safety. They haven't been in the past and you should know that. You're going broke fighting a battle you can't win and when he's out and you're penniless, you're at the court's mercy."

"Then what should I do, Frank? Just forget about it all? Live in denial or dementia, like it was a bad dream?"

"Don't spend another penny on a hearing you can't win, Jane. If you want another court appearance, I've told you all along you should hire a litigation attorney and file suit against the city that let Michael out of jail with outstanding warrants. At least you'd get a cash settlement instead of throwing your money away."

"I can't!" I thundered. "Remember, the statute of limitations ran out while I was living in my car. I only had one year to file suit and I couldn't do that without an address!"

"Then go underground," Frank said, shrugging his shoulders as if it was the only sensible thing to do.

"Then I'll be in contempt of court!" I objected.

"Yes, but that's better than being dead!" Frank said loudly, prompting the few people at the bar to look at us curiously. "The court doesn't care about you and the kids, Jane. That should be obvious to you by now."

"It's painfully obvious, but shouldn't I try to get justice?"

Frank laughed and then gazed at my serious face.

"You don't have long until Michael gets out," Frank softly reminded me. "Every state has laws for good behavior of prisoners. When Michael serves his mandatory sentence, as long as he hasn't made big mistakes in prison, he's out, sprung, free, done-his-time-outta-there!"

"That's part of the problem, Frank. Why don't they reward prisoners with good behavior from within the system? If they have a month of good behavior, let them have a television pass, let them watch the Super Bowl, or somethin' other than turnin' a convicted killer out into the streets before he's served his sentence. Isn't that threatenin' the people in the community? Endangering their lives and security?"

"Jane, in a sense, you're right." Frank shook his head. "But it's more economic than that. It comes down to dollars and cents. It's cheaper to turn prisoners loose than to keep them locked up. The chance a prisoner gets out and kills one person out of a few million people in the state, well, that's pretty good odds to those calculating them. It's worth the risk. The rest of us are safe, and the state has saved money. And if government can save the taxpayers money, guess which option they take?"

"Save the money."

"Exactly," Frank said. "Jane, you can't spend all your time and money trying to fix the system. Why do you think I'm drinking draft beer? I've spent a bundle trying to change it!"

"I have a responsibility to do everything I can to keep Michael behind bars for as long as possible since we're the ones at risk."

"I agree," Frank assured me, "but not if that means putting yourself and your family in povertyville. Wake up, Jane! You're going to lose this one. You don't stand a snowball's chance in hell of terminating his parental rights! Life. Liberty. Property. The pursuit of happiness. Does any of that ring a bell? There's nothing more sacred than a man's property rights."

"Women and children aren't property," I said.

"There are many flaws in the system," Frank answered. "People know that. But don't think for a second that you can change the world, Jane! The legal system is a living, breathing machine, a monster out of control! It's bad DNA, Jane, and it keeps regenerating."

"Like incest," I countered.

"You said that, Jane," Frank pointed out. "Don't accuse me of blasting your heritage."

I knew Frank was right. I was running out of strength. Slumping back into my chair, I thought for a few minutes about the bitter truths Frank had pointed out. It didn't make much sense to keep throwing my money away. I knew I should call Pat and tell her not to proceed. I'd be spending money I didn't have, and for what? To be ruled against by a judge who already said he didn't see the harm in Michael's actions.

Frank lit a cigarette and stared at the smoke he exhaled, blowing small rings into larger ones as I fought back tears.

"Frank," I said in a shaky voice as I wiped my eyes with the already moist napkin. "Where do I find hope? How do I keep believin' in life?"

"Jane, there's not a simple answer. It's a question that perplexes many of us. You just keep going. I've waited all my adult life. I get a small victory now and then. Those are the good days. I have a few good days in a row, and I think maybe there's hope."

"How do I give my children hope?" I asked. "I can't sit day in and day out and wish for something that never comes and probably never will."

"You give them a way to escape," Frank advised. "How do you relax and let your frustrations go?"

"Through music and humor," I answered.

"Well," Frank said. "Here's a buck, go play your favorites on the jukebox."

Silently, I took his dollar and walked toward the jukebox.

"And, Jane," Frank yelled just as I was about to put the dollar in the slot, "next time that judge asks you if you read those letters to Megan, you say, 'Yes, Your Honor.' Just don't tell the judge you read them to her at four o'clock in the morning with a sock in your mouth!" He chuckled. "He won't ask why and how you read them. He doesn't need to know she was asleep! You gotta find your own kind of justice, Jane."

I got the laugh I needed to break the day's stress.

I didn't stay at Vito's much longer, partly because I felt the urge for a good long cry and I wanted to get some of it out before I picked up the girls. I knew it was best to stop my current legal actions, but I couldn't take the rest of Frank's well-meaning advice. I had a mission. I could not live with the abuse dished out by Michael. And, if the legal system was a continuation of Michael's mistreatment, I was going to have to find a better way to confront it.

After I said goodbye to Frank and paid our tab, I got in my car. As I drove, I thought about my legal quagmire. There was no use fighting a losing battle. Yet, how could I give up? I had Erica and Megan to consider. Maybe I had some fault in the way my life had turned out, but they had none. To give up. To sit in a chair as Frank suggested and wait for better days. What kind of an example did this set for them? What kind of world was I leaving for them? One where injustice triumphed and those who were wronged, battered, or slaughtered had to endure whatever they were dealt.

All night I tossed and turned, thinking, pondering, and when morning came, I had begun to formulate an answer with which my children I and could live.

I called Pat and said, "Pat, I talked this over with Frank. He feels I should not go on with the termination hearing."

"Jane, as much as I hate to admit it, I think he might be right, but that's your decision. I'll do whatever you decide. You heard Judge Chin. The only way he would let us continue with the hearing was if we could prove that Michael had not supported you during the pregnancy or hadn't supported Megan for a period of six months. How are we going to do that?" Pat asked.

"We can't," I answered. "Megan was several weeks old when I went into the shelter and she was six months and one day old when Michael killed Johnny and went to jail. We just can't win this one."

I paused, gathered my thoughts, and then went on. "But there are other ways, Pat. So far in this case, both judges have agreed that as long as Michael is in prison, Megan does not have to visit him."

"You're right," she said.

"Well, I'm going to do my damnedest to see that he stays there."

"We all want that, but how?" she asked.

"I need to find that out. But if the system can be utilized by the criminals like Michael and his prison buddies to continue to beat their victims, then it can be used by victims to stop their perpetrators from inflicting more torment."

In the midst of these tense legal complications, I had my family to protect and care for and a challenging school schedule to maintain, as well as a sensitive job at the battered women's shelter. A little relief came after I explained my court appearances to my professor of women's history, Andrea. Andrea suggested I write up my legal experiences and present them in an oral report to the class. Andrea had assigned a research project on women in politics and said my real life story would be important for other students to hear.

I felt guilty not being able to put as much work as I would have liked into my project. I was living the experience though, and it was one I felt deeply about conveying. When I presented it and saw the horrified faces of my stunned classmates, I knew Andrea's suggestion had been a good one. The students asked question after question about how something like what had happened to me could occur, most of them believing as I had once, that there was truth and justice for all.

After my class presentation, Andrea gave me the phone number of her friend, Dr. Teresa Brimmer, a criminal justice professor. Andrea urged me to call her, explaining that Dr. Brimmer taught classes dealing with battered women and her area of expertise was police response. Dr. Brimmer had published many articles on the subject. Her work had earned her an appointment to the Warren Christopher Commission for the Rodney King hearings. Andrea had told her about my ordeal and she wanted to meet me.

At first I felt intimidated by Dr. Brimmer's title and accomplishments and couldn't get up the nerve to call her. When I finally did, I found she was not only approachable, but we shared a similar sense of humor. Both of us relied on humor to keep our spirits up during what seemed to be overwhelming hopelessness when trying to remedy the problems battered women face.

Dr. Brimmer told me that my experiences reflected many of the problems that most battered women contend with in the criminal justice system. After we had discussed my life, I told her about some of my experiences working in the shelter. She praised my work and emphasized how important it was for me to speak out about violence in the home, not just to other domestic violence survivors, but to people in our community and to our political leaders.

Dr. Brimmer invited me to speak to her "Women and Crime" class, which was composed of graduate and undergraduate students. "Students," she said, "are more profoundly affected by firsthand accounts than by reading statistics on battered women." I felt a little nervous about speaking to a class that had graduate students in it, but she pressed me and finally I agreed.

The 9:00 A.M. class was filled with criminal justice students, many of whom would be future police officers. My heart pounded as I began to speak to them. I felt an urgency to explain the need for police and criminal justice officials to respond quickly to the needs of battered women and children. I wanted them to understand how Michael had been so viciously violent one minute and so confident a minute later when a police officer knocked on our door. "It was a Jekyll and Hyde technique that resulted in the police usually siding with him, leaving me and the girls in danger," I explained. I wanted to convey the importance of the damage and the dangers of leaving the scene of these crimes without intervention by the authorities. "Michael would always beat me more intensely after the police had left. His threats to kill me increased each time the police were involved, when the threat of his abusive behavior could be discovered and prosecuted. Unfortunately for us, that intervention never came."

I stressed the dangers to the class, detailing the tension building phase of the abuse and how dangerous leaving was for me and most other battered women I'd met. I tried to accentuate the problems women have in prosecuting their abusers. "Many women are afraid to stand before their abusers and judges and court personnel and detail their violations. Since most cities rarely have stiff penalties for the battering of women, most abusers will be back on the street, or in their homes, after the court hearings. Because of this, it's imperative for police to defend these victims, in the name of human rights and justice, if this horrible crime against women and children is ever going to stop."

As my speech went on, a blond young man raised his hand and said, "This is how it's supposed to be, men ruling over women, as prophesied in the Bible. You are wrong and unchristian for stepping on our God-given duties." As I watched, a gang of cronies patted their outspoken buddy on the back for standing up for what they thought was right. I cringed at these comments and felt sad that some had interpreted scripture in ways to justify violence. I remained frustrated and confused, thinking that the premise of most religions was supposed to be the betterment of life, to spread peace, love, and kindness, not hate, rage, abuse, and control.

Dr. Brimmer took me to lunch after I spoke and said to me, "The telling of your experiences, Jane, is very important, not only for you, but for the millions of other women and children trapped in violent homes." She urged me to write and publish my story and become more politically involved in order to create change.

"It's hard to think of the greater good when I feel such extreme dread for the girls and I as Michael's parole date grows near," I said.

"Have you thought of sending petitions to the parole board and writing to your representatives for help?" she asked. She gave me a few names of some local legal advocates and suggested that I contact them.

Her words fueled my courage. During the next weeks I gathered as many supporters as I could. I called shelters, spoke to classes and groups, told them about the injustices, and asked for signatures at every meeting at which I spoke. Initially I tried to stir interest on a state level, but as I went on I realized the problems were national, and gradually changed my focus.

Crime had become a central topic of concern and debate in political campaigns. It was appalling to me that most politicians focused on street crime. Never had I heard a politician allude to violence in the home as a problem or say that violent behavior may be learned in the home and carried into the street. Children learn by what they see and hear, and if violence in the home is accepted, or not cut off, it only stands to reason that children would use these learned skills in the streets as a method of resolving conflicts. This combined with the accessibility of handguns was a recipe for destruction. The number of murders of family members by other members in this country compared to any other democratic, supposedly civilized nation, are disproportionately high, avoidable, and embarrassing.

I spent hours each day trying to spread the message, hoping that someone would listen and try to help. I went to the library and found the addresses of women's organizations, senators and representatives, and even scanned the newspapers and television news programs for information on women's and children's issues and proposed legislation. I sent hundreds of letters and made innumerable phone calls to everyone that could help or sounded like they were interested in change.

My efforts seemed to have little effect. I was becoming discouraged when one day Ann Wilson called me at home. She was a staffer from the Washington office of Representative Constance Morella of Maryland. She asked me to submit a written summary as testimony for the Judicial Training Act. The deadline for submission was only two weeks away. The House Judiciary Committee was conducting a hearing on why judges needed to be educated about the dynamics of domestic violence. I knew it wasn't enough to train police officers and prosecutors, much as that training was needed. But if a judge didn't understand the issues, the case was hopeless. One of my letters had reached

Representative Morella's office, and her staff thought my experiences were perfect examples for their cause.

I spent long days and nights putting the sequence into readable form. I was exalted by my success in reaching these people, but when I began to write, I realized that not only was writing an invigorating challenge, it was also enormous work. I wrote and edited, rewrote, threw out, edited. It was a merciless process, and the deadline was closing in. But I wanted my report to be clear and show the need for change. Finally, I had my paper shaped and ready for review. Then I gave it to Frank, who helped me revise and polish it once more. Within two more days it was ready. I mailed my testimony express to Washington, making the deadline by one day.

I told Andrea what I'd done and gave her a copy of my congressional testimony to read. She suggested I get it out to as many groups as possible. She told me to call Carol Bartlemy, of the university's department of women's studies. Andrea thought Carol might be interested in publishing my testimony in their quarterly magazine, *Forum.*

She was. Carol asked me to come to her office and approve a few minor revisions. Later that month when *Forum* appeared, the testimony became my first publication.

After following Andrea's other suggestion and sending out the testimony to groups, I received several calls asking me to speak at various events. One was a candlelight vigil in memory of women who were killed as a result of domestic violence. It would be held on the steps of the Hamilton County Courthouse. I quickly accepted and attended.

After the ceremony I stayed on for a reception. I shook hands with many well-wishers and greeted several local politicians who seemed interested in helping. One of those I met was a detective who expressed his concern.

"My name is Detective John Ladd," he said in introducing himself. "I couldn't believe the horrible story you told tonight. Did this happen to you in Ohio?"

"No, it was eastern Kentucky. But I've worked at one of the local shelters for nearly a year, and I can tell you that similar stories happen here every day."

"I'm sorry to hear that. Could you tell me what you're seeing?"

"Just the other day a woman called our shelter because she couldn't get the police to help her. I called nine-one-one, and the police dispatchers told me to call her a cab, because they were too busy with other calls to send an officer."

"Well, I can assure you that doesn't happen around here," Detective Ladd stressed. Then he added, "You let us know when your abuser is going to be released from jail. We'll talk to our city officials and look into getting a security system installed in your home before he gets out."

Detective Ladd handed me his business card and told me to call him if I ever needed help. When I got home that night, I stuck the card on my bulletin board above the phone, next to Dr. Brimmer's home and office numbers.

I soon learned that Dr. Brimmer and Detective Ladd were people of their words. Whenever I called either one for help they always had worthwhile advice. Their commitment and dedication helped not only the other victims I was trying to aid, but they gave me hope for my own case. They helped restore my faith in a system that had largely ignored the needs of my family.

When I called Pat again, I had good news. "I've collected several hundred signatures for his parole hearing," I told her.

"Good work, Jane. That's your means of protection. If you can convince the parole board to keep him inside, you're safe."

"But the prison system has awarded him good behavior already. They'll probably give him an early out"

"Because they don't know the history of the case," Pat said. "They only know what the murder trial transcripts say. It's your job to let them know what happened. What about your daughter?"

I bit my lip nervously and then went on. "I think Erica should be heard," I said quietly.

"I agree. You have the evidence that was denied use in the murder trial. Show them it was clearly premeditated murder! It's your only hope."

When I picked up the girls from day care that day, I struggled to keep my emotions from showing. When I saw their innocent faces and thought about the things they'd been through, especially Erica, and knowing the uncertainty of our future, it seared my soul.

That night I read them several bedtime stories and played a game of cards with Erica after we tucked Megan in snugly. I wrestled with asking Erica how she felt about testifying. I didn't want to burden her. She was still a child with her life in front of her. She shouldn't have to worry about our safety. Somehow I managed to tell her. I was surprised to learn from Erica that she wanted to speak. Maybe they'll listen to me and we'll be safe. She'd been through enough, but we had to speak out when Michael's parole hearing came up and let the truth be known.

Until that time I didn't like the idea of breaking the law and going underground as Frank had recommended, but I had come to feel it was better than taking Megan to visit Michael and watching Erica suffer needlessly knowing her sister was visiting her father's killer.

It was weeks later before I heard from Pat. When she called to explain that Judge Chin had agreed to dismiss our case without prejudice, she warned me not to get too excited until I heard the rest of his order.

Michael's attorney had requested I pay more money to cover Michael's legal fees. Judge Chin ordered me to pay Mr. Gotler an additional $500 for Michael's legal expenses. I didn't have that much money. I wasn't going to try to borrow it, either. I had borrowed enough.

Then, a few weeks later, Pat called me and said Mr. Gotler had asked Judge Chin to issue a warrant for my arrest for failing to obey the court order to pay him for Michael's attorney bill. I had to appear at another hearing and explain my financial circumstances! Judge Chin had agreed not to arrest me as long as I appeared in court. At the hearing I pleaded with him not to make me pay, but Judge Chin decided that I could pay after I graduated from college. I explained to him that by the time I graduated Michael would be eligible for parole and he could pay his own attorney fees. The judge opposed my suggestion. He said there was no guarantee Michael would be released, and Judge Chin and Mr. Gotler both knew I had monthly income: Johnny's Social Security benefit until Erica's eighteenth birthday. Judge Chin gave me until my expected date of graduation to pay Gotler. When I explained the decision to Frank, he said, "I suggest you stay in school until you earn a Ph.D."

The revictimization never ends, I thought. Had I pursued the termination it might have cost me thousands of dollars I didn't have. Now I was expected to pay a killer's lawyer. For a few days I again felt like giving up, but I realized no one loved Erica and Megan like I did. There was no institution that would love them and meet their needs and provide them with understanding like I could. The courts had failed them when Michael continued to batter me and eventually killed Johnny. The welfare system had fallen short when we lived in our car and needed food and Erica needed therapy. Time and time again the legal system had failed all of us.

Our only source of safety was the signatures I'd started collecting. Our only hope for a future was the parole board.

I called several victims' rights groups and asked how many signatures had stopped the paroles of other convicted killers. The numbers were not specific, they said. A few hundred could do it. I didn't want to take any chances. I'd aim for a thousand, I decided.

I bought a ream of paper and wrote in large bold print at the top of each page:

By their signatures, the citizens listed below, all of legal age, are adamantly opposed to the early release of Jerry Michael Haney, prisoner #104986, who was sentenced to thirteen years for the murder of John T.R. Eidson. At present, he has served less than half his sentence. We believe justice would only be served if Jerry Michael Haney serves out his entire sentence.

This was my only chance for justice.

I pulled out my address book and sent letters with several blank petitions to everyone I knew asking them to help. I mailed hundreds of letters. Every time I spoke to a classroom of students or other groups that were interested in learning about domestic violence issues, I passed around the petitions and asked for their signatures. As soon as I filled a sheet, I mailed it ahead to the parole board. I gave petitions to my friends to collect more signatures.

For two years I carried the petitions with me everywhere I went.

The day came when I explained to Erica that the time had come to speak. She was excited knowing she would finally have the opportunity to have her voice heard. We talked about how she would feel most comfortable addressing the board, not to discourage her and make her nervous, but to lend her advice on the inevitable stress that such an experience could bring. Erica was still a child but wise beyond her years. She knew her statement alone would show that there was no fight or argument before Johnny was killed and that therefore Michael's crime was not a case of self-defense. We knew the crime Michael had committed was premeditated murder, not "only manslaughter."

As Michael's parole hearing approached, other obstacles and dangers emerged. I researched the parole process and found that prisoners usually aren't released from prison directly to the streets. Sometimes prisoners were placed on home incarceration and equipped with electronic ankle bracelets and monitors and were reintroduced into society gradually. Knowing that Michael's whereabouts could be monitored twenty-four hours a day was a relief, but it was not foolproof. News reports of the malfunctioning of some ankle bracelets haunted me. I was not willing to take that chance with our safety.

The most common release program involved the prisoner going from maximum security to a halfway house. Prisoners could also be sent to minimum security and then to a dormitory-style building without a fence where each prisoner had their own room and extra privileges and lived on the honor system but were still supervised and had to observe curfews.

Halfway houses were more common. Prisoners could obtain daily passes to leave and look for work or to handle business off the grounds, unguarded. These facilities were located throughout the state, and prisoners could be sent to any of the 120 counties in Kentucky. Most disturbing for me was that Michael could ask the parole board to release him into a certain county. Many prisoners request release into the county where their parents, wives and children live, and sometimes the parole board will accommodate their wishes.

My greatest fear was that Michael might ask for a location in northern Kentucky. Since we lived in Cincinnati and Michael knew our address from our numerous court appearances, the danger of him moving somewhere just across the Ohio River would put him within a twenty-mile drive from my family. Commuter buses traveled back and forth many times a day. I'd felt safe here and enjoyed the distance between us over the last few years, but the thought of Michael living so close to us threatened me, gave me bad dreams, and brought back the terror of Johnny's death and the abuse I'd suffered. I felt I could no longer sleep peacefully. To allow Megan or Erica out in the neighborhood to play would be dangerous. What if after the hearing Michael was granted parole and he was transferred to our area? Was it possible for me to get early word of the news and get us out of town quickly enough?

I couldn't bet on it.

I didn't want to go to the hearing, relive our repulsive past, and again be failed by the system. If Michael was released, I didn't want to have to come home, grab the children, and flee town. Not knowing where to go, there were more worries in addition to moving to a new town and the burden of finding the money to pay for the move. What if my dream of graduating from college were lost? Then running for our lives would also guarantee that we would remain poor. Without a degree, good paying jobs would stay out of my reach. Living on a small Social Security check, working a minimum wage job and whatever government assistance we could qualify for at a time in history when poor people are despised and misunderstood did not sound inviting, but neither did becoming a sitting duck for Michael. All of his letters had promised in that deceptively snide way that he would come for us. He even insisted that he couldn't wait.

The hardest part would be leaving many good friends behind, people who had helped us and given me direction. We would miss the comfort of friendship and family. I knew leaving their playmates would be difficult for the children. We could never contact any of them again. It would not be safe for them or me, especially if Michael returned to his previous occupation selling long-distance phone services.

Michael had worked as a salesperson at several phone companies. His job was to analyze a phone bill and determine how to save the potential customer money. He would brag about his ability to get confidential information. It would be easy for him to look up the phone number of one of my friends or close relatives, examine their incoming as well as outgoing calls and, by process of elimination, figure out where we were living. If he returned to that line of work, it would be simple for him to request someone's phone records under the guise of finding a way to save the person money and could then trace their calls to my location.

My heart was heavy, but I decided even if he forced us to run again, somehow I would keep going to school. Somehow I would not relinquish our dreams. If we moved we could not tell anyone where. I could not leave a trace. I could never change my driver's license or register to vote for fear of being easily traced by Michael. I'd have to maintain a low profile. The children and I would have to keep our past behind us, never letting anyone know who we were or what had happened. We'd have to give up our personal history, remain silent, and become anonymous, but we would persevere in our struggle for a better life free from harm.

CHAPTER 25

One Final Plea

Michael's parole hearing had been set for January 3. At Christmas we had almost no money. I couldn't afford a tree, but I did manage to hang a few lights around a tall bookcase. Erica and I tried to string the lights into a tree-shaped outline. We moved books and stacked them under our beds and placed small dime store gifts on the shelves. The kids thought this yule structure was interesting, but I felt hurt for them when once again we couldn't have a traditional celebration. Each night after the children were tucked in, I would sit on the floor at the foot of this depressing symbol and cry out my misery. All I could think of was how much I hated Michael and the system that protected him.

After the new year rang in, I became more hopeful, even confident that Erica and I could convince the parole board to keep Michael jailed. As long as we could tell the truth about the abuse and not be gagged as I had been at the murder trial, I felt sure they'd understand how dangerous it could be to free Michael.

I'd moved to a different state in the late summer before school started. I'd chosen to move for security reasons, but this

this meant we had to drive three days to reach Michael's parole board hearing. It was hard saving money for the trip during the holidays: yet another example of me having to divert money from my children to spend it on dealing with Michael.

The kids loved missing school for a few days. I'd convinced a co-worker, Lisa, to come along for the drive. I felt safer having another adult with me during the wintry travel. We decided she would wait in the hall with Megan while Erica and I went into the hearing. I wanted to shield Megan from the proceedings. She was still too young to understand what had happened, and talking about the murder in front of her would only create emotional problems for her. It was bad enough that Erica had damaging memories of her father's murder and my being abused.

We packed lunches and snacks and had plenty of blankets and water and other emergency gear in the trunk of my car. We sang along to songs on the radio and tallied license plates from various states while I tried hard not to think of losing again. I remembered the inadequate feelings I experienced after the murder trial and how easily I'd become rattled on the witness stand. Since then, I had gone to school and, although the traces of my "hill girl" accent were still apparent, I could now articulate the tragedy that began with Michael abusing me and led to Johnny's murder. I could explain the hardships on my children and the continued failure of the legal system.

While driving, I prepared my speech with specific phrases, sentences, and paragraphs. Every time I stopped for gas, I'd jot down the memory of a court decision and the confusion that followed. I tried not to think about the violence, but those repulsive memories seldom left me. I knew I did not have to make notes on them. There was no way to forget. I could answer questions or recall vivid details of the beatings and torture Michael had put us through. Those images stayed with me. I also knew I needed to reveal to the parole board how Michael had manipulated the legal system. I knew he'd use his charm to try to win them over, try to get his release, and continue his abuse and harassment of the children and me.

I felt confident until I crossed the Kentucky state line. Then uncertainty took over. I struggled to remember my statement and worried I'd get tongue-tied or omit an important issue. What if this was another failed attempt at justice? But worse, what if Erica experienced more trauma? Was I doing the right thing in bringing her? I had to believe I was. For as long as I could remember, Erica had been asking for her turn to tell what happened, in hopes of purging her own guilt.

Despite all my words of comfort, my attempts to tell her she had no fault, for all this time Erica had blamed herself. Weeks before the hearing, she recalled the day before her father's death when Michael asked her who the man was with Mommy. She told him it was her daddy. "Why didn't I tell him it was only a neighbor? If Michael hadn't known who was with us, maybe he wouldn't have gone to get a gun and killed Daddy."

We found the courthouse easily and parked within walking distance of the door. We had fallen behind schedule along the trip, and, when I parked the car and checked my watch I realized we were a few minutes late. I bundled the girls snugly, locked the car, and raced with them and Lisa to the courthouse.

The winter wind felt bracing. I pulled in the cold air and took a few relaxing breaths. I needed to be calm. This was our day in court, maybe our last chance. I tried not to think about how we had to spend our lives begging for protection. As we climbed the courthouse stairs, I noticed how pale Erica was, and I could sense her apprehension. I clasped her hand tightly.

Once inside, I was directed to Mary Whitaker's office. We took the elevator up and found her office at the end of the crowded hall, but she wasn't in. I felt faint when I thought we'd missed our appointment and wouldn't be able to testify. A receptionist directed me to a room at the other end of the hall where the hearings were being held and where I might find Ms. Whitaker.

Like other courthouses, benches lined the walls where anxious people waited to be heard. I couldn't help but wonder how their lives had been destroyed by violence. Had they watched a loved one killed? Had they lost more than one family member or friend? Had their victimization been rape, domestic violence, theft, or some other offense that can leave you jaded, exhausted, broke, and spiritually vacant? Had they experienced a loss of security? Did their children also face frightening futures complicated by the decisions made within these walls?

When the white frosted glass door opened at the end of the hall and people filed out of the room, I noticed a red-haired woman with a name tag and carrying a clipboard. I edged closer to read the tag. It was Mary Whitaker.

"Hello," I said. "I'm Jane Wells. I'm sorry we're late."

"Hi, Jane. I'm Mary," she announced as we shook hands. "Glad you made it safely. To stay on schedule, we sent another family in before you. Don't worry. You're next. Come this way."

Erica grabbed my hand and squeezed it tightly as we walked through the door. I felt her body shake. I placed my arm on her shoulder and pulled her close to me. I looked down and saw her eyes swell with tears as she bit her lower lip.

"Are you sure you want to do this?" I whispered. "You look scared. I'm a little scared myself. We can go home if you want. Erica, look at me. We don't have to do this."

"No, Mom," Erica said softly. "I'm not a little girl anymore. Besides, what happens if they let Michael out?"

"I can tell them, Erica," I assured her. "I can explain to the board what happened."

"No. I need to tell them what I saw. If Michael gets out early, he might kill you or steal Megan! I've waited a long time for this, Mom. I'm just scared I won't say the right thing, or the parole board won't believe me."

"Tell the truth and you'll do fine," I said as we took our seats at the table. I understood her fear of being ignored and discounted by the courts. I wasn't surprised by her "big girl" attitude either. Deprived of her youth by violence, she stood just a few inches shorter than me and already she could wear my shoes, but her size hadn't caused her loss of innocence. I knew how empty and suspicious our experiences had left us both.

My thoughts were interrupted when a fiftyish woman with tortoise-shelled glasses at the table introduced the members on the panel as I nodded reassuringly to Erica. I turned back and looked at all the strangers on the panel. Some were shuffling papers and others looked curiously at me. I didn't catch their names and was startled when one of them asked me to speak.

"We would appreciate it if you could limit your comments," a loud voice boomed. "We need to know why you believe Jerry Michael Haney should remain in prison." I glanced nervously Erica's way, trembling.

"Do you want to go first, Erica?" I asked.

"No. You go, Mom," Erica answered.

As I took a deep breath, images of Michael's abusive fists punching me, blood flowing from Johnny's mouth, and Erica's shrieking voice exploded through my mind. A few minutes would not be time enough to explain the days, weeks, months and years Michael had abused us before he killed Johnny. My time had come and my future safety rested on the decision of the small group of people sitting across the table from us. I clenched my teeth, swallowed, laid my notes in front of me, then exhaled slowly. My one chance at justice and security depended on this moment and my words that followed.

"My name is Jane Wells, and I am a survivor of homicidal domestic violence," I began. "I have come here today to explain why Jerry Michael Haney should not be released and I will keep my explanation as short as possible. From the beginning of my marriage to Mr. Haney, I have painfully learned how tenuous freedom is when women and children are the victims of crime and systematic abuse. I went from economic self-sufficiency to financial ruin and from independence to dependence on an inadequate and myopic legal system that not only failed to respond to my dangers and life-threatening needs, but aggravated my plight. I went from owning my own home to living in my car with two children. Mr. Haney took all of my money and other assets while I was staying at a battered women's shelter."

The faces before me were a blurred mass of shapes and colors. I felt an adrenaline rush throughout my body as I tried to focus and make eye contact with each of them as the words surged from my mouth.

"The events leading to the homicide began when I married Jerry Michael Haney, a man who, when I became pregnant, began to abuse me. Incidents of choking, punching, being tied up and isolated from my children, including being separated from Megan when I was nursing her, were some of the torturous violations I was forced to endure. Countless times my clothes were ripped off my body by Michael in front of his teenage sons and my daughter, this very child sitting next to me. His excuses for such behavior ranged from dinner being late to showing the children how disgusting a pregnant woman looked.

"I contacted an attorney shortly after this abuse began, trying desperately to protect myself and my child from the danger. I was advised that in Kentucky, as in other states, a pregnant woman cannot be granted a divorce. I was forced to remain domiciled with my abuser. I was not eligible for public assistance because I was married and owned property which further crippled my ability to leave him.

"Over the next few months, Michael began to pawn or sell my personal belongings. Sometimes it was to finance his pleasures, sometimes as a blatant exercise of power over me. My attempts to stop him were always met with a beating. I began to call the police. When they arrived, the police would not arrest Michael. They instructed me to contact a judge so that he could help us work out our marital differences while I stood pregnant and bleeding, pleading for protection while Erica, then five years old, looked on in horror. This cycle continued vindictively.

"After our daughter was born, tension between us intensified. Michael knew I wanted to leave. I worked hard to maintain peace until I had healed from the delivery. I wanted to be prepared to move what was left of our furniture, find work, find a place to live, and find child care for Erica and her newborn sister. A few weeks after Megan's birth, I was tortured for over thirty hours and isolated from my children. I managed to catch Michael off guard and flee with my children to safe shelter and was treated at a local hospital for injuries.

"The following day I went to the courthouse and filed a domestic violence petition and asked for a restraining order. Michael appeared while I was there and filed charges against me in an attempt to further victimize me. A court date was set. We were both ordered to stay out of the house until after the hearing. I felt good that we had entered a shelter for protection and my property would be safe with the order in effect.

"Unbeknownst to me, Michael went to the judge's chambers immediately following the hearing and requested the order be reversed, emphasizing the fact that I was in a safe shelter and he could not physically harm me there. The judge removed the order without considering my personal possessions. Michael helped himself to my belongings and when the court date came around, Michael failed to appear. Warrants were issued, but Michael was never apprehended. My belongings, which had filled a three-story house, had disappeared. Justice was beginning to sting.

"While in the shelter I found a job and was stalked by Michael. He called the business where I worked so frequently that after only a few days on the job, my boss fired me because of Michael's harassment. He was determined to starve us and force me to be economically dependent on him. The rental property I'd once relied on for income was nearing foreclosure. Michael had spent the rent checks as he pleased, leaving me with more than a few months of past due bank notes. All I could do to save myself from bankruptcy was sign the property back over to the bank.

"With no relief available, I decided to relocate in order to find work and peace of mind. While I made arrangements to move, my first husband, John Eidson, Erica's father, the man Michael killed, learned of our traumatic experiences and contacted me to offer his support.

"Johnny and I stayed in close contact during the next few months. After I'd been living in a hotel with my children for several weeks, Johnny offered to help us get settled into an apartment. Meanwhile, Michael stalked me and eventually tracked me to my new address.

"Michael followed me daily and harassed me at both of my new jobs as well as my new residence. I called the police and disclosed to them the history and the danger. They informed me I would have to go back to the county in which the warrants had been filed, gather the documents, and begin proceedings in this county of the same state. The reason for this leg work was: wife beating was a lesser offense and in some counties seemed perfectly legal, and an accepted way to keep a woman in line. Therefore, these seemingly unimportant warrants did not show up on the police computers. And it cost Johnny Eidson his life.

"I took two days off from both my jobs and traveled over one hundred miles each way to get the paperwork. I returned with some furniture my family had given me and copies and numbers of four outstanding warrants for Michael's arrest. Johnny, my first husband, accompanied us. That evening, Michael showed up at my new residence and began to demand a place to sleep and verbally and physically abused me and Johnny, with the children looking on.

"Johnny ran to a phone to call the police. When they arrived, Michael fled. The police eventually captured him and brought him to my front door and asked me to confirm his identity as my abuser. I then gave the arresting officer copies of the outstanding warrants for Michael's arrest. The office instructed me to call the jail and give them the information, which I did, and begged them not to release him. After settling the children to bed, Johnny slept on the couch and I went to my room and drifted to sleep thinking justice would finally be served.

"Early the next morning I was awakened by gunfire and screams of pain and panic. Michael had been released after being held only a couple of hours." I paused and looked at each member of the panel in turn. "I think you should hear from Erica what happened next.

"Are you ready?" I asked Erica. The room was void of sound or stir. When Erica nodded her head yes, I turned to our audience and saw all eyes fixed on us. Some of their mouths gaped. Others had raised brows and painful expressions.

Erica shifted in her seat and cleared her throat. I could tell she was gathering her thoughts.

"Tell them what happened when Michael came to the house that morning," I whispered. I could tell the thought of speaking to the board was intimidating. So much had happened to her. I thought it might be difficult for her to pick a place to start.

"That morning, ah, Michael knocked on the door," Erica said. "My dad and I were in the living room. He was reading the paper, and I was . . . was playing in the living room with Dad, while he read. He said he would look for a job nearby. He was going to stay here and help us. Then he was going to ask Mom to marry him again."

Looking at me, Erica looked sad but managed to smile. She'd often wondered what if, just as I had.

"Well, then, when we heard the knock, my dad went to the door and looked out. Dad told me it was Michael. My dad took my arm and led me upstairs and into my room. He said we needed to hide from Michael. I ran and got in my closet. Dad looked out my window and looked down to see if Michael was still at the front door. But Michael wasn't there. Dad told me Michael was gone.

"Then Dad looked at me and smiled and turned around to walk out of my room and I followed him. That's when I saw Michael with a gun. I heard the gun shots. I don't know how many, but my dad started screaming 'Oh my God, Oh my God!'

Then, that's when my dad fell on the floor. Michael kept firing his gun at him. Blood was coming from my dad's mouth. When Mom opened her door, Michael put the gun in her face and said he was going to kill her next. I . . . I started screaming. When Dad and I went to get the paper, I forgot to lock the front door. Maybe we could have stopped . . ." She began to weep.

"Erica, it was not our fault," I interrupted as I put my arms around her while she cried. Unable to watch her continue with her painful testimony, I took over, more determined than ever.

"There was not a fight or struggle as Michael testified at the murder trial. That was fabricated for his defense. But Erica wasn't allowed to testify in court. And, at the time, I didn't want her to. Maybe I was wrong. Maybe this information would have convinced the jury of premeditation, instead of them buying into Michael's self-defense story. But I was trying to spare my young, wounded child from suffering more pain.

"According to court testimony, Michael and an accomplice, whom he'd met in jail just the night before Johnny's murder, spent several hours obtaining a gun. Then Michael came to my home, entered it, and shot Johnny in the back three times while Erica watched in horror. That's when I came out of my room as Erica described, holding my six-month-old daughter, and was introduced to Michael's gun. He aimed his gun between my eyes and threatened to kill me and then himself.

"I clutched the girls close to me. I stepped over Johnny's body. I hope none of you ever have to experience that eerie feeling of stepping over a loved one's body. But I had to get us to safety. I tried to flee for our lives, but I was held at gunpoint by Michael and could not escape. I pleaded with Michael for the safety of my children. When the police arrived after the neighbors had called them, they knocked on my door, distracting Michael, and that allowed me to maneuver my way to the door. When I tried to open it, Michael slammed my fingers in the door and shoved the gun in my ribs, inches from our child, and pulled the trigger. Michael was going all the way with his plan to kill me, except that the gun jammed.

"Sensing that he was off guard, I shoved him back, knocked him to the floor, and ran outside to safety with my children. Several hours later, the bomb squad flushed him out of the apartment, and Michael was finally captured.

"Michael was tried for murder but convicted only of manslaughter and misdemeanor burglary. None of the history of his abuse that my children and I had suffered was permitted to be presented to the court as evidence. Yet, testifying as a murder witness, oddly, I was questioned about my sexual past.

"In subsequent child custody hearings, Michael has been proclaimed a 'fit' father. The court has ordered me to accept his collect phone calls from prison. Try to imagine how frightened Erica would feel if she answered the phone only to hear the voice of the man who killed her father. Child support from Michael has been suspended because the judge felt a large arrearage would be an unnecessary burden on him. I am still amazed at the sympathy given to such a ruthless man.

"I, on the other hand, have been ordered to read his letters to my younger daughter. These letters contain thinly veiled threats couched in language beyond her comprehension. Moreover, every foray into domestic court brings more financial burden on me as I am ordered to pay my attorney fees, Michael's attorney fees, and my daughter's guardian ad-litem fees plus court costs every time Michael moves the court for some custodial modification. The judicially sanctioned letters and fee obligations are forms of abuse. I believe that justice and compassion should not be antithetical concepts in a civilized society.

"As a result of these injustices, my children and I were forced to live in our car for some time. When I tried to get food, medical, and financial assistance from the Department of Human Services, I was told I could not apply if I did not have an address.

"Somehow, through all of these injustices, while many people told me to give up, to crawl in a hole, or leave the country,

I've managed to overcome these obstacles. I've returned to school at the University of Cincinnati and have worked my way up from a student with an inferior academic background to the dean's list.

"I could not end this plea without giving a few examples of the effects this tragedy has had on my children. Following a court appearance to decide if Michael should have visitation with Megan, I had broken my glasses and sat at the kitchen table crying. Erica came to me and put her arms around my shoulders and asked me what was wrong. I explained that I had broken my glasses, which I needed to drive and for school, and didn't have the money to get a new pair. In an attempt to console her mother, she said, 'Don't worry, Mom. All we have to do is *kill* someone and the government will buy you a new pair. Remember what nice clothes Michael had at the trial, and new glasses? They even pay for him to go to school. Remember, Mom? They said he makes straight A's.'

"What are we teaching our children in this country? In her fifth grade social studies class last year, Erica studied the constitution. When her teacher explained that our country guaranteed truth and justice for all, Erica raised her hand to inform her teacher that she was wrong. 'Children don't get justice in this country,' Erica told her.

"Unfortunately, Erica knows she may be forced to come face to face with her father's killer. Worse yet, she may soon be put through the torment of knowing that her baby sister is forced to see the man who not only killed her father, but who beat her mother on a regular basis and would have killed her if the gun hadn't jammed. I realize that this board has no control over these child custody decisions, but the judge has ruled that once Michael is released he will be granted visitation rights. No court in the country can overturn the State of Kentucky's decision. The Full Faith and Credit Clause in our constitution keeps every state from overturning another state's rulings.

"I have fought hard to keep my family together and safe, but I am at the end of the line as I speak to you today. I have no legal remedy for these terrifying legal dilemmas. I am left to dread the day I am ordered by the courts to allow Michael Haney to come into our home. My children and I need to believe that our home can remain safe. Had the truth of the murder been exposed, we would not be sitting here today. Michael would have been convicted of murder and a harsher sentence imposed.

"Although these mistakes cannot be reversed, one thing is sure: if Michael remains behind bars, we will be safe from his violence.

"I beg you to keep Jerry Michael Haney jailed until his sentence is served for killing Johnny Eidson. I beg you to grant my family freedom from fear."

Epilogue

On January 3, 1995, Erica Eidson and Jane Wells told their experiences to the Kentucky State Corrections Parole Board. Over one thousand signatures of protest for Jerry Michael Haney's parole were on file.

On January 9, 1995, Megan's seventh birthday, the Kentucky State Corrections Parole Board denied Jerry Michael Haney's release.